ENCYCLOPAEDIA OF WOMEN IN SOUTH ASIA
(Sri Lanka)

ENCYCLOPAEDIA OF
WOMEN IN SOUTH ASIA
(In 8 Volumes)
Sri Lanka
(Volume 5)

Editors
Dr. (Mrs.) Sangh Mittra
Dr. Bachchan Kumar

KALPAZ PUBLICATIONS
DELHI-110 052

ENCYCLOPAEDIA OF WOMEN IN SOUTH ASIA
(International Studies, Women)

Rs. 7000 (Set)

ISBN: 81-7835-187-0 (Set)
81-7835-192-7 (Vol. 5)

Published in 2004 in India by
Kalpaz Publications
C-30, Satyawati Nagar
Delhi-110 052
E-mail: Kalpaz@hotmail.com

Lasertypesetting by: Varsha Graphics, Delhi
Printed at: Mehra Offset Printers, Delhi

Contents

1

Historical Background, Geography and People

The glimpses of Sri Lanka through the ages provide merely a hint of the rich and variegated history of the island—a history which not only helps us to understand how people lived in the past, but also explains many of the present-day attitudes, policies and aspirations. Yet the relationship between the past and the present is not always clear-cut. Each historian looks back at earlier ages and seeks to interpret them in the light of his own knowledge and experience. Historians can introduce bias not only by their interpretations of events, but even simply by the selection of the 'facts' they seek to record. Perceptions of the past are therefore often subjective. Moreover, in terms of current attitudes and aspirations perceptions could become more important than reality. These problems, however, are not peculiar to history but rather are common to all social sciences. The solution to them is not to turn away from history—for it pervades all our lives—but to seek a balanced and comprehensive understanding of the past. It is in this spirit that this book has been written.

The Religions of Sri Lanka

Sri Lanka presents a mosaic of religions. Buddhism, which was introduced to Sri Lanka well over 2200 years ago, remains the religion professed by almost 70 per cent of the people today (see Table 1). The Buddhists are a cohesive community, for while the Buddhist *sangha* (order of monks) is divided into a number of sects, each with a separate leadership, there is no serious doctrinal dispute amongst them. The Buddhists have strong memories of discrimination against them during the period of colonial rule

Table 1
Population of Sri Lanka by Religion (in thousands)

	1946		*1953*		*1963*		*1971*		*1981*	
	Number	*Per cent*	*Number*	*Per cent*	*Number*	*Per cent*	*Number*	*Per cent*	*Number*	*Per cent*
Buddhists	4294.9	64.5	5209.4	64.3	7003.3	66.2	8536.8	67.3	10,292.6	69.3
Hindus	1320.4	19.8	1610.5	19.9	1958.4	18.5	2238.6	17.6	2,295.9	15.5
Muslims	436.6	6.6	541.5	6.7	724.0	6.8	901.8	F7.1	1,134.6	7.6
Christians	603.2	9.1	724.4	8.9	884.9	8.4	1044.3	7.9	1,111.7	7.5
Others	2.3	—	11.9	0.1	11.4	0.1	8.2	0.1	15.3	0.1
Total	6,657.3		8,097.9		10,582.0		12,689.8		14,850.0	

Sources: Statistical Abstract of the Democratic Socialist Republic of Sri Lanka, 1979, pp. 42, 43: Preliminary Report of the Census of 1981, p. 3.

and sometimes tend to look suspiciously at the influential Christian minority. The more extreme among them have continued to campaign for the recognition of Buddhism as the state religion, but most appear content with the current situation where Buddhism is accorded a special place while religious freedom and equality of treatment for adherents of all religions is assured to all.

Relations between Buddhists and Hindus have been traditionally cordial though these bonds have been adversely affected by the recent rise of Sinhalese-Tamil ethnic tension. The proportion of Hindus in Sri Lanka has declined in recent years (see Table 1), but they are still more than twice as numerous as the next largest religious community, the Muslims. The Muslims have gained increasing self-consciousness, with the emergence of oil-rich Islamic states in West Asia. A significant proportion of them have worked in West Asia and their remittances have helped to uplift the economic status of many of their community. The recognition of the sensitivity of Hindus and Muslims led the government of Sri Lanka to establish separate government departments to deal with Hindu and Muslim affairs in 1980.

The fourth largest group are the Christians who form just 7.5 per cent of the population. About 90 per cent of the Christians are Roman Catholics, the rest being composed largely of Anglicans, Calvinists, Methodists and Baptists. Sixty years ago Christians made up 10 per cent of the population. The indigenous elite under colonial rule was made up almost entirely of Christians. After independence, they have had to contend with Sri Lankan governments which were dependent on the Buddhist majority. However, Christians have by and large successfully made the adjustment. Christian services are conducted in local languages and Christians are no longer seen by Buddhists and Hindus as agents of Western colonial dominance. However, in recent times fissures have arisen between Sinhalese Christians, who form over 60 per cent of the community, and Tamil Christians. There are also some differences between the Roman Catholics, who made up 90 per cent of all Christians, and the numerous Protestant groups, and indeed among the Protestants themselves, but these denominational rivalries have become less important in more recent times.

Indeed, one of the trends of the past few decades has been increasing cooperation among religious dignitaries of all faiths in attempts to ensure greater cooperation and understanding among the different ethnic and religious communities living in Sri Lanka.

Sri Lankan History: Some Forces and Themes

The history of small islands is often the story of adaptation to external influences. Sri Lanka is no exception. The island, just 25,332 square miles in extent, is located off the southern extremity of the Indian subcontinent. Indeed, the Palk Strait which separates Sri Lanka from India is only twenty-five miles wide at its narrowest point and the open beaches on either shore have always made the crossing a relatively easy one. Thus, the strongest influence on Sri Lanka throughout the ages has been that of India.

As we have seen earlier, the two chief ethnic groups are almost totally of Indian origin. Indeed, so are the two major religions, for both Buddhism and Hinduism were born in the Indian subcontinent. In fact, Indian religious influence cannot simply be measured in terms of the numbers of people professing these religions. For centuries Sri Lanka has been drawn into the religious and ideological movements that have affected the Indian subcontinent.

Indian influence has also been strong in the social sphere. Indian social customs, styles of dress and the Indian caste system have left their mark on Sri Lanka. Continual contact with India has also led to a strong Indian imprint on Sri Lankan cultures. Indeed, as will be illustrated in later chapters, the influence of India in relation to literature and the arts has been overwhelming until fairly recent times.

Proximity to India has had important political consequences. It is not merely that political concepts and models of political organisation were often borrowed from India. Whenever most of peninsular India or a major part of South India has been dominated by a single power, that power has sought to extend its political domain to Sri Lanka. Sri Lankan rulers have generally been apprehensive of such efforts because of the great disparity in power and resources between their small island and the dominant power in the neighbouring subcontinent. Thus, the admiration and acceptance of Indian ideas and culture has often existed side by side with fears of Indian political dominance.

One should not, however, exaggerate the element of Indian influence in Sri Lankan history and culture. The sea has provided Sri Lanka with some isolation from the vagaries of Indian politics. In over two thousand years of recorded history Indian-based powe rs have maintained direct control over Sri Lanka in whole or in part for less than a hundred and fifty years.

Elements of Sri Lankan society and culture have evolved in ways that are distinct from what can be seen in most parts of India. For example, Buddhism continued to flourish in Sri Lanka long after its decline in neighbouring India. The Sinhalese caste system too developed in a form far less rigid than in South India.

A key element of the distinct civilisation that developed in ancient Sri Lanka was the evolution of an irrigation technology which has no parallel in India. The earliest agricultural settlements were established mainly along river valleys in the northern and south-eastern plains (Rajarata and Rohana). Both these regions fall largely within what is known today as the dry zone of Sri Lanka, a region where the rainfall is usually less than 75 inches annually and where there is an effective dry period of at least three months. Rain-fed agriculture in the dry zone was a hazardous venture due to the high annual variability of rainfall. In some years the rain would fail and the smaller streams would begin to run dry. In response to this challenge the settlers gradually evolved in intricate system of reservoirs, great and small, fed by canals which not only tapped the water of the rivers of the dry zone but even conducted water from the wetter parts of the country. This complex irrigation system which reached its zenith by the twelfth century A.D. necessitated an elaborate administrative apparatus for its maintenance. The development of the hydraulic system went hand in hand with the strengthening of royal power, and income from the enhanced production enabled rulers to be lavish in their patronage of religion and the arts. These elements in their turn contributed to the evolution of a separate national identity.

Buddhism appears to have made a significant contribution towards the moulding of this national identity. For many centuries many Tamils as well as most Sinhalese were Buddhists and, as will be described later, Buddhist literature and art played a major role in moulding Sinhalese culture. The *sangha* appears to have had considerable political influence and thus the Buddhist polity of ancient Sri Lanka came to be somewhat distinct from the Hindu kingdoms which developed in South India after the seventh century A.D.

The evolution of a separate identity was also facilitated by the flow of peoples from other parts of Asia and Africa. External influences on Sri Lanka, therefore, have not been confined to those from India. From very early times the central location of the island in the Indian Ocean has laid it open to the impact of other peoples of the littoral. Sri Lanka is just one thousand five hundred miles west of the Straits of Malacca and the Sunda Strait, the two major gateways from the Pacific to the Indian Ocean. The Straits of Ormuz and Bab-el-Mandal, the main arteries of maritime trade from Europe and West Asia to the East, are just two thousand miles to the north-west and west respectively. Thus in the centuries when winds and ocean currents determined maritime trade routes, Sri Lanka lay athwart the major sea lanes of the Indian Ocean. The advent of the steamship did little to change this, for with the opening of the Suez Canal in 1869, Colombo gained in importance as a wayside stop and a refulling station on the shortest sea route from the western shores of the Pacific to Europe.

The hydraulic civilization of Rajarata lasted well over a millennium but finally collapsed by the early thirteenth century. Thenceforth there was gradual drift of population and of centres of Sinhalese political power to the south-western regions. The lowlands of the south-west are narrower than those of the north and moreover are dissected by a series of ridges running parallel to the coast. However, this was not the reason why states based on the south-west were generally less powerful than the old kingdoms of the Rajarata. Most of the area covered by the south-west lowlands fell within the wet zone and a large part of it had over 100 inches of rainfall. Thus elaborate irrigation works were no longer necessary for the cultivation of rice. Correspondingly, the dependence of the farmer on the central government was less and loyalty to the centre was weaker. Centrifugal tendencies were stronger. However, agriculture remained by far the most important source of revenue to the state, though the central administrative bureaucracy became much less complex and the political organisation more feudalistic. The construction of monumental public and religious edifices became rarer.

While the centres of Sinhalese power moved to the south-west, a Tamil-Hindu kingdom based on the Jaffna peninsula and its environs became firmly established in the thirteenth century. The rulers of this kingdom clearly saw themselves as potential rulers of the whole of Lanka, but their failure to achieve this objective in the fourteenth centuries limited them to the largely Tamil north. It was the existence of this independent Tamil kingdom from the early thirteenth to the early seventeenth centuries that later provided the basis for Tamil nationalist claims to a separate national identity.

Throughout the period of Sri Lankan history upto about the fifteenth century the central highlands of the island did not play a prominent role. Indeed the highest parts of the mountainous region—forming an anchor-shaped region above 5000 feet in elevation—were almost totally uninhabited until a hundred years ago. Even the two plateau regions that flank the mountain core—the Hatton plateau and the Uva Basin—were sparsely settled. Indeed, until the arrival of the Europeans in Sri Lanka the major areas of settlement in the hill country seem to have been in the areas under 3000 feet in height. However, in the seventeenth century when the conquest of the lowlands by the Westerners confined indigenous political power to the mountainous region, the central highland region began to play a key role in the preservation of indigenous culture and traditions. There was a marked increase in the population in the central highland region and its rulers came to wield influence beyond the strict limits of their territorial domain.

European colonial powers began to exert influence on Sri Lanka from the sixteenth century onwards. The western impact on Sri Lanka's history and culture was a wide-ranging one. Their coming added another minisule ethnic group—the Burghers—to Sri Lanka's plural society.

A key change which occurred with the establishment of colonial rule over parts of the lowlands relates to the economic basis of the state. All indigenous states had derived a major part of their revenue from land. Western colonial powers on the other hand financed their rule largely from profits derived from the control of trade and commerce. The transition can clearly be seen in the time of the Portuguese rule in south-west (1597-1656) and in Jaffna (1619-1658). The Dutch (1638-1796) and the British (1796-1948) administrations in Sri Lanka were clearly based on revenues generated from commercial crops. An inevitable consequence of this policy was the concentration of state attention on commercial rather than subsistence agriculture. Over time this led to a change in the entire economic pattern of the country, with the production of crops such as cinnamon and coconut and later coffee, tea and rubber obtaining more state encouragement than the cultivation of paddy.

Another element of the Western legacy was Christianity. The spread of Christianity, especially in coastal areas, has led to the introduction of Western and Christian values. On the other hand, though parts of the coastal areas had been in European hands since the sixteenth century, the small number of Christian missionaries and priests in Sri Lanka ensured that Westernisation was confined to an elite group among the Christians until well into the nineteenth century. It was the growth of newspapers and the establishment of Western-type schools in the late nineteenth century that exposed the majority of Sri Lankans to Westernization, and the Buddhist, Hindu and Muslim religious revivals of the period have to be understood in this context. The continued exposure of Sri Lanka to Western values and concepts has stimulated the growth of cultural revivalist movements aimed at preserving indigenous traditions and values.

Much of this volume is concerned with the British impact on Sri Lanka and developments since independence. Historians of Sri Lanka have on the whole been less critical of the economic impact of British rule than their counterparts in the Indian subcontinent. There is reason for this. Unlike in India, there were no major industries that were adversely affected by British policy. There is considerable evidence that the construction of a network of roads and railways originally designed to consolidate British rule in the island and to promote the spread of plantation enterprise eventually had an important positive impact on the economy as a whole. Indeed, unlike in India, the development of an indigenous entrepeneurial class in Sri Lanka owes much to the rise of the plantation economy in the country. Despite its limitations, it was the plantation economy that enabled Sri Lankan politicians to lay the foundations of a welfare system during and after the last years of British rule.

This is not a portray a picture of a wholly benevolent colonial administration. The British derived considerable economic benefits from the colony through their control of commerce and trade. British investors in Sri Lankan plantations made large profits while living conditions of the plantation workers remained abysmal. British neglect of domestic agriculture is a factor that aroused criticism from nationalist leaders for many years. At the end of British rule Sri Lanka was left dependent on foreign sources for a very large proportion of its basic food requirements and after independence Sri Lankan governments have had to invest considerable resources to correct this imbalance.

Whatever judgement is made regarding the benefits or negative effects of British rule, it is clear that what happened during the 150 years of British dominance was an acceleration of the pace of change in Sri Lanka's economy. In the early nineteenth century the area under commercial crops—cinnamon, coconut and arecanut—was very small in comparison to the area under subsistence farming. By independence, commercial crops, mainly tea, rubber and coconut, accounted for two-thirds of the area under permanent cultivation. Some implications of this growth of commercial agriculture such as the growth of an entrepreneurial class have already been touched upon. It is worth noting at this stage that it also led to the growth of internal and external trade. India ceased to be Lanka's major trading partner, perhaps for the first time in history. Sri Lanka became increasingly tied to the world economy. With increasing population, problems of landlessness and land hunger emerged. Indeed, the changes brought about by the rise of commercial agriculture are so widespread that many historians identify the beginnings of the modern period of Sri Lanka's history with the growth of the plantation economy in the 1830s.

The political legacy of British rule has also been the subject of some debate. British policy in bringing in cheap Indian labour to the plantations in the highlands left a problem that was to complicate internal politics in Sri Lanka as well as Indo-Sri Lankan relations. Even more important is the question of the introduction of democratic institutions. There is little doubt that for a century or so the British merely continued the tradition of autocratic rule. Sri Lankans or rather a miniscule minority of Sri Lankans became involved in choosing their representatives to the legislative council only in 1911. After that, however, development accelerated, with representation rapidly increasing in the 1920s. By 1931—seventeen years before the end of British rule —Sri Lanka had obtained universal franchise and some element of responsible government. It is possible to argue that even this brief experience in the working of democratic institutions proved invaluable in persuading the people that responsible government was an experiment worth trying.

The thirty years that have passed since independence have seen many changes in Sri Lanka despite considerable strands of continuity with the past. Sri Lanka's political structure has been substantially modified. The Westminster-style constitution with a prime minister and a nominal head of state has been replaced by a presidential system. The British-style system of elections largely through single-member constituencies with a single ballot where the winner was decided on a plurality of votes has been replaced by a system of proportional representation. On the other hand, the principle of responsible government based on universal suffrage has been retained. Sri Lanka has been seven parliamentary elections and one presidential election after independence. Six of these elections have resulted in a change of government.

The nature of the political system prevailing in Sri Lanka has been the subject of considerable controversy. Some critics have argued that whatever freedoms and fundamental rights are enshrined in the constitution frequently have been abridged by the use of 'emergency powers' by successive governments and that of a study of the actual working of the political system presents a picture much less attractive than that given by the constitutional documents. Moreover, it is also contended that what obtains today is merely a thin veneer of democratic practices which disguises a political culture dominated by a dependence on patron-client links rather than legal rights, respect for high social status rather than an insistence on equal rights and an acceptance of authority—all elements that are traceable to feudalistic social relations in pre-modern times. There is some truth in this contention. On the other hand, there is considerable political activity at all levels in Sri Lanka today and much of it is organised by opposition groups. The high rate of voter participation (it has been over 69 per cent in every general election after independence) and the readiness of the Sri Lankan voter to reject incumbent parties as well as the acceptance of the parliamentary system by almost all political groups seems to suggest that democratic forms of government have taken root in Sri Lanka.

However, there are two major problems that cast a shadow over the future of democratic rule in Sri Lanka. One of them is the growth of ethnic conflict between the Sinhalese and the Tamils. The two communities are divided not only by language and culture but also by memories of conflicts in the past. These divisions did not prevent cooperation between the elites of the two groups at the time of independence. However, in the decade that followed, the demand of the minority Tamils that their language should have equal official status with Sinhala was rejected by the majority Sinhalese and Sinhalese politicians were forced by pressure from rank and file to advocate that Sinhalese should be the sole official language of Sri Lanka. The status accorded to language was close to the hearts of both communities for it not only symbolised the survival of their respective cultures but also represented an avenue to state employment and access to the lucrative professions. Extremist politicians on both sides were quick to rouse each group against the other. Hostility grew and the conflict broadened into other areas such as employment, education and land grants. Four major ethnic riots—in 1958, 1977, 1981 and 1983—drove the communities further apart. From the mid-1970s extremist Tamil groups began to resort to arms and virtually all these Tamil groups began to campaign for the establishment of a separate Tamil state of Eelam in the north and east of the island. Tamil guerilla units began to attack banks and government institutions. They were financed by expatriate Tamil groups living in the West and found a ready sanctuary in the neighbouring Indian state of Tamil Nadu. Increased violence led to further hardening of attitudes and imposition of anti-terrorist legislation which abridged some fundamental rights. A political solution to the Sinhalese-Tamil conflict seems to be a pre-requisite not only to the survival of democracy but also to the unimpeded economic development of Sri Lanka.

The second major problem is that of economic growth and redistribution. The first thirty years after independence saw successive governments attempting to increase production in the domestic agricultural sector and to promote import substitution industries. From about 1958 this policy was combined with an expansion of state control over the economy including increasingly rigid import control and exchange control mesures and a state takeover of the plantations producing export crops. The result was a low level of foreign investment and a slow rate of economic growth. Much of what economic growth was achieved was eroded by a rapidly rising population. All governments, however, maintained an extensive welfare system including free education and health facilities and subsidised food. However, throughout these thirty years unemployment grew apace and when international trade was disrupted in the early 1970s with sudden increases in the prices of fuel and grains, the government was forced to cut back on welfare programmes and faced increased discontent among the people.

A major change of policy was inaugurated by the government elected to power in 1977. This government continued to invest heavily in developing domestic agriculture. However, private foreign investment was encouraged, particularly in the field of industry, and restrictions on trade were largely dismantled. It was hoped that this policy would increase employment, stimulate the development of new exports and eliminate the scarcities and shortages that had been the rule in Sri Lanka from the early 1960s.

In some ways the new policy has led to positive results. Unemployment has fallen and the net growth rate after 1978 has been more than double what it was in the previous decade. On the other hand, while many groups appear to have benefited by the quickening of the economy, the widening gap between the rich and the poor seems to give increased scope for political discontent.

Today, as in the past, Sri Lanka is making an effort to adapt what it receives from the outside world to suit local circumstances. It is also seeking to overcome internal divisions and tensions. Many of Sri Lanka's reactions to these problems are influenced by its heritage from the past. History is certainly not the sole determinant of current attitudes but it provides a perspective which influences the actions of both individuals and groups. It is for this reason that a knowledge of Sri Lankan history could well be a key to understanding much of what is happening in the country today.

The Early Settlements

The earliest days of man in Sri Lanka are shrouded by the mists of antiquity. The ancient chronicles, such as the *Dipavamsa* written in the fourth century A.D. and the *Mahavamsa* composed some time later, recount the island's history from the time of the North Indian colonisation of Sri Lanka about the fifth century B.C. The North Indian settlers are said to have encountered spirits—*yaksas* and *nagas*—but no human beings. Yet prehistoric archaeology proves beyond doubt that man had arrived and had lived in the island long before the North Indian migration. Sir Lanka is separated from South India only by a narrow stretch of sea. The beaches on most of the north-east and north-west coasts of Sri Lanka are open and inviting. They are occasionally broken by the estuaries of rivers, and rivers in those days provided the easiest access inland either by various types of river craft or along the river bank.

Specific evidence relating to the earlier inhabitants, however, is very meagre. There are just a few objects which might relate to the Old Stone Age. Evidence in India seems to indicate that man lived there some 500,000 years ago and that he could have arrived in Sri Lanka soon after this, but there is no firm evidence on which we can base the date of the arrival of *homo sapiens* in Sri Lanka. We are on much firmer ground when we come to the later stone cultures. Skeletal remains and some implements of stone and bone have enabled archaeologists to build up a picture of what is generally known as the 'Balangoda cultures'. This culture prevailed over most of the island from perhaps 10,000 B.C. to the sixth century B.C. and indeed survived in the remoter forested regions of the island up to the Christian era. The Balangoda man had Australoid characteristics and lived in caves. He evidently knew how to make fire but originally seems to have eaten his food—including meat—without cooking. At some point in the first millennium B.C. the Balangoda man seems to have acquired some knowledge of agriculture, the art of pottery, the ability to shape stone tools and the technique of drilling. By this time their culture resembled that of the people living in neighbouring South India and there was probably considerable interaction across the Palk Straits.

There has been some speculation that, apart from settlers from India, Sri Lanka might have been colonised by people of the Hoabinhian culture of South-East Asia. It is known that people of this ancient culture invented the outrigger canoe by about 4000 B.C. and found their way by accident or design to islands in South-East and East Asia. In the west they reached Madagascar perhaps by the end of the first millennium B.C. It is possible that these people would have touched at Sri Lanka and even settled on its coasts. However, no definite trace of such settlement has yet been found.

The coming of the North Indians was a fearsome blow to the people of the Balangoda culture. The newcomers had iron tools and were traders and sedentary agriculturists. The older community had to adopt new ways or retire even further inland to the forests. There is little doubt that many were absorbed by the newcomers but some continued their livelihood by haunting and probably evolved to become the Vadda community which has lived as a group of hunters down to the present century.

The *Mahavamsa,* the most important of the early chronicles, records the coming of the North Indians in some detail. According to this account the immigration was led by Vijaya, son of Sinhabahu, ruler of Sinhapura in Latadesa. The conduct of Vijaya and his companions had so incensed Sinhabahu that he placed them on a ship and sent them to exile. Vijaya and his companions are said to have met with a hostile reception at a port on the west coast of India and to have eventually landed in Sri Lanka near Puttalam. Relieved at making a safe landing, they are said to have touched the earth and found that their palms became red through contact with the soil. They, therefore, named the landing place Tambapanni or 'copper-coloured hand', and this name was later used to denote the whole island.

Whether Vijaya himself was a historical figure is open to some doubt. His very name signifies 'victory' and might well symbolise the successful migration of North Indians to Sri Lanka but this itself is an important item of information. By the sixth century B.C., the Indo-Aryans had established themselves in the Indo-Gangetic Plain in India and had penetrated into some areas of the Deccan, south of the Vindhya mountain range. They had developed a complex social organisation with a division of people into the four basic *varnas* or castes. Though wheat was grown in some of the drier areas, they had developed a widespread cultivation of rice. The use of metal was well known and the iron plough was in common use. Though most Aryans lived in villages, trading centres had developed and trade and communications were flourishing both along the river valleys and the coastal areas. The Vijayan legend gives a distinct indication that these Aryans had made their way along the coast to Sri Lanka by about the fifth century B.C. The name of the port where Vijaya met with a hostile reception, variously identified as Supparaka (Sopara, north of Bombay) or Bharukaccha (Broach), together with other evidence seems to indicate that one wave of the initial migration was from north-west India.

The *Mahavamsa* itself seems to provide evidence that settlers arrived from the north-eastern parts of India too. It reports that Vijaya, towards the end of his reign, sent message requesting his younger brother to come to Sri Lanka to assume power but the latter who had already become king at Sinhapura was unwilling to come and sent his youngest son, Panduvasudeva, instead. Panduvasudeva himself arrived safely and is said to have succeeded Vijaya as king but the significant fact in this acount is that Panduvasudeva is said to have landed at Gokanna (Trincomalee). Gokanna, which has one of the finest natural harbours in the world, was a natural gateway to the island from the eastern coast of India and some historians have interpreted the Panduvasudeva legend as the symbolic representation of a parallel migration from north-east India. These are probably the people who brought the word *ganga*, the name of the chief river in north-east India, and used it as a generic name for rivers.

These initial groups of North Indian migrants were probably supplemented by another stream of migrants who settled in the south, probably on the banks of the Walave Ganga. All these early migrants may well have been grouped in various clans—for in ancient Sri Lanka we do hear of various clans or groups—the Lambakannas, Moriyas, Taracchas, Balibhojakas and so on. These clan names appear to have had a totemistic origin. For example, the Moriyas used the peacock as their emblem. It has been suggested that in course of time the strongest of these clans—the Sinhalas or the people of the lion—appear to have gained dominance and in time the whole group of migrants became known as the Sinhalas or the Sinhalas.

Others have advanced alternative explanations. For example, it has been convincingly argued that the term 'Sihala' was initially used for the ruling family and that it was only in course of time that the others acquired the Sinhala identity. According to this view the extension of the Sinhala identity over all the settler groups took well over a millennium. At the early stages Sinhala consciousness was merely that of a social group. This could explain why the *Mahavamsa* reports that Vijaya accepted Kuveni, daughter of a local chief, as his first consort. The *Mahavamsa*, of course, does record that Kuveni was eventually rejected and exiled, but significantly Vijaya's second consort was a princess from South India, the daughter of the Pandyan ruler of Madura. This Pandyan princess is reported to have brought a number of maidens as wives for Vijaya's followers. These stories seem to indicate that whatever was the origin of the Sinhala identity the people whom it eventually encompassed were not just settlers from North India alone but also the product of some intermarriage with the earlier inhabitants of Sri Lanka and with migrants from South India.

Indeed, there is some archaeological evidence from excavations made around Pomparippu in north-west Sri Lanka that the South Indian Megalithic culture had considerable influence over that region of the island at least by the third century B.C. The style of urn burials, the pottery and other objects found in Pomparippu are similar to objects found at the Adichchanallur site across the Gulf of Mannar in India. While cultural influence does not necessarily imply migration or intermarriage, it is important to remember that time the ethnic identities of these groups of people were not developed strongly enough to keep them distinct. Another feature of the Vijayan legend is the emphasis on settlement by groups of colonists led by warrior chiefs. This is quite likely to have happened. However, some historians point to the possibility of settlement originating as a result of trading connections. By the fifth century B.C. important seaports had developed both on the eastern and the western coasts of India. The pearls found in the shallow seas of the Gulf of Mannar as well as the precious stones—chiefly sapphires and rubies—found washed down the river beds in central Sri Lanka seem to have attracted merchants from early times. The early references to the island in Buddhist Sanskrit literature term it *Ratnadipa* or the 'land of gems' while one of the oldest stories relating to settlement records that the island was colonised, not by a prince called Vijaya but by a merchant called

Sinhala. It is more than possible that trading settlements supplemented or even preceded those of colonists.

Finally, we may conclude our analysis of the Vijayan legend by noting that Vijaya is supposed to have landed in Sri Lanka at the exact time of passing away of the Buddha. The *Mahavamsa* records that the Buddha predicted that Buddhism would be established in Sri Lanka and protected there. It also records that the Buddha himself visited the island thrice in his lifetime. The authors of the *Mahavamsa* were Buddhist monks (*bhikkhus*) and they were naturally at pains to emphasise the special role of Sri Lanka and the Sinhalese in fostering Buddhism. This theme of the close connection between the island, the Sinhalese and Buddhism was repeated in the course of the island's long history and became a key element in the island's tradition.

Introduction of Buddhism

The chronicle would have us believe that Buddhism was introduced to Sri Lanka in the reign of King Devanampiyatissa (250-210 B.C.), over two hundred years after North Indian migrants arrived. It is almost certain that these migrants had originally brought some form of Brahmanism with them. The earlier inhibitants of the island had of course adhered to various forms of primitive religions.

Buddhism itself originated in North India, Siddharta Gautama (563-483 B.C.), the son of a Kshatriya prince of the Sakya tribe who was disillusioned by a life of luxury was its founder, Gautama left his palace at the age of thirtyfour to seek salvation. After six years of extreme asceticism he became convinced that neither extreme indulgence nor its opposite was the way to salvation. After a long period of meditation he finally worked out the Middle Path. From then on he was known as the Enlightened One.

He preached that life was suffering and that suffering was caused by desire. Thus the cessation of suffering could be achieved only by the cessation of desire or covetousness. The ony way to end desire was to follow the eightfold path of right views, concepts, speech, conduct, livelihood, effort, mindfulness and meditation. This would lead to *nirvana* or freedom from the cycle of rebirth. The popularity of Buddhism in India rose from a combination of factors. Its message was clear and rational. It provided a path of salvation through one's own efforts without any need of intercession by priests. It thus provided the perfect foil to the ritualistic practices of Brahmanical priests in India at that time. Moreover, while Buddhism accepted the doctrine of *karma*, it also held that real nobility was a matter not of birth but of purity of mind. The Buddha accepted disciples from all castes. They were required to give up all their worldly wealth, live a calibate life and wear garments made from rags and dyed in saffron (so as to make them unattractive). Their mission was to be to seek to understand the way to salvation and to show it to others, and they were to live with what food they received from begging.

The members of the Buddhist Order were known as *bhikkhus* or mendicants and the order itself as the *bhikkhu-sangha* or association of mendicants. However, though no individual *bhikkhu* could accept and own property, the *sangha* as a body could accept gifts. Before long it was given parks and residences. A body of rules or *vinaya* was also formulated to ensure that the original parity of the *sangha* was not vitiated.

In the two centuries after the passing away of the Buddha Buddhism spread to many parts of India and it is possible that Buddhists visited and even settled in parts of Sri Lanka. However, we have no evidence of this. Meanwhile, in India schisms had arisen within the *sangha*. Buddhist tradition records that Councils were held from time to time to ensure the purity of the doctrine and the *vinaya* and in the second such Council there appears to have arisen a split between the *Sthaviras* (elders) and the *Maha-sangikas* (members of the Great Order). At the Third Council held at Pataliputra in 250 B.C. the *Sthaviras* managed to exclude their rivals and this led to the eventual schism between the more orthodox Theravada sect and the Mahayanists who laid greater emphasis on the ideal of the *bodhisattva*—the Buddha-to-be—towards which all were supposed to strive. One of the results of the Third Council was a missionary effort to convert outlying regions and one such mission was that sent to Sri Lanka.

The Buddhist tradition strongly links Asoka, the ruler of most of India with this missionary effort. Asoka had become a convert to Buddhism after he saw the havoc caused by the war in which he had defeated the Kalingas; although he remained a monarch tolerant of all religions in his empire, he supported the Buddhist missionary effort. His own son (or brother) Mahinda has deputed to bring the doctrine to Sri Lanka and won a great initial advantage by converting King Devanampiyatissa. The religion spread swiftly and by the first century B.C. was the major religion in the island. During the reign of Devanampiyatissa himself, Sangamitta, a daughter of King Asoka, brought the Buddhist Order of Nuns to Sri Lanka. A sapling of the Bo-Tree under which the Buddha attained enlightenment was also sent with Sangamitra to Sri Lanka and planted amidst great ceremony at Anuradhapura. Devanampiyatissa himself donated a royal park, Mahamegha near the capital city and this resulted in the founding of the Mahavihara which developed as the major centre of orthodox Buddhism in Sri Lanka. Another important Buddhist centre grew up around the caves of Mihintale where Mahinda and his disciples originally resided.

Origin

The *Mahavamsa* (begun in the 6th century A.D.) and its sequel, the *Culavamsa,* chronicle Sri Lanka's early history. According to the *Mahavamsa,* before the 6th century B.C. there existed two tribes. Yakas and Nagas. Stone objects found indicate that *homo sapiens* were probably present about 500,000 B.C. in Sri Lanka. From 5,000 B.C. till about 500 B.C. a people called Balangoda practised stone-working. They dwindled with the arrival of the first settlers from India.

The Sinhalese Arrive

The first royal dynasty was started by Prince Vijaya (543-505 B.C.). This Indian price was banised from his father's North Indian kingdom because of his bullying ways. His father, Sinhabahu, was believed to be the offspring of a lion (*sinha*) and a princess, hence the name Sinha (or Sinhalese) for the race founded by Vijaya in Sri Lanka.

Vijaya landed on the northeast coast of Sri Lanka. The legend goes that a witch, Kuveni, fell in love with him. Abandoning her people, she transferred her realm to the newcomer but after they had produced two children, Vijaya decided to start a blue-blooded dynasty. He ordered Kuveni and their children into the wilderness and married a South Indian princess. His dynastic dreams, however, did not come true for him.

Vijaya therefore invited his brother to the new land, but it was a nephew who finally arrived to produce the children of the

Sinhala race. Vijaya's two children by Kuveni survived and are believed to be the ancestors of the aboriginal dwellers of Sri Lanka, the Veddhas.

Anuradhapura

What do tanks (artificial reservoirs) and monuments have in common in Sri Lanka? The answer to this riddle is that both were built by kings.

Currently, Sri Lanka is closely linked with India. Buddhism was brought to the Island by Mahinda, son of the great Mauryan Emperor Asoka in the 3rd century B.C. This was during the reign of Devanampiya Tissa whose capital was at Anuradhapura.

With the entry of Buddhism Sri Lanka's Classical Era began. Art, architecture and stone sculpture flourished. Immense hemispheres called *dagoba* were built to enshrine relics of the Buddha. They are venerated even today and never fail to inspire the beholder, being simple in shape, serene in appearance and magnificant in size.

This ancient civilisation of Sri Lanka emerged in the island's dry zone, the extensive north central plains and a smaller area in the southeast. At the same time that temples were being erected and exquisite statues carved out of solid rock, irrigation reservoirs and channels were being constructed. An ingenious tank covering 4,560 acres was built by King Mahasena (A.D. 274–302). Approximately 200 years later King Datusena (A.D. 460–478), built the Kalawewa (*wewa* means "tank"), a reservoir covering seven square miles with a dam three miles long and 36–58 feet high. Little did he realise then that it would one day be his grave.

The Tamils

During Devanampiya Tissa's reign in the 3rd century B.C., a large number of Hindu Brahmins whom the Sinhalese called Bamilas arrived in Sri Lanka. The word "Tamil" is derived from *Bamila*. They spoke a Dravidian language and did not convert to Buddhism.

In the 2nd century B.C., the kingship of Anuradhapura fell into Tamil hands. One of the Tamil kings, Elara, tried to unite the Sinhalese and the Tamils. Elara's kingdom co-existed peacefully for a time with a Sinhalese kingdom in the south ruled by the father of a prince called Gamini. When Gamini proclaimed himself King Dutugemunu, he routed the Tamil chieftains and King Elara. After ruling from Anuradhapura for a period, he turned deeply religious and devoted himself to building monasteries and temples at Anuradhapura and elsewhere.

Tamil rule prevailed now and then when the Pandyans, Cholas and other invaders from India swept across the land. The central hills and southern areas, however, never came under Tamil Rule. The northern part of Sri Lanka remains a Tamil stronghold.

Sigiriya

A violent king, yet dear to the Sri Lankan heart, is Kasyapa, eldest son of King Datusena of Anuradhapura. Kasyapa was afraid his half-brother, Mugullan, would inherit the throne because Mugullan's mother was a princess whereas his own mother was a commoner. He killed his father by walling him in the very tank he had built, Kalawewa. Seizing the throne, Kasyapa built himself a palace fortress on Sigiriya, a tall plateau-like rock, to protect himself from the anger of the rightful heir.

Halfway up the sheer rock face are wonderful frescoes: paintings of beautiful women, some holding lotus flowers. Beside the hewn steps winding up the rock to the palace fortress is a remarkable feature, a lime-coated wall which has a mirrored surface to protect the climber moving up or down the hewn steps. Sigiriya's mirrored wall carries graffiti of crisp verses written by visitors down the ages either in praise or ridicule of the bare-bosomed fresco beauties.

Polonnaruwa

The seat of the kingdom moved from Anuradhapura to Polonnaruwa. King Parakrama Bahu I (A.D. 1153-56), a Sinhalese king, gained control of nearly the entire island. During his reign several Buddhist shrines and monuments were added to Polonnaruwa. King Parakrama Bahu I is best remembered for the tank he constructed, Parakrama Samudra (Sea of Parakrama), of which he said, "Let not a drop of water flow into the sea before it is used in the service of man."

Then with the decline of the Classical Era, kings moved their capitals to various places on the island, until finally the last kings had their capital in Kandy in the hill country. This remained the capital till the middle of the 19th century, in the British era.

Sri Lanka lies at the southern tip of India. In the days of sailing vessels its position was immensely important, straddling as it did the major sea routes.

The island shares the same continental shelf with India and is a mere 30 miles away from its gigantic neighbour. Romantics call Sri Lanka the "Teardrop of India." To the south of the island is the vast Indian Ocean, and to its east is the Bay of Bengal.

Roughly pear-shaped, Sri Lanka measures 270 miles from Point Pedro in the north to Dongra Head at the southernmost tip; and 140 miles from its eastern to its western coast. It covers an area of 25,332 square miles.

Geologists believe that Sri Lanka lay beneath the sea. A series of earthquakes probably thrust the island up, producing in the process a terrain of central hills crowned with mountains whose sides plunge sharply down to valleys below. The highest point is Pidurutalagala (8,329 feet). The central hills are surrounded by plains, very broad ones in the north and fairly narrow in the south.

Rivers, Falls and Tanks

Most of the rivers start in the central hills and radiate outward, seeking the sea. The largest river is Mahaweli Ganga (208 miles) and the smallest is Gal Oya (67 miles). In their journey the rivers of Sri Lanka tumble over rock faces, forming waterfalls. The most famous is the Diyaluma, the world's sixth highest waterfall with a drop of 670 feet. Its name is derived from *diyahaluma,* which is Sinhala for "spilling waters." The waterfall best known for its legends is the Dunhinda, which is believed to be full of mysterious caverns and treacherous depths.

Sri Lanka's rivers were tamed by the Sinhalese kings. Through marvelous feats of hydraulic engineering, they turned arid scrubland into fertile fields, earning for Sri Lanka the title of "Granary of the East." Among the many man-made lakes, called tanks, are some dating from the Anuradhapura period over 2,000 years ago. The latest hydroelectricity project is the Mahaweli, begun by the government in the 1980s.

Legendary Waterfalls

Sri Lanka's grand waterfalls have inspired poets, painters, musicians and naturally storytellers. A few of the waterfalls are described below.

The turbulent waters of *Dunhinda Falls* wash over a number of fantastic beings. One is a beautiful fish who wears a golden earring (totally ignoring the fact that fish do not have earlobes) and surfaces only once a year. It swims over the buried treasure of

Kumarasinghe, the prince of Uva, which is guarded by men armed with gold swords. Swimmers must beware as these guardians look for a human sacrifice once a year. The most romantic legend of Dunhinda Falls is the one about the princess from the Gampola dynasty who eloped with a commoner. The unfortunate couple was down to a village near the falls. Determined not to be separated, they fled to the highest ledge of he falls and jumped to their death. That night, a terrible storm wiped out the surrounding villages. The shrieks of the lovers are heard even today when storms reach their peak—so they say.

Lover's Leap in Nuwara Eliya has its source in Pidurutalagala, Sri Lanka's tallest peak. This waterfall is haunted by the ghosts of another runaway couple, who jumped to avoid an angry father.

The aptly named *Laxapana*, derived from *laksapahana* (Sinhala for "a million lights"), generates power for a hydroelectric project which supplies the island's electricity. *Bridal falls* is the name given to St. Clair Falls in Talawakelle whose waters resemble a bride's veil.

Baker's Falls is named after Sir Samuel Baker, the famous explorer who discovered the Nile. He founded an experimental farm in Sri Lanka where he introduced vegetables.

Climate

Sri Lanka's climate is tropical, that is, mostly hot and wet. Temperatures in the northwest reach 100°F and higher, while Nuwara Eliya, a town nestling in the central hills, the mercury hovers around 50°F. Humidity is high in some places, making daytime unpleasant. Nights are generally cooler and in the hot and dry arid zones nights are delightful, preceded by balmy evenings. From December to January, the entire island has a welcome break from the heat, the hill country enjoying an almost temperature climate. The hottest months are March and April; the driest is February.

The island is divided into the wet and dry zones, with an arid zone that is even drier than the dry zone. The wet zone includes the western, southern and central hills which face the rain-carrying southwestly winds. The wind, after shedding its rain, blows across the eastern plains as the dehydrating *kachchan* winds. The southwest monsoon, active from May through August, is the major rain-giver. The northeast monsoon brings rain to the northern and eastern areas from October through January. It brings less rain than the southwest monsoon but sometimes causes floods and wreaks havoc.

Everything Sprouts Green

The first impression a visitor gets is green in all its hues, blazing here and there with the brilliant crimson of bougainvillea and flame-of-the-forest. The island has its brown patches, which sadly increase with deforestation. Much of the land is under cultivation. The Sinharaja is a primeval forest with thick undergrowth and tall trees. It is home to the fast disappearing Vesak orchid and is now a protected area.

The vegetation, the result of climate and relief, varies from the dense tropical evergreen rainforest of the lowland wet zone and the mangroves of the coastal areas to the thorny trees of the dry zone and the tough grasslands called *patana,* dotted with red rhododendron.

Animal Life

Sri Lanka is famous for its wildlife, despite the fact that many animal species have been pushed by extensive land cultivation to the few remaining forests. There, particularly in Sri Lanka's national parks, they can be observed in their natural environment.

The two biggest national parks are the Ruhuna (popularly called Yala) in the southeast and the Wilpattu National Park in the northwest. Ruhuna National Park is a semi-arid thorny scrub forest while Wilpattu is a lush, thick secondary forest. Three other parks are the Gal Oya, Uda Walawe and Lahugala national parks. At the Lahugala Tank (artificial reservoir) in Lahugala National Park, elephant grass grows wild. Herds of wild elephants are drawn to this sanctuary on their migration through the island.

Some of the animals in Sri Lanka's national parks are the Asian elephant, the spotted leopard, the sloth bear, three species of monkey (the shy gray, black-faced langur, the aggressive brownish red macaque and the rarely seen ape called the purple-faced leaf or bear monkey), and several species of deer including the elk, barking deer, spotted deer and mousedeer. The reptile family in Sri Lanka is represented by the crocodile of jungle tanks and rivers, the monitor lizard near rivers of the dry zone, and the iguana. There are also several snake varieties.

More than 400 species of indigenous and migrant birds are found in Sri Lanka, the prettiest preferring the woody areas. Thus, in the Yala National Park one may see the beautiful peacock dance in the right season (December to May). Among the indigenous birds are the Ceylon lorikeet and the Ceylon blue magpie.

Cities

Colombo. The capital city of Sri Lanka, which is also its commercial and maritime centre, lies on the western coast. The harbor, enlarged and built up, bustles with merchant and cargo vessels. The international airport at Katunayake, a 30-minute drive from Colombo, has recently been revamped to meet international standards.

Colombo teems and steams, sweats and toils. Slums have grown up a stone's throw away from five-star hotels and palatial private residences. Sleek, air-conditioned limousines maneuvre for road space with belching, groaning buses. At one street corner a visitor may have his or her pockets picked, and at another meet the friendliest and warmest smiles.

A few miles east of Colombo lies Kotte, the ancient royal capital. There, at Sri Jayewardenepura, is the new parliamentary complex tranquilly sited in the Diyawanne Oya.

Kandy. The seat of the last kings of Sri Lanka is 72 miles from Colombo. Though cooler and more beautiful than Colombo, it is no less congested.

Galle and Trincomalee. Galle on the southwestern coast and Trincomalee to the northeast are natural harbors. Both are quaint and Dutch-fortressed, with a distinctly sleepy air. Trincomalee is the site of a major historical attraction, Swami Rock. The ruins of a *kovil* (Hindu temple) sit squarely on the top of the rock, which has a sheer drop to the deep blue sea below. Closenburg in Galle is a swimmer's paradise and another tourist attraction.

Jaffna. The principal city in the northernmost part of Sri Lanka is, like the peninsula that bears the same name, unique and very different from the rest of the island. It is where most Sri Lankan Tamils have their roots. Crossing Elephant Pass, the narrow bit of land that joins the Jaffna peninsula to the main island, is like entering another country. The palmyrah palms take the place of the "texture of coco-nuttery" (in the words of the English landscape painter, Edward Lear) of the rest of the island. Closely enclosed

Table 2
Population of Sri Lanka by Ethnic Groups (in thousands)

	1946		*1953*		*1963*		*1971*		*1981*	
	Number	*Per cent*	*Number*	*Per cent*	*Number*	*Per cent*	*Number*	*Per cent*	*Number*	*Per cent*
Low country Sinhalese	2,902.5	43.6	3,469.5	42.8	4,470.3	42.2	5,425.8	42.8	10,985.7	74.0
Kandyan Sinhalese	1,718.0	25.8	2,147.2	26.5	3,042.6	28.8	3,705.5	29.2		
Sri Lanka Tamils	73.3	11.0	884.7	10.9	1,164.7	11.0	1,424.0	11.2	1,871.5	12.6
Indian Tamils	780.6	11.7	974.1	12.0	1,123.0	10.6	1,174.6	9.3	825.2	5.6
Sri Lanka Moors	373.6	5.6	464.0	5.7	626.8	5.9	828.3	6.5	1057.0	7.1
Indian Moors	35.6	0.5	47.5	0.6	55.4	0.5	27.4	0.2		
Burglers and Eurasians	41.9	0.6	46.0	0.6	45.9	0.4	45.4	0.4	38.2	0.3
Malays	22.5	0.3	25.4	0.3	33.4	0.3	43.5	0.3	43.4	0.3
Others	48.9	0.7	29.5	0.5	19.9	0.2	15.5	0.1	29.0	0.2
Total	6,657.3	100.0	8,097.9	100.0	10,582.0	100.0	12,689.9	100.0	14,850.0	100.0

Sources: *Statistical Abstract of the Democratic Socialist Republic of Sri Lanka*, 1979, pp. 38, 41: *Preliminary Report of the Census of 1981*, p. 3.

houses and compounds with intricate cadjan fences made of palmyrah leaves replace the more open and less organised homesteads of the rest of the island.

Adam's Peak. Sri Pada or Adam's Peak rises 7,360 feet as a colonial rock in Maskeliya in the central hills. It is visible even from Colombo on a clear day. At night from December through March it is visible as a string of lights reaching almost to the sky.

On the summit is a giant footprint variously attributed to Adam, the Buddha and Shiva. Adam is supposed to have been compelled to stand on one foot at this spot after his expulsion from Paradise (a double punishment for the poor man). The Buddha, according to a legend, rested here during one of his three visits to the island. No one, however, believes it is his footprint since Buddha was only mortal. Claim is laid on behalf of the Hindu god Shiva too. Hence the peak is venerated and visited by Christians, Moslems, Buddhists and Hindus. To further enhance its religious role, Adam's Peak is the site of a *dagoba* or Buddhist temple, a shrine, and a temple to the god Saman.

Three routes lead to the summit. The easiest and most popular is a two-mile climb through tea estates and rocky terrain followed by another two-mile trek up sheer rock-hewn steps. The trekker passes a Japanese peace shrine (for luck, discarding a needle and a ball of thread), souvenir kiosks and restrooms. Even water is sold, the price escalating as one's climbing stamina decreases!

Most people climb through the night to reach the summit at dawn—in time for the spectacular sunrise which throws the shadow of the peak across mountain and plain for miles beyond. The wonder is that so many (standing) can be accommodated on the pinnacle top. A bell tolls continuously as pilgrims register the number of times they have climbed the peak by tugs at the bell-rope.

Ethnic Groups

The major ethnic group in Sri Lanka today is the Sinhalese. They comprise 74 per cent of the population (1981 Census figures—see Table 2) and are descended partly from migrants who arrived from North India as early as around 500 B.C. However, in time these migrants became considerably intermixed with the original proto-austroloid inhabitants of Sri Lanka and absorbed many later migrants from both North and South India. They are thus biologically mixed group. The Sinhalese identity as it gradually evolved became centred round two factors—the Sinhalese language and the Buddhist religion. The relative importance of the two factors has changed with time, but even today some 93 per cent of all Sinhalese are Buddhists and there are few non-Sinhalese Buddhists in Sri Lanka—thus strengthening the concept of a Sinhalese Buddhist identity.

The Sinhalese are broadly divided into the Low Country Sinhalese, who comprise about 60 per cent of the group, and the Kandyan Sinhalese, who make up the rest. This distinction arose as a result of the prolonged Western occupation of the south-west coast which exposed the Low Country Sinhalese to Westernization and modernisation, while the Kandyans remained a more conservative group defending indigenous tradition and culture. In the past few decades, with increasing internal migration, this distinction has tended to become less valid and less important, though by and large there is a higher percentage of Buddhists among the Kandyan Sinhalese than among the Low Country Sinhalese.

The most important ethnic minority in the country are the Tamils, of whom the Sri Lanka Tamils (12.6 per cent of the population in 1981) are partly descendants of immigrants who arrived in Sri Lanka in very early times. Like the Sinhalese the Tamil community has grown through the ages by the absorption of later immigrant groups to the island. The Tamil element in Sri Lanka increased substantially with the arrival of the Indian Tamils largely in the late nineteenth and early twentieth centuries. Since the Indian Tamil community came largely as workers first for the coffee and then later for the tea and rubber estates in the highlands, they have also been called up-country Tamils. By 1921 the Tamils in Sri Lanka made up 24.8 per cent of the total population; of this percentage over half, 13.4 per cent, were Indian Tamils.

The physical isolation of the Indian Tamils in the largely Sinhalese areas has delayed their fusion with the Sri Lankan Tamil community. However, the proportion of those who identify themselves as Indian Tamils has fallen rapidly in the last two decades partly due to the absorption of many of them into the Sri Lanka Tamil community and partly due to the repatriation of about 300,000 Indian Tamils to India in the last twenty years. By 1981 Indian Tamils in Sri Lanka acounted only for 5.6 per cent of the total population. Over 85 per cent of both groups of Tamils are Hindus.

The other important ethnic minority are the Moors. The Moors of Sri Lanka have no direct connection with the people of North Africa from whom they derive their name. They are called Moors mainly because the Portuguese gave this name to all the Islamic communities they encountered on the Indian Ocean littoral. The Moors of Sri Lanka are really descendants of Arab, Russian and Indian settlers who intermarried with the local people of the areas they came to live in. In time, they moved from the seaports to villages in the interior and today they include a large agricultural community on the eastern coast of Sri Lanka. They make up over 7 per cent of the total population and virtually all of them are Muslims. They are linked by religion to a small community of Malays who form just 0.3 per cent of the total population. The Malays are descendants of Javanese and Malay immigrants who arrived largely during the time of Western colonial rule. (see Table 2).

Two other small groups remain to be considered. The larger of the two are the Burghers—descendants of European settlers, many of whom intermarried with other ethnic groups. The Burghers were an influential community during colonial rule and made up about 0.6 per cent of the total population at the time of independence in 1948. Since then, however, immigration, chiefly to Australia, Canada and the United Kingdom has reduced their numbers and by 1981 they made up only 0.3 per cent of the total population and had lost most of their power and influence.

Finally, there are the Vaddas—descendants of the proto-austroloid peoples who were in Sri Lanka before the arrival of the Sinhalese and the Tamils. These people lived for many centuries as hunters but have now become agriculturists and have been largely absorbed by the Sinhalese and the Tamils. Those who continue to call themselves Vaddas live largely in the north-central and eastern parts of the country and number less than a few thousand.

By and large, contemporary relations amongst these different ethnic groups hve been peaceful. The exception has been the growing tension between the Sinhalese and Tamil communities, especially between the Sinhalese and the Sri Lanka Tamils. The two communities have gradually drawn apart in the last three decades leading to a bid for secession by the Sri Lanka Tamils of the north and the east.

Both the Sinhalese and the Tamils are divided by caste. Today, however, caste is significant only in two major areas—marriage and politics. Caste groups are largely endogamous, though intercaste marriage is becoming increasingly common. Caste linkages are also used by politicians as a means of mobilizing popular support. It is likely that the rise of ethnic tension and ethnic consciousness has muted caste conflict in Sri Lanka.

2

Education and Employment

From a gender perspective, education is widely perceived to be one of the 'success stories' of Sri Lanka. Employment is seen as an area of relative failure in which the majority of women could not achieve the benefits they anticipated from education. As this perception implies, education and employment are interrelated, both in holistic framework of human development and in the narrower focus of the development and utilisation of human resources. Development in both education and employment cannot be isolated from the socio-economic and political context in which women have lived in the past five decades. Women made significant social gains in the 'welfare state' of the immediate post-independence decades. The shift to a closed economy in the 1970s, and to an open economy with an agenda of growth without equitable distribution in the 1980s, exacerbated the social exclusion of the poor, particularly of women in low-income families. Women were caught up in the frustrated aspirations of the beneficiaries of education, the widening fissures in the social fabric created by ethnic tensions, and the trauma of violence, displacement and deprivation caused by the youth insurgencies of 1971 and 1987-89 in the south and the ethnic war in the north and east since the mid-1980s.

External forces, both positive and negative, has impinged on women's lives in Sri Lanka. For instance, globalisation and its corollary, economic interdependence, have incorporated more and more women in the international labour market on unequal terms. Gender became an international issue only in the 1970s. But a succession of international conferences and activities from 1975 onwards and international instruments such as the UN Convention on the Elimination of All Forms of Discrimination Against Women have contributed to the increasing visibility of women's issues in the country. The Women's Charter, formulated and accepted as policy in 1993, has two sections—on the right to education and on economic rights. Women were not visible in any national development plans before 1972, and while the national machinery for women's affairs has existed since 1978, gender issues have not yet been integrated in the national planning process.

It is important to note, too, that women are not a homogeneous group. Their paths from schooling to occupational mobility may be affected by class and ethnicity. However, these trends are underpinned by gendered norms and related behavioural patterns that affect all women in their interactive economic, domestic and community roles and in gender relations and resource allocation within the family.

This contexualisation of women's issues is a prelude to the broad analysis of women's experiences in education and in employment in two phases: (*a*) from political independence to the mid-1960s; and (*b*) from the late 1960s to the present. The two phases do not represent a rigid demarcation in trends. They have been identified to facilitate analysis without creating undue discontinuities.

Towards Gender Equality in Access to Education in the 1960s

Political independence in 1948 did not lead to significant changes in the education sector in Sri Lanka, as the most seminal policies had been introduced in the 1940s during the period of transition under the state council administration. Local policy makers, elected on the basis of universal franchise introduced in 1931, had sought to reduce the socio-economic, regional, ethnic and religious disparities in education secondary education attempted in 1950, 1951 and 1966 (Jaysuriya, 1969). State expenditure on education rose from 2.7 per cent to 4.6 per cent of GDP from 1950 to 1964, and to nearly 5 per cent by the end of the 1960s—the highest point during the five decades under review.

Consequently, the number of schools increased from 5,726 in 1945 to 9,550 in 1965, and there were 10,088 schools in the country in 1997. The number of co-educational schools rose from 77.6 per cent of all schools in 1945 to 89.2 per cent in 1963, and was over 90 per cent by the end of the 1960s. The number of teachers doubled between 1953 and 1963 and half these teachers were women (*Annual School Census*, 1953, 1963).

Student enrolment burgeoned during these years (Jayaweera, 1988). The participation rate of the 5-14 age group had been 57.3 per cent at the 1946 Census and less than 40 per cent of those enrolled had been girls. Gender equality was virtually achieved by 1963 with male and female participation rates of 76 per cent and 72 per cent respectively in the 5-14 age group (Table 1). Enrolment rates between 1946 and 1963 exceeded population growth rates in this age group. Gender differences in national literacy rates declined as male literacy rose from 76.5 per cent at the 1946 Census to 85.6 per cent at the 1963 Census, and female literacy from 46.2 per cent to 67.1 per cent (Table 2).

The most significant expansion took place in senior secondary education as a consequence of the cumulative impact of free education and the change in the medium of instruction in secondary education to the local languages in the 1950s. Enrolment in Grades 9-10 doubled from 1952 to 1957 and again from 1957 to 1965. Enrolment in Grades 11-12 that provided access to higher education increased sixfold during this time, and the number of candidates for the Grade 12 public examination increased from 2,026 in 1952 to 31,185 in 1965. Male and female participation rates in the 15-19 age group were 43.3 per cent and 36.6 per cent respectively in 1963 (Table 1) as compared with an overall rate of 11 per cent in 1953. By 1963, 42.9 per cent of urban girls and 33.3 per cent of the rural girls in this age group were enrolled in secondary schools. The proportion of girls in total enrolment increased from 42.4 per cent in 1946 to 46 per cent in 1963, and was 45.5 per cent in Grades 1-5, 47.2 per cent in Grades 6-10 and 47.9 per cent in Grades 11-12 in 1963. By 1963, the trend of more girls than boys being enrolled in secondary grades was already manifest in Grade 11 (50.04 per cent).

Table 1
Educational Participation Rates, 1963 (per cent)

Age Group	*Total*	*Male*	*Female*
5-11	76.2	77.6	74.6
5-14	74.4	76.7	72.0
15-19	40.0	43.3	36.6
20-24	4.6	5.3	4.0
5-19	65.2	67.7	62.5
5-24	53.8	56.2	51.3

Source: Based on *Census of Sri Lanka*, 1963, Department of Census and Statistics, Government of Sri Lanka, Colombo.

Table 2
Literacy by Sector and Sex (per cent)

	1946	*1953*	*1963*	*1971*	*1981*	*1985-86*	*1991**	*1994**
All-Island								
Total	62.8	69.0	76.8	78.5	86.5	84.2	86.9	90.1
Male	76.5	80.7	85.6	85.6	90.5	88.6	90.0	92.5
Female	46.2	55.5	67.1	70.9	82.8	80.0	83.8	87.9
Urban								
Total	76.2	82.6	87.7	86.2	93.3	89.1	93.2	93.2
Male	84.5	88.5	91.8	90.3	95.3	92.4	94.0	94.8
Female	65.7	74.1	82.7	81.5	91.0	86.1	84.3	91.8
Rural								
Total	60.1	66.4	70.1	76.2	84.5	84.6	87.1	89.5
Male	74.7	79.0	83.9	84.1	89.0	88.5	89.9	92.1
Female	43.0	52.4	63.6	67.9	79.9	80.7	84.3	87.1
Estate								
Total						59.4	66.1	
Male						74.5	79.0	
Female						45.9	52.8	

Sources: *Census of Sri Lanka*, 1946, 1953, 1963, 1971, 1981; *Labour Force and Socio-Economic Survey*, 1985-86; *Household Income and Expenditure Survey*, 1991; and *Demographic Survey*, 1994, Department of Census and Statistics, Government of Sri Lanka, Colombo.

* Excludes north and east.

Higher education saw a similar 'explosion' in the early 1960s, responding to pressure from the products of secondary schools. In 1942, the Medical College (established 1870) and University College (established 1921) set up under the colonial administration were amalgamated to form the University of Ceylon, an autonomous liberal institution, envisioned in the Oxbridge tradition to nurture an academic and professional elite. The introduction of free education had a minimal impact as entry was confined till the end of the 1950s to a limited number of applicants from English-medium secondary schools.

The use of Sinhala and Tamil as the medium of instruction in senior secondary grades from 1958-59, however, and a more liberal stance on admission to universities after the change of government in 1956, transformed the prevailing elitist ethos. The university student population increased from 2,950 in 1958 to 14,210 in 1964.

Two new universities were established in Colombo in 1959 to meet the demand, and in 1967 the University of Ceylon was restructured to form the University of Peradeniya and Colombo in order to accommodate the 'bulge'. The proportion of women students increased from 10.1 per cent in 1942 and 24.4 per cent in 1959, to 36.9 in 1966, 40.3 per cent in 1967, 43.3 per cent in 1968 and 44.4 per cent in 1970—the peak till the 1990s (Table 3). The first women students entered the veterinary science, dental, agriculture and engineering faculties in the late 1950s and early 1960s. The social composition of the university student population lost its urban bias, as 73 per cent of the men and women students were from the rural sector by 1967. The percentage of students from professional families declined from 81 in 1950 to 34 in 1967 (Strauss, 1951 Uswatte-Aratchi, 1974). Ethnic disparities created by colonial education policies declined in arts faculties.

Table 3
University Education, Demand and Supply

Year	*Grade 12 Enrolement*	*No. of Candidates GCE A/L Exam. Applicants*	*No Admitted to University*	*Percentage Entered University*	*Enrolment in University*	*Percentage Females*	*Percentage Arts-Based Courses*
1943	n.a.	350	197	56.3	904	11.5	37.2
1946	n.a.	1,171	372	31.7	1,302	13.7	39.7
1950	n.a.	1,443	438	30.3	2,036	18.7	38.5
1955	2,900	2,096	658	31.3	2,431	26.7	40.8
1959	6,173	3,938	1,189	30.0	4,039	24.4	55.0
1965	26,250	31,199	6,359	20.3	14,422	32.2	76.1
1970	23,075	30,973	3,457	10.9	11,813	44.4	71.2
1975	41,054	48,432	3,482	8.4	12,648	40.7	60.4
1979	82,973	101,015	5,255	5.2	16,032	39.9	62.8
1985	67,722	105,500	5,630	5.3	18,217	42.8	55.6
1990	105,239	120,471	8,970	7.4	31,447	42.9	49.6

Sources: Ministry of Education, *Annual Reports*, 1943-65; *Annual School Census*, 1970-90; University of Sri Lanka, *Annual Reports*, 1953-70; University Grants Commission, Planning Unit, Basic Data 1975, 1979, 1985, 1990.

What was significant in the developments in education was that a rapid increase in participation took place within a short span of time in a low-income country. Women were major beneficiaries of these changes. Only a privileged minority of girls, chiefly from western-oriented families, had a complete secondary education before the 1940s. But the central schools of the 1940s in their rural locations and the upgraded rural schools of the 1960s enabled over one-third of all rural girls, who had hitherto been denied access to senior secondary education through lack of economic resources and English proficiency, to avail themselves of educational opportunities by the early 1960s. In contrast to the ninety-one women university students from professional families in 1942, nearly 6,000 young women from middle and 'working-class' families emerged annually with university degrees in the mid-1960s. In the general population in 1963, the percentage of women who had never been to school (29.2) was still more than double that of men (13.5), but in the 15-19 age group. 9.8 per cent young men and 10 per cent young women had had at least ten years of education (*Census of Sri Lanka*, 1963).

Within this positive scenario, however, distortions in the development process had reinforced inequalities or created new inequalities. Despite the financial incentives offered by the state to promote educational participation, middle-class families were the earlier beneficiaries of free education, and poverty continued to deny both girls and boys access to education, chiefly to secondary and higher education. Retention rates among the cohort of Grade 1 entrants in 1962 were 46 per cent in Grade 6 in 1967 and 28.1 per cent in Grade 9 in 1970. In 1969, 61.9 per cent boys and 61.9 per cent girls in the 5-9 age group and 65.3 per cent boys and 64 per cent girls in the 10-14 age group from families with the lowest incomes, and 86.5 per cent boys and 85.3 per cent girls in the 5-9 age group and 70.5 per cent boys and 83.7 per cent girls in the 10-14 age group from families with the highest incomes, were enrolled in school. Both socio-economic and gender disparities were wider in particiption in the 15-19 age group—34.2 per cent boys and 25.2 per cent girls in the highest income group (*Socio-Economic Survey*, 1969-70)—perhaps pointing to both economic and socio-cultural constraints. In terms of ethnicity, for instance, in 1963, the proportion of girls in total enrolment was 47.1 per cent among the Sinhalese, 45.3 per cent among the Sri Lankan Tamils, 46 per cent among Burghers, 38.7 per cent among Moors and Malays and 37.3 per cent among Indian Tamils (*Census of Sri Lanka*, 1963). Girls were therefore disadvantaged in the Muslim and plantation communities. In the plantation community, an enclave of educational disadvantage before and after independence, 69.2 per cent boys and 49.5 per cent girls in the 10-14 age group and 20.8 per cent boys and 6.7 per cent girls in the 15-19 age group were in school in 1969, compared to national statistics of 72 per cent and 36.6 per cent girls in the two age groups respectively.

Regional imbalances in the provision of education received low priority with the abandonment of the policy of central schools in underserved locations, and inequality in the allocation of resources in favour of large and often prestigious urban denominational schools nationalised in 1960-61. The most critical imbalances were created by the expansion of mainly the arts streams in rural secondary schools, which resulted in an increase in the percentage of university students enrolled in arts faculties from 42 in 1958 to 76.1 in 1965. Secondary schools in four of the twenty-four districts in the country had no science education facilities in the late 1960s. Girls were more disadvantaged than boys by both lack of provision and course preferences influenced by socialisation in gendered norms. In 1949, 34.7 per cent of entrants to arts-based faculties and 15.2 per cent of entrants to science-based faculties were women. In 1966, 54.6 per cent of arts entrants but only 18.3 per cent of science entrants were women. The concentration of women students in the arts faculties of universities during this time had far-reaching implications for their career options.

Diversification of educational opportunities within and outside the system of general education failed to take off during these years, leaving women with largely cognitive skills fostered by an academic education. Efforts to diversify the structure of the secondary school system were not acceptable as they were likely to widen inequalities and reinforce social exclusion. Attempts to make crafts compulsory in the 1950s and agriculture in the 1960s in secondary schools failed because they were in conflict with prospects for remunerative employment.

The vocational education sector received low priority in policy direction, operating in isolation from the school system. Perceptions of gender-appropriate jobs prevented women from utilising even the limited facilities available. An agricultural school in Kundasale (established 1948) and a few practical farm schools for girls (set up in the 1960s) were hardly adequate in an agrarian society in which nearly two-thirds of the female labour force were in the agriculture sector in the 1960s. Few women were enrolled at this time in technical related courses in the Technical College established in 1893, or in the new institutions opened in the 1950s and 1960s—the Hardy Institute in 1956, junior technical schools in urban centres from 1957, and the Institute of Practical Technology in 1961 which developed into the College of Technology in 1966. Women were confined to the mobile training programmes in sewing organised by the Department of Labour in the 1950s for school dropouts and to the gender-differentiated training-cum-production courses in what were chiefly cottage industries. Vocational education during these years reinforced and even widened gender division in the labour market.

Women's Economic Activities, 1948 to the Mid-1960s: From Subsistence to Professions

Women in Sri Lanka have traditionally been economic producers, working side by side with men in fields and in domestic industries. Despite the influence of nineteenth-century colonial norms of domesticity on the upper and middle classes, the mobility of low-income women was reflected in the way many rural women moved from subsistence agriculture in landless families or families with minimal assets to enter the labour market as workers in domestic service, in factories and in petty trade, before and after independence.

The export-oriented colonial economy based on tea, rubber and coconut plantations continued to dominate in the decades after independence without significant structural changes. Ideological differences, however, led to a policy shift to a socialist perspective, state or central economic planning, and inward-oriented import substitution in industry after 1956 (Lakshman, 1997). State infrastructure expanded after 1948 with the extension of education and health services and state control of the economy. However, the fall in commodity prices in the international market from the end of the 1950s, deterioration in terms of trade and slow economic growth created resource constraints that affected employment opportunities adversely from the mid-1960s.

The access of women to employment in the two decades after independence was determined by these parameters of economic development. Women in home-based economic activities in the informal sector have been invisible in labour force statistics computed on the basis of narrow definitions of 'gainful employment'. In the 1960s, the percentage of women in the labour force in official statistics increased from 20 to 26, as a consequence of population expansion as well as of the increasing participation of women in secondary and higher education.

It appears that the majority of women continued their traditional economic activities during these years. Of the total female labour force, 62.8 per cent were in the agriculture sector at the 1963 Census. The major development strategy in this sector was the large-scale agricultural development of the dry zone through settlements—the Gal Oya Scheme in the 1950s and the Walawe Scheme in the 1960s. Women lost their traditional land rights in these settlements with the imposition of the British practice of primogeniture under the Land Development Ordinance of 1935. In these settlements, in village expansion schemes, and in their small plots, in cultivation off paddy land, *chenas* (slash and burn cultivation) and home gardens or in wage labour, there was no change in the economic activities and lives of women. Among the immigrant plantation families in colonial economic enclaves, women comprised half the labour force but continued to receive unequal wages for equal work with men, and had a poor quality of life in a male-dominated domestic environment.

In the underdeveloped industry sector left behind by the colonial administration, women were engaged chiefly in traditional, home-based, gender-differentiated economic activities, such as the coir industry, working with primitive equipment in low-skill, low-income tasks. The women's societies established in villages by the Department of Rural Development from 1954 onwards domesticated them in consonance with the gender role assumptions of policy makers. The only new development was the reliance on import substitution industries—the large capital-intensive state industries, and the smaller industries which offered some employment opportunities for women. The most significant of these was the handloom industry, which was virtually feminised in the mid-1960s by the distribution of a large number of looms to women producers and the establishment of handloom training and production centres in villages. For large numbers of rural girls from secondary schools who joined these centres, handloom weaving became their life-line over the next decade (Jayaweera, 1998).

The immediate impact of the increasing access of girls to secondary and higher education was, however, the entry of women in large numbers in professional and middle-level jobs in the services sector, jobs which had expanded with the growth of state infrastructure in the social and economic sectors. Two trends need to be noted. Educated women in families with economic resources 'escaped' from the conventional lives of their mothers, circumscribed by the limits of domesticity, to urban-based employment. Women in rural and less affluent families emerging from universities and secondary schools in the early 1960s achieved upward socio-economic mobility in professional and middle-level employment. As early as in 1953, 38.7 per cent of the labour force in professional and semi-professional employment consisted of women.

The majority of these women continued to seek entry to conventional jobs in the health and education services, associated culturally with their ascribed servicing and nurturing roles. But they began during this period to seek entry also to high-level employment. The prestigious foreign service was opened to women in 1958 and the elite administrative service in 1963. There were women lawyers but still no women engineers, architects, biologists, veterinary surgeons and agronomists in 1963. At a lower level, the promotion of tourism created employment opportunities in the travel trade, and women began to enter into the clerical and sales services, with a concentration of the less educated and the poor in low-income service occupations. Education and employment were perceived by parents and students as agents of socio-economic mobility, although the proportion of women who achieved this goal was determined by their family resources and the limited access to higher education.

Gender, Equity and Human Resources Development since the 1970s

From the late 1960s, policy priorities shifted from concern for extending educational opportunity to diversifying education to meet the needs of the economy. This preoccupation with the needs of the labour market was influenced by two forces. The flow of expertise from overseas reflected by the dominance of human capital theories in vogue from the 1960s that popularised in local policy circles theories of 'mismatch' dysfunctionality, 'diploma disease' and the practice of unsuccessful manpower projections in a narrow conceptual framework. Local concern was accelerated by the increasing inability of a sluggish economy to absorb the products of the education system after the mid-1960s. The change in stance was reflected in planning documents of the time (Ministry of Education, 1972; Ministry of Planning and Economic Affairs, 1967, 1971). Yet, social demand and a democratic polity ensured that the commitment to free education was not lost. The 1978 constitution, for instance, contained a broad policy directive to eradicate illiteracy and to ensure universal access to education at all levels. Free textbooks were distributed to all students below Grade 11 in 1981. Sri Lanka was able, therefore, to retain its 'outlier' status in social development in a low-income country, as seen in its relatively high physical quality of life index in the 1970s, and high ranking in the human development index in the 1990s (UNDP, 1994).

Both quantitative and qualitative development of education were, however, affected adversely by the imposition of IMF-World Bank structural adjustment policies after the new government in 1977 initiated a radical shift in macro-economic policy towards liberalisation of the economy and reliance on market forces for growth. In consonance with the objective of reducing social sector expenditure, the proportion of state expenditure on education declined to 2.2 per cent in the mid-1980s, and allocations from the national budget to around 6-8 per cent as compared with allocations of 16-20 per cent in the 1960s. Income disparities widened and poverty increased, creating hardship among the poor (Lakshman, 1997).

The concern for extending educational opportunity resurfaced in the 1990s. The UN Conference on Education for All in 1990, the ratification of the UN Convention on the Rights of the Child in 1991 and its sequel, the Children's Charter of Sri Lnka, in 1992, and the SAARC summits gave this concern a new momentum. The continuing incidence of poverty and social unrest compelled the state to implement special poverty alleviation programmes from 1989, including allowances for school meals and distribution of free materials for school uniforms from 1993. In January, 1998, as a part of the ongoing education reforms, compulsory education regulations were introduced for the 5-14 age group under the Education Ordinance of 1939, after a lag of sixty years.

Some of the consequences of the low priority given to extending educational opportunity before 1990 were the stagnation of literacy rates at around 90 per cent for men and 82 per cent for women in the 1980s (Table 2), the Marginal increase in enrolment rates among the 5-14 age group from 83.7 per cent for boys and 83.6 per cent for girls in 1981 to 88.3 per cent and 87.4 per cent respectively in 1991, and the static enrolment rates among the 15-19 age group during these years (Tables 4 and 5a and b). Literacy centres for out-of-school children between 5 and 14 years were opened from 1981 onwards, but received the lowest priority and failed to meet the educational needs of even 5 per cent of out-of-school children. The tribulations of girls in domestic service and those trapped in commercial sexual exploitation are some of the visible manifestations of the consequences of non-schooling.

Table 4

Educational Participation Rates: Urban, Rural, 1981 (per cent)

Age	*Total*			*Urban*			*Rural*		
	Total	*Male*	*Female*	*Total*	*Male*	*Female*	*Total*	*Male*	*Female*
5-9	84.4	84.5	84.2	86.6	86.4	86.9	83.8	84.1	83.6
10-14	82.4	82.9	81.8	85.2	86.4	84.4	81.6	82.1	81.1
5-14	83.7	83.7	83.6	85.9	86.4	85.6	82.7	83.1	82.4
15-19	41.9	41.2	42.7	46.7	44.9	48.0	40.6	40.0	41.3
20-24	8.9	8.7	9.0	9.7	9.4	10.2	8.7	9.1	8.7
5-24	55.8	56.0	55.6	56.6	55.3	57.3	55.7	56.3	55.1

Source: Based on *Census of Sri Lanka*, 1981, Department of Census and Statistics, Government of Sri Lanka, Colombo.

Table 5a

Age-Specific Enrolment Rates in Schools by Gender, 1991 (per cent)

Age Group	*Male*	*Female*	*Total*
5-9	90.1	87.3	88.7
10-14	86.6	87.5	87.1
5-14	88.3	87.4	87.9
15-19	37.5	42.6	39.9
20-22	3.1	4.6	3.8
5-22	62.1	63.4	62.4

Source: *Annual School Census*, 1991, Ministry of Education, Statistics Division, Government of Sri Lanka, Colombo.

Note: Data exclude north and part of the eastern province, and are based on population projections.

Table 5b
Educational Participation Rates, 1994 (per cent)

Age Group	*Total*	*Male*	*Female*
5-9	94.6	94.6	94.6
10-14	94.4	94.3	94.4
5-14	94.4	94.5	94.4
15-19	54.5	53.4	55.3
20-24	4.7	4.7	4.6
5-24	61.8	62.2	61.4

Source: *Demographic and Health Survey*, 1994, Department of Census and Statistics, Government of Sri Lanka, Colombo.

Socio-economic disparities rather than gender determine the educational opportunities of girls in Sri Lanka. In the school system in 1997, 96.6 per cent of all schools were co-educational and 68 per cent of all teachers were women; 48.4 per cent of enrolment in Grades 1-5, 49.3 per cent in Grades 6-8, 51.6 per cent in Grades 9-11, 56.8 per cent in Grades 11-12 and overall, 49.9 per cent of total school enrolment consisted of girls—a trend that has continued since 1970 (Table 6). The percentage of girls in total enrolment in

Table 6
Enrolment in Schools by Level and Sex, 1997

Educational Level (Years)	*Total*	*Male*	*Female*	*Female (%)*
1-5	1,799,211	928,047	871,164	48.4
6-8	1,047,177	530,629	516,548	49.3
9-11	1,026,368	496,449	529,919	51.6
12-13				
Science	47,811	26,799	21,012	43.9
Arts	117,996	39,196	78,800	66.8
Commerce	59,407	31,231	28,176	47.4
Total	225,214	97,226	2,0466,788	49.9
Total	*4,100,810*	*2,054,022*	*2,046,788*	*49.9*

school was slightly lower in two districts—48.6 in Ampara and 48.5 in Nuwara Eliya, with cncentrations of rural Muslim and plantation population groups respectively. Girls in plantation schools have been the most educationally disadvantaged, but as a result of donor-supported programme interventions introduced in the mid-1980s, the percentage of girls in the total enrolment in plantation schools increased from 45.9 in 1984 to 48.3 in 1994. More boys than girls 'drop out' of schols; this is true even in most plantation schools currently. In the general population, more women than men between 15 and 30 years of age have had at least 10 years of education.

On the other hand, socio-economic disparities affect the access of girls to education. In the metropolitan city of Colombo, for instance, girls in middle-class residential locations and those in low-income shanty and 'slum' neighbourhoods belong to two or two different educational worlds. There has always been a congruence between the socio-economic background of parents, school facilities, and performance in achievement tests and public examinations. Since the late 1980s, a new vulnerable group has emerged from the ethnic war in the north and east: victims of trauma, displacement and exclusion from the school system. Educational policies have not been able to compensate for the deprivation caused by this environment. Nor they have attempted to promote mutual understanding, national harmony and social cohesion and stability in a multi-ethnic society.

In the 1960s, the access of girls to senior secondary education was seen to be a significant step in their advancement. The low priority given over the years to a more equitable distribution of secondary science education facilities and to the reduction of regional imbalances in provision has limited the proportion of senior secondary schools with a science stream to 5 per cent of the country's schools and to 1-2 per cent in educationally disadvantaged districts such as Moneragala. In 1997, 66.8 per cent of students in the arts stream and 43.9 per cent in the science stream in all schools were girls (*Annual School Census*, 1997). The participation rate of rural girls does not differ from that of urban girls, but it appears that girls in non-affluent rural families have access only to ill-equipped secondary schools. These imbalances are reflected in admissions to universities.

In the 1970s, policy makers abandoned the task of eliminating disparities in education facilities and introduced the artificial mechanism of district quotas to equalise educational opportunity at the point of entry to universities. Quotas are at best a temporary device, and over reliance on this mechanism for over twenty-five years has palpably delayed the reduction of inequalities in the provision of education. Some disadvantaged students have gained admission to universities, but the most disadvantaged districts have been unable to fill their quotas in the absence of adequate facilities. The problem of intra-district disparities remains unsolved as shown by the fact that the social composition of the university student population has not changed significantly after 1967 (Jayaweera, 1984; UGC, 1996). Many Year 5 scholarship winners placed in prestigious urban schools were disadvantaged in competition in developed districts. Critical outcomes of this were the frustrations and resentment aroused among able Tamil students in the well-developed districts of Colombo and jaffna. Their exclusion from universities by high cut-off points contributed to fuelling the ethnic conflict.

In higher education, too, the brakes were applied to expansion by freezing university admissions from 1967 to 1976 through a ceiling imposed in order to restrict the number of graduates entering the labour market. The universities lost their autonomy by successive Acts of Parliament in 1966, 1972 and 1978, and their admission policy came under state control, although academic freedom in teaching, examination and research survived. In the 1980s, however, the University Grants Commission, created in 1978, promoted the expansion of universities. Enrolment that had stagnated at round 12,000 increased to around 18,000 in the 1980s and, given the backlog created by the disruption in university programmes during the social unrest in 1987-89, to 32,800 in 1995. The number of universities increased to twelve including the open university established in 1980s, and two more are in their formative stages. Seven postgraduate institutes and three undergraduate institutions function in different universities.

The percentage of women students in universities declined to 40.7 in 1975 with the elevation of the male-dominated College of Technology to university status in 1972. Since then, their percentage has fluctuated between 40 and 45, and 49.9 per cent of entrants in 1997 were women. Admission statistics (UGC, 1984-96) indicate that more women students than men students qualify for university education, but that a higher proportion of men than women reach the cut-off points for admission for reasons that are yet unclear. Overall, only 3-4 per cent of all women and men in the relevant age cohort are in higher education institutions. Over 40.3

per cent of students qualified at the GCE A/L examination, and 40 per cent of all applicants, around 10,000, entered universities.

The competition to enter universities has promoted excessive learning by rote, and has spawned an extensive private tuition industry that has increased the private costs of education within a free education system. Girls in the rural sector are disadvantaged in access to private tuition and have had to opt for arts courses through lack of school and extra-school facilities in science education. At the same time, pressure on the universities for admission has intensified in the absence of adequate alternative opportunities in higher education. Large numbers of women are in colleges of education and nursing schools, but fee-levying programmes in law, accountancy, library sciences and computer skills and minimally in technology, that are concentrated in the capital city, reinforce socio-economic and gender inequalities in access to diverse opportunities in higher education that could enhance the life chances of women.

Despite the endorsement of 'mismatch' theories by policy makers, it cannot be averred that the 'corrective' measures taken to diversify education programmes since 1970 have widened opportunities. The 1972 curriculum reform had its positive aspect in the incorporation of mathematics and science in the common secondary school curriculum from Grades 6 to 9, irrespective of geographical location and status of school. But the two pre-vocational subjects that were part of the common curriculum foundered in efforts to foster 'local' skills in the context of an unequal society and a sluggish economy. The vocational options of girls were limited conceptually and operationally by the home science syndrome that pervaded schools.

Job-oriented university courses, introduced in 1972 for around half the students of arts faculties in two universities with the approval of the planners, petered out by the end of the 1970s, as the output of students of these courses were more disadvantaged than students in conventional courses in access to employment in a shrinking labour market (Marga Institute, 1983; SLFUW, 1980). In the late 1960s, six junior university colleges were established to offer alternative employment-related opportunities for aspirants to higher education. The colleges were closed down in 1970 as they could meet neither the educational aspirations nor the employment needs of students. A similar exercise in 1991 established eleven affiliated university colleges in nine districts to extend opportunities in higher education with anticipated potential for employment. These institutions suffered the same fate of disjuncture in educational and employment expectations. Six of them survived to become two new universities in 1997, and two campuses that are expected to develop into new universities with relatively more employment-oriented programmes. The percentage of students enrolled in arts faculties has been reduced purposefully to 40. Women students were caught up in all these changes as equal participants, without perceptible improvement in their future prospects.

Outside the general education system, the vocational educational sector expanded from 1970 onwards, and new institutions and programmes were organised, often under pressure in the context of high unemployment rates. The establishment of the Tertiary and Vocational Education Commission for policy and programme formulation in 1992 was a belated measure of recognition of inadequate facilities to meet the needs of over 50 per cent of school leavers and of weak or non-existent linkages with the labour market. Around 3,000 institutions or programmes are said to exist (Kelly and Culler, 1990; TVEC, 1992), but the differential rewards for the products of these institutions relative to higher education institutions have devalued them in the perception of students and parents. Employers, too, are said to have taken little note of these institutions and to have preferred to recruit directly from schools for on-the-job training (Kelly and Culler, 1990). The state is the lead agency in this immediate sector in education, as the private sector provides chiefly on-the-job training or fee-levying, urban-based centres.

Girls seek secondary level vocational training in these institutions in significant numbers, but their internalisation of gender role stereotypes and the analogous tacit assumptions of policy makers and administrators have created wide gender imbalances in enrolment in programmes (Jayaweera, 1991, 1995a and b). Around 40 per cent of students in technical colleges are women, but over 70 per cent of these women are enrolled in secretarial, business administration and home science courses, and they are severely under-represented in technical-related courses. In the programmes of the Department of Labour, which was taken over by the Vocational Training Authority (set up in 1995), the

National Apprenticeship Board established in 1971 and reconstituted as the National Apprenticeship and Industrial Training Authority in 1971, the National Youth Services Council set up in 1968, and the non-formal technical units started by the Ministry of Education in 1974, 40 to 75 per cent of the trainees are women, but over 80 per cent of these women trainees are found to be enrolled in dressmaking, secretarial or beauty culture courses and a minuscule number in technical skills development programmes.

Women who have traditionally sought training in small industries such as weaving, coir, pottery, embroidery, lace making and handicrafts continue to do so as few other non-farm options are available in the rural environment, but these industries are still depressed since their collapse with abrupt market liberalisation at the end of the 1970s, and only a few 'centres of excellence' cater to the tourist and export markets. Currently, only around 25 per cent of the total student enrolment in agricultural schools are women. The Institute for Construction Training and Development was established in the 1980s to meet the needs of a booming construction industry in the early 1980s, but only 1.3 per cent of its trainees were women, relegating women permanently to the status of unskilled workers.

Social class determines access to different levels of skill development (Gunawardena, 1994), but gender inequality in the distribution of skills confines women to a narrow range of conventional 'feminine' or 'gender-appropriate' skills in an economy in transition. The depressing experiences of women seeking training successively in different programmes in search of elusive economic rewards underscore their marginalisation in productive training (Gunawardena, 1994; Jayaweera, 1991). A few NGOs have implemented programmes for women in technical-related training to diversify their skills, but they lack the resources to replicate these efforts.

Employment and Unemployment Since the 1970s

As in the 1960s, female employment increased in the 1970s and 1980s at an even faster rate than that of men. But with market liberalisation and the implementation of structural adjustment programmes, the quality of employment opportunities available to women deteriorated. As may be seen from table 7, the percentage of the female labour force in paid employment, which had risen from 66.9 in 1953 to 79.4 in 1981, declined to just over 50 in the 1980s, and rose again to 67.8 only in 1994 with the expansion of the financial and services sector in the 1990s. Around half the women who had access to paid employment were shunted to low-paid, casual and marginal economic activities. Overall, increase in employment in the 1980s occurred chiefly in the agriculture sector, in self-employment or in unpaid work. The percentage of unpaid women family workers, in fact, rose from 6.5 in 1981 to between 20 and 25 in the 1980s. The pervasive impact of globalisation on the economy during the 1980s and 1990s created a demand for low-cost female labour that virtually reversed earlier trends despite the rising educational levels of women. In the 1980s, labour laws reinforced equal wages among workers in the formal sector, and maternity leave was extended to eighty-four days for the first two pregnancies. There is, however, pressure to deregulate, and the

Table 7
Employment Status by Sex (per cent)

Year	*Employers*		*Paid Employers*		*Own Account Workers*		*Unpaid Family Workers*	
	M	*F*	*M*	*F*	*M*	*F*	*M*	*F*
1953	3.7	1.3	59.4	66.9	33.6	18.9	3.3	12.9
1963	2.9	0.5	60.6	82.2	31.3	8.9	4.7	6.7
1971	3.8	0.8	63.7	76.9	28.9	11.2	3.5	11.2
1981	2.4	1.2	62.3	79.4	32.5	12.9	2.8	6.5
1985-86	3.0	0.9	58.2	58.4	29.6	17.7	9.2	23.0
1990	4.4	1.2	59.5	55.6	28.4	18.1	7.7	25.1
1994*	4.1	1.1	56.9	67.8	24.2	16.5	4.7	14.6
1996*	3.0	0.3	59.4	64.6	31.7	16.9	5.9	18.2

Sources: *Census of Sri Lanka*, 1953, 1963, 1971, 1981; *Labour Force and Socio-Economic Survey*, 1985-86; *Labour Force Survey*, 1990 (1st Quarter), 1996 (4th Quarter); *Demographic and Health Survey*, 1994, Department of Census and Statistics, Government of Sri Lanka, Colombo.

* Excludes the north and east.

large numbers of women in the informal sector remain outside the ambit of labour legislation.

The narrow range of vocational skills acquired through the education system meant that there was no significant change in the gender-based occupational crowding in the labour market. Women 'pioneers' made inroads into hitherto male occupational preserves, but in 1990 less than 10 per cent of managers, engineers, surveyors and technicians, and even fewer judges, were women, in consonance with the gender role assumptions of 'appropriate' jobs on the part of administrators, employers and women.

Women continued with their traditional economic activities in the agriculture sector. The percentage of women in the agriculture labour force in labour force statistics increased from 24.9 in 1963 to 29.5 in 1994, although the percentage of the female labour force involved in agriculture declined from 63.5 to 42.1 in the same period with expansion of employment opportunities in other sectors.

Several important developments took place in the agriculture sector which increased women's involvement without a commensurate improvement in their economic status. Land reform in 1972 and 1974 had little impact on women in terms of ownership or participation. The Accelerated Mahaweli Development Programme translocated over 100,000 families from the mid-1970s to the end of the 1980s to newly planned irrigated land and settlements in the heartland of the ancient irrigation-agriculture system in the dry zone. Settlers were envisaged to develop small commercial family farms. State land was also transferred to landless families in different parts of the island and Allima (1997a) estimates that 31 per cent of the population benefited from land distribution during these years.

Women in these lands allocated by the state under the Land Development Ordinance (1935) lost their inheritance rights. In the Mahaweli settlements women were perceived by policy makers to be farmers' wives and not women farmers. Land was allocated chiefly to male heads of household; training and extension reached women through male 'contact farmers' for several years; farmers' organisations were male-dominated; and home development centres contributed to the 'housewifisation' of women economic producers, a process that was observed also in the district-based

Integrated Rural Development Programme implemented from 1978 (Jayaweera et al., 1994; Kumar, 1987; Rajapakse, 1996).

In reality, the workload of Mahaweli women increased with their status as pioneer settlers, and as cultivators and managers of their home gardens. They have not been displaced by mechanisation as yet, but their participation in the programmes of the Farm Mechanisation Centre is minimal. Women have borne the brunt of the adverse consequences of structural adjustment programmes, such as the withdrawal of the fertiliser subsidy in 1989. In the face of rising production costs of Green Revolution technologies and inputs, the unpaid labour of women has been used by small farmer families to adjust to constraints.

The plantation sector also saw radical changes. Land reform and displacement, repatriation, and citizenship rights for those who remained in the country affected women in immigrant plantation labour families. The pendulum swung from private enterprise to state ownership and management in 1974, and again to privatisation of management in 1992. Gender equality in wages was achieved in 1984 as a consequence of the political clout of the main plantation trade union. While donor-supported programmes improved access to health and education services, women's economic activities as tea pluckers and rubber tappers continued unchanged. With repatriation, more village women sought to escape from impoverishment by seeking employment on plantations. As education levels rose, young plantation women no longer wished to be employed in the jobs that women had been engaged in for generations, and consequently sought employment outside the sector, or were unemployed.

The most visible and extensive changes have taken place in the industry sector, with market liberalisation in 1977, the policy shift from import substitution industries to export-oriented industries, and the rapid increase in the share of manufacturing of exports from 5 per cent in 1978 to 72 per cent in 1994. Women workers in this sectors have had different experiences. Women engaged in handloom weaving and other local small industries that had been protected and subsidised in the 'closed' economy of the 1970s suddenly found themselves vulnerable in 1977, with decontrol of prices, removal of subsidies and consequent rising production costs, and competition in an open market with better-quality imported goods. Many small industries collapsed in the aftermath, and around 40,000 women lost their livelihood in the handloom industry between 1977 and 1980 (Atukorale, 1986). The impact on women village producers as major contributors to family income was devastating (Jayaweera, 1998). Efforts made in the mid-1980s and 1990s to revive these industries have been abortive: a few 'centres of excellence' and export-oriented entrepreneurs flourish, but women in the rural sector continue to lack non-farm income earning opportunities in their local environment.

Despite the occasional rhetoric, macro-economic policies promoted since 1977 have failed to provide a conducive, enabling and supportive environment for the development of loal small industries and for utilising local resources for industrial production (Ariyabandu and Hiddelege, 1995; Jayaweera, 1996). The garment industry now dominates the rural scene. The rural economy remains undiversified, and the majority of women primary and complementary income earners engage in a struggle for family survival and maintenance, as they have done through much of the five decades under review.

On the other hand, a transformation has taken place in the lives of a large number of young women between 18 and 30 years with the expansion of export-oriented industries as a focal point in national policy. The relocation of labour-intensive industries in Sri Lanka, as elsewhere in economically developing countries, and the consequent international division of labour, as well as the use of the 'comparative advantage' of low-cost female labour created new employment opportunities for women. Since 1978, young women from relatively low-income rural and urban family have moved to the export processing zones (EPZs) in Katunayake (established in 1978), Biyagama, a district contiguous to the Colombo district (1985), Koggala in the south (1990), to other factories outside the zones and, in the 1990s, to garment factories in rural locations island-wide. Around 80 per cent of the labour force in the EPZs are young women. The garment industry has been feminised with 90 per cent of its employees being young women workers. Men, however, predominate at the management and the technical levels in these enterprises. (Table 8)

Table 8
Employment in the GCEC Industries, 1996

Occupational Level	*Male*	*Female*	*Total*	*Female (%)*
Administrative staff	2,362	841	3,203	26.3
Executive staff				
Technical	1,697	277	1,974	14.0
Non-technical	1,840	247	2,087	11.8
Supervisory				
Technical	2,139	938	3,077	30.5
Non-Technical	1,637	2,212	3,849	57.5
Clerical and allied	3,120	3,815	6,935	55.0
Skilled	9,307	15,105	24,412	61.9
Semi-skilled	8,500	52,475	60,975	86.1
Unskilled	8,560	15,580	24,140	64.5
Trainees	5,558	23,400	28,958	80.8
Other	3,813	1,721	5,534	31.1
Total	*48,533*	*116,611*	*165,144*	*70.8*

Source: Greater Colombo Economic Commission (GCEC).
Note: The GCEC includes three EPZs and factories outside the zones.

Women have been able to earn an independent cash income in a burgeoning area of employment. Around two-thirds of the women workers have had a complete secondary education and have sought employment in these factories as semi-skilled assembly line operators in the absence of alternative employment opportunities. Their prospects for upward occupational mobility are stymied by the labour-intensive rather than skill-intensive technologies transferred to these factories. Their working conditions have been secondary considerations in most workplaces, exposing them to excessive working hours, occupational health hazards, lack of job security, lack of protection by labour legislation and trade unions, and substandard living conditions in boarding houses in the vicinity of the zones (CENWOR), 1994; Goonatilake; Voice of Women, 1983; Weerasinghe, 1989).

Bereft of income earning opportunities in their local environment, women have responded to the demand for home-based workers in subcontracting industries that have proliferated around major industries (Jayaweera and Dias, 1989), and in the short-lived experiment in export production villages in the 1980s

(CENWOR, 1988). While these economic activities have enabled women with child care responsibilities or without employment avenues to support their families, the 'big investors' and their intermediaries tend to thrive at the expense of the 'small producers' and piece rate workers through an inequitable distribution of profits in a 'semi-formal' sector of the economy that is outside the operation of labour legislation.

The services sector has been the 'forte' of women in the modern state, and was a channel of upward mobility in the 1960s. The percentage of women in professional and sub-professional categories was 49.5 by 1985-86, and 41.5 in clerical-related occupations in 1994. Women's niche in professions and in the public service is, however, being threatened by the implementation of policies to reduce the public sector in the second wave of structural adjustment programmes after 1989. Around 120,000 employees have sought 'voluntary' retirement with a 'golden handshake' in the public service and with the privatisation of public enterprises. Gender-disaggregated data are not available, but given the involvement of women in professions in the social sector and in secretarial employment, their employment opportunities appear to have been restricted and women 'domesticated' involuntarily.

At the highest administrative levels and managerial positions in the public and private sectors, there is minimal movement towards the recruitment of women to decision making positions, and high visibility for the few women who have been able to bypass the 'glass ceiling'. The percentage of women in Class 1 in the Sri Lanka administrative service increased from 1.8 in 1978 to 17.5 in 1992. The percentage of women professors in universities rose from 2.4 in 1973 to 11.6 in 1996, and currently 12.2 per cent of the Class 1 employees in the education service are women. But only one professional woman reached the position of secretary to a ministry, and only one woman in the elite administrative service has been appointed secretary to a ministry, albeit in the marginalised Ministry of Women's Affairs. The juxtaposition of gender equality in educational participation and inequality at the administrative level is clearly illustrated by the fact that in the conventionally 'feminine' education sector, 68 per cent of all teachers but only 25 per cent of all principles are women. Male dominance operators at decision making levels except in the political system.

The majority of women in the services still remain concentrated in lower-level employment. A phenomenon that has dramatically increased the resources of women at this level is the outflow of women as migrant domestic workers to meet labour shortages overseas. The percentage of women among migrant workers has increased sharply from 0.4 in 1976 to 52.5 in 1981 and 78.9 in 1994. Gender inequality is reflected in the fact that the majority of technical and skilled workers have been men and the majority of unskilled workers have been women.

Women domestic workers have been pushed by poverty and unemployment to brave the uncertainties of employment in an alien environment. Until a few years ago, they were exposed to 'market forces' and laissez-faire policies, and were vulnerable to exploitation by recruitment agencies and employers, to sexual abuse overseas, and family dislocation and abuse of children left behind. Nearly 95 per cent sought employment in West Asia, and have returned there despite their traumatic experiences during the Gulf crisis. A minority have gone to Singapore and Hong Kong, and to Cyprus, Italy and Greece in Western Europe, and have been joined in recent years by garment workers employed in factories in the Maldives, Mauritius and Seychelles (Dias and Weerakoon, 1995; Hettige, 1991; Yapa, 1995).

These women are the second highest contributors to foreign exchange revenue. They have reduced unemployment in the country and a substantial number have become primary income earners in the family, increasing land and housing assets, educating their children and improving their quality of life. Some of them have been victims of sexual abuse, physical assault and even death in their work environment. Hardly any of these women have been able to acquire new skills to improve their employment prospects on their return, but many have been clearly empowered by their experience. Belatedly, the Foreign Employment Bureau established in 1985 has moved to implement supportive programmes since 1995, encompassing insurance, credit, training, protection from unscrupulous agencies, and even plans for child care.

Most women have been compelled over the decades to fall back on self-employment to augment family resources. Self-employment has been seen by policy makers as a panacea for unemployment since the 1970s and as a mechanism for promoting entrepreneurship in the market economy. The state, NGOs and donor agencies have promoted self-employment to reduce poverty and to 'integrate women in development' as a legacy of the UN Decade for Women (1976-84), oblivious perhaps of the fact that women have been integrated in development programmes on an unequal basis, but have not been integrated in development planning in a holistic framework of gender equality.

Self-employment projects have increased exponentially since the 1970s. Women in impoverished families, those displaced or marginalised from local industries, or confined to the home by child care responsibilities, or without access to the formal sector or to overseas employment, constitute around 70 per cent of the participants in self-employment programmes. Their involvement is visible in women in development projects since 1976, in the Change Agents Programme since 1978, in Grameen Bank model credit-cum-savings programmes from the 1980s, and in poverty alleviation self-employment programmes in the 1990s.

These women form the residual sector in employment programmes, and their activities are expected to grow into micro-enterprises en route to economic viability. They have access to credit, although the small size of the loans available precludes any feasible expansion of enterprises. They have been mobilised and are articulate particularly in their collective strength. Many groups, such as the Janashakthi banks in the south, have accumulated substantial savings. They have, however, had minimal access to technology, to vocational and managerial skills, and to market 'know-how', and have by and large been unable to utilise credit and resources optimally to 'take off' from subsistence levels to viable economic activities or to entrepreneurship. Self-employment programmes appear to have perpetuated poverty, particularly among the large number of secondary-educated women whose potential for skill-intensive development has yet to be tapped.

The women entrepreneurs who have prospered in the market economy have been those, such as the members of the Women's Chamber of Commerce established in 1985, who have had the initiative and the family resources to use the incentives offered by macro-economic policies and the market economy. A few NGOs have assisted resourceless women to acquire the skills necessary for profit-oriented production and entrepreneurship. But micro-enterprises lack adequate conditions for success in the context of macro-economic policies that favour large-scale industries.

The most disadvantaged group are perhaps the women engaged in low-skill, low capital, low-income economic activities in the urban informal sector. They have continued to live in low-income neighbourhoods for decades, with spatial limitations for home-based economic activities. They have been bypassed by development programmes. They are not able to access jobs in the formal sector unlike men in their communities, and are engaged in producing low-quality goods for the 'poverty market' in their environment as a survival strategy. It is apparent that these economic activities are seen as an alternative to unemployment in pockets of disadvantage within and at the periphery of the capital city (Jayaweera, 1998; Kottegoda, 1991).

Looking back over these fifty years, it is clear that the most acute problem confronting the youth, especially young women from secondary schools and universities who have been entering the labour market since the end of the 1960s, has been the high incidence of unemployment. The genesis of unemployment was the imbalance between population growth and ecconomic growth. Population growth rates of 2.8 per cent in the 1950s and 2.2 per cent in the 1960s resulted in high labour force growth rates of 2.5 per cent and 2.2 per cent in the 1970s and 1980s. Concomitantly, external economic pressures led to the decline in economic growth rates from an average of 4.6 per cent of the GDP in the 1960s to 2.3 per cent in the early 1970s, reducing the absorptive capacity of the economy and increasing unemployment (Alailima, 1992, 1997b). The absence of sustained economic growth, with fluctuations from high growth rates in the early 1980s to very low rates in the late 1980s and again to relatively higher growth rates with variations in the 1990s, prevented the reduction of unemployment rates till the mid-1990s.

Women were more vulnerable to unemployment than men because the female labour force increased at a faster rate than the male labour force, particularly in the 1980s when both educational gains and economic pressures brought more women into the labour market. The percentage of women in the labour force increased from 26.2 in 1971 to 37.3 in 1990, declining in the early 1990s for reasons that have not been identified as yet, and rising slightly to 31.5 in 1996. Female labour force participation rates were 26.0 per cent in 1971, 39.4 per cent in 1990 and 30.7 per cent in 1996. Consequently, women's unemployment rates have been at least double those of men consistently since the end of the 1960s—7.3 per cent male unemployment and 8.9 per cent female unemployment in 1963, 11.4 per cent and 21.2 per cent in 1969-70, 7.3 per cent and 21.4 per cent in 1981, 9.1 per cent and 23.4 per cent in 1990, and 8.9 per cent and 16.2 per centin 1996 (Table 9).

Table 9
Unemployment Rates by Sex, 1963-96 (per cent)

Year	*Total*	*Male*	*Female*	*Source*
1963	7.3	8.9	7.6	*Census of Sri Lanka*, 1963
1963-70	13.9	11.4	21.2	*Socio-Economic Survey*, 1969-70, Department of Census and Statistics
1971	18.7	14.3	31.1	*Census of Sri Lanka*, 1971
1973	24.0	18.9	36.3	*Consumer Finances and Socio-Economic Survey*, 1973, Central Bank
1975	19.9	14.3	32.9	*Land and Labour Utilisation Survey*, 1975, Central Bank
1978-79	14.7	9.2	24.9	*Consumer Finances and Socio-Economic Survey*, 1978-79, Central Bank
1980-81	15.8	12.4	23.0	*Labour Force and Socio-Economic Survey*, 1985-86, Department of Census and Statistics
1981	17.8	13.2	31.8	*Census of Sri Lanka*, 1981
1981-82	11.7	7.8	21.3	*Consumer Finances and Socio-Economic Survey*, 1981-82, Central Bank
1985-86	14.1	10.8	20.8	*Labour Force and Socio-Economic Survey*, 1985-86, Department of Census and Statistics
1990	14.0	9.1	23.4	*Labour Force Survey*, 1990-91 (1st Quarter), Department of Census and Statistics
1994*	13.3	11.4	17.9	*Demographic and Health Survey*, 1994, Department of Census and Statistics
1996*	11.1	8.8	16.2	*Labour Force Survey*, 1994 (4th Quarter), Department of Census and Statistics

* Excludes the north and east.

In Sri Lanka, unemployment is a youth problem and the highest rates have been among women and men entrants to the labour market in the 15-29 age group. By education levels, the highest unemployment rates have been among secondary school leavers and, within this group too, the unemployment rates of women have exceeded those of men (Table 10). The poorest are inevitably the most affected, with a male unemployment rate of 21.9 per cent and female unemployment rate of 33.6 per cent.

Table 10
Unemployment Rates by Educational Level (per cent)

Eductional	*1981-82*		*1985-86*		*1994**	
Level	*M*	*F*	*M*	*F*	*M*	*F*
No Schooling	2.1	2.6	7.7	4.8	4.6	2.3
Grades 1-5	3.8	7.8	7.0	9.4	3.8	3.7
Grades 6-8			9.5	16.5		22.9
	9.6	33.5			14.9	
Grades 9-10			15.4	34.9		
GCE (O/L)	14.5	42.0	14.4	35.6	16.3	28.3
GCE (A/L)	22.0	52.2	18.7	44.9	15.6	30.7
Degree			3.3	10.2		
	8.1	12.1			2.5	4.0
Postgraduates			4.2	3.2		
Total	*7.8*	*21.3*	*10.8*	*20.8*	*11.4*	*17.9*

Sources: *Consumer Finances and Socio-Economic Survey*, 1981-82, Central Bank, Colombo; *Labour Force and Socio-Economic Survey*, 1985-86; *Demographic and Health Survey*, 1994, Department of Census and Statistics, Government of Sri Lanka, Colombo.

* Excludes north and east.

Educational expansion without structural changes has been blamed, often exclusively, for the high incidence of unemployment, especially by proponents of mismatch theories. Undoutedly, education increases capabilities and aspirations and raises the educational levels of men and women in the labour force. The rapid expansion of educational opportunities for women in secondary and higher education in the 1960s resulted in a situation in which the educational levels of the female labour force were higher than those of male labour force from 1971. Eduaction expanded faster than employment opportunities in a sluggish economy but, whereas vocational aspirations are determined by the reward structure, employment opportunities increase with economic demand. In the case of women, the skills developed by the educational and vocational sectors are limited to a narrow range of conventional skills that also restricted the range of employment opportunities available to them. At the same time, the demand for female labour was for low-cost women workers, including 'nimble' skills for factory employment. The imbalance between the supply of and demand for skills exacerbated the unemployment situation created by slow economic growth. In 1994, 73 per cent of GCE (A/L) unemployed and 57 per cent of GCE (O/L) employed were women (Alailima, 1997b).

The relationship between education and employment/unemployment has been complex through the decades. The highest economic activity rates and equal participation with men in the labour force are found among the educationally most disadvantaged group, plantation women. Higher education facilitates access to high-level employment but does not guarantee it, as illustrated by the plight of unemployed university graduates. The interface of class, gender and macro-economic policies and structures has ensured that equal access to education has not led to the equal access of women to employment.

Women university graduates have been specially frustrated in their aspirations. A study of women graduates over 1972-78 found that 40 per cent were unemployed, and that the products of job-oriented courses were relatively more disadvantaged in access to employment (SLFUW, 1980). A study of men and women graduates during 1974-79 found that 20.3 per cent men and 36.3 per cent women were unemployed in 1980 (Marga Institute, 1983). Graduate unemployment was contained by state intervention programmes from time to time. The Graduate Training Scheme in 1970 placed 5,000 graduates in the public sector, but preference was given to men in consonance with the concept of 'male breadwinner'. Unemployed graduates were absorbed as teachers on a mass scale in 1976. In the Graduate Placement Programme implemented from 1979 to 1984, 95.8 per cent of the graduates were given appointments as teachers. In 1991, the teaching profession was still able to absorb a significant proportion of unemployed graduates who were not acceptable to the private sector. The public sector that is being reduced now was the main instrument used to relieve unemployment.

University graduates, whose access to higher education was facilitated by free education and the use of the mother tongue as the medium of instruction, now face a bleak future in the context of the diminishing role of the public sector and the expansion of the private sector as a major source of employment. The dethronement and devaluation of English in the education process since the 1950s has deprived them of a language skill that is in high demand in the private sector. English remains a 'badge of distinction' (*Report of the Special Committee on Education*, 1943), as it was in the colonial era. The failure of the state to successfully implement graduate placement programmes in collaboration with the private sector in the 1990s is symptomatic of a deepening crisis in unemployment. The fate of current 'Tharuna Aruna' Scheme to provide internships for graduates in state, private and NGO establishment is as yet uncertain.

Social class, therefore, operates as the most powerful determinant of employment for those with secondary and higher education attainment. Women, however, have always had an additional disadvantage. Not only have gender role stereotypes limited their skills development, but the bias of employers and administrators surfacing from their gender role assumptions of appropriate jobs also tends to influence recruitment and promotions. In a study in 1979, 60.7 per cent of employers said that priority should be given to men as 'breadwinners', 78.6 per cent felt that there were 'suitable' jobs for women, presumably irrespective of abilities and aptitudes, and a few did not like to see women in positions of authority. They perceived women as docile and pliant reproductive role was seen to increase production cost and reduce profits (University of Colombo, 1979). In a study conducted in 1996 (Aturupane, 1996), employers were found to have a strong preference for male employees. Their image of women and men workers was based on stereotypical perceptions of gender-appropriate occupations and differential behavioural profiles.

After five decades, gendered norms will underpin employment-related policies and attitudes, and in the case of less affluent, the interface of class and gender tends to affect the occupational history of women, irrespective of their educational attainments.

Education and Empowerment

Education is envisaged to develop potential and to strengthen capabilities and a sense of individual worth in terms of human rights and dignity. Human rights connote social and gender equity in a free society. Sociologists, however, have pointed out that education operates in practice as an agent of social reproduction, reinforcing unequal social relations (Bourdieu and Passeron, 1990; Macdonald, 1980). While in Sri Lanka the access of girls and women to education has increased, it appears that the content of education and the 'hidden' curriculum in educational institutions have tended to perpetuate unequal social and gender relations, thus assisting in disempowering many women through the education process.

Over the decades, education has expanded the horizons of women and men, but since colonial times the curriculum has been examination-dominated. In the 1960s, uniform syllabuses were developed with the objective of democratising education through a common curriculum. In practice, a rigid curriculum, the practice of rote learning and the promotion exclusively of cognitive skills did not provide space for the autonomous growth of a student's personality and the development of self-confidence, initiative, creativity, flexibility, cooperation and other personality attributes that are necessary for individuals as citizens, workers or effective members of society.

While boys and girls share this narrow learning culture, a gendered process of socialisation through the education process has reinforced asymmetrical gender relations in the family, economy and society. Stereotypical child rearing practices have been carried over to the school, widening gender differences. Gender-based diversification of courses have prevailed in practical subjects. Despite the common life-skills programme introduced in 1982, the earlier practice of channelling secondary school boys to woodwork and metal work and girls to home science, irrespective of aptitudes, continues in conformity with perceived norms. Gender role stereotypes in textbooks and educational materials are less obtrusive than in the past, but they are still reflected even in ongoing curriculum revision. A significant proportion of teacher education students were found to have negative attitudes to gender issues (de Mel, 1994). A study on the socialisation of girls noted that two agendas prevailed—motivation to develop the highest educational and vocational aspirations, juxtaposed with the imposition of behavioural norms that required girls to be passive, quiet and obedient, thereby eroding their self-confidence and self-esteem. It was seen that girls had internalised gendered norms that limited their aspirations and options and their life chances (Jayaweera, 1993).

The outcomes of this socialisation process have been documented in studies. Green (1952), Jayaweera (1976), Jayaweera and Rupasinghe (1998) and Rupasinghe (1988) have recorded that the vocational aspirations of secondary school girls over nearly five decades have been, in order of preference, teacher, doctor and nurse, while those of boys have been engineer, doctor and teacher. Girls opt for arts courses in preference to science courses, for biological sciences in preference to physical sciences, seen as male areas of 'excellence'. The percentage of girls enrolled in university engineering courses has been between 12 and 14 since 1975. It was seen earlier that women trainees selected secretarial courses in technical colleges and conventional 'feminine' courses in non-formal vocational training programmes.

In terms of performance, a study of the entry competencies of 5-year-olds found that there were no gender differences in language, numbers or social skills (Abhayadeva, 1991), and studies of abilities of secondary school students confirm his finding (Rupasinghe, 1991). At the GCE (O/L) examination there appeared overall to be more differences within the sexes that between them, although girls had a slight edge in language and boys in mathematics (Jayaweera et al., 1991). Nevertheless, the performance of girls in the GCE Advanced Level examination has been lower chiefly in mathematics and physics, showing marked gender differences.

It is apparent that the education system has made no effort through its organisation or content to counter the social construction of gender in the education process (Jayaweera, 1993, 1997a and b). At neither the secondary school nor the university level are girls empowered to question or challenge oppressive social practices, to envisage social change towards more gender equity, or even to develop the self-confidence to share in decision making on equal terms with men (Liyanage, 1996). Consequently, women still seek employment that is consonant with their servicing and nurturing roles, employers have conscious and unconscious gender biases in recruitment, and the gender division in the labour market is reinforced. Unequal spousal relations lead to domestic violence and sexual abuse. Household work is still seen as women's work by both men and even some women. Nearly half the university student population are women, but many women eschew leadership and management positions through lack of confidence or time.

Education has been so ineffective in directly empowering women that research indicates that the major agency of empowerment for women has been employment and control of an independent income, with or without education.

Education and Socio-Economic Mobility

A major goal of free education in the 1940s was the promotion of socio-economic mobility to the highest level on the basis of individual abilities (*Report of the Special Committee on Education,* 1943). It is relevant, therefore, to examine the extent to which this objective has been achieved over the last fifty years and the gender dimensions of positive and negative trends. Socio-economic mobility in the context of an analysis of change in education and employment is examined chiefly in terms of upward occupational mobility with all its implications for economic advancement and social prestige.

While the immediate beneficiaries of free education were the middle classes, there is no doubt that a large segment of the population which was outside the education system was brought into its ambit in the 1960s. As shown by Alailima (1997a), the difference in educational participation rates of the 'poor' (the bottom 40 per cent of households classified according to household income) and the 'non-poor' declined to 10 percentage points by 1969 and to 5 percentage points by 1985, with participation rates of over 80 per cent in both groups.

However, universal primary and junior secondary education was not achieved despite expectations. Consequently, the non-schooled and the early school-leavers, chiefly among assetless rural families, the urban informal sector in the low-income neighbourhoods and plantation families have been confined to inactivity or unskilled labour at the bottom of the occupational hierarchy as the outcome of a process of social exclusion.

Parental and student aspirations have focused on secondary and higher education as agents of upward socio-economic mobility through occupational-cum-social prestige. The central schools of the 1940s and 1950s were effective agents of this process, producing men and women who reached the highest levels of professional excellence within and outside the country. The Year 5 scholarships at the end of primary education opened vistas of advancement for the able children of the poor. Yet, the education participation rates of the 15-19 age group rose from 29 per cent in 1969-70 to 43 per cent in 1985-86 among the poor and from 43 per cent to 59 per cent among the non-poor (Alailima, 1997a), underscoring the existence of socio-economic constraints to participation among the former group. Regional imbalances in the provision of secondary science education facilities have reinforced socio-economic disadvantage through educational disadvantage. In the case of girls, gender-based differentiation in course options reflected in a penchant for arts courses has distanced them from many economically rewarding occupations.

Universities functioned as agents of socio-economic mobility in the 1950s and 1960s as free education reduced the privileges of the affluent and offered educational opportunities at the tertiary level to students from rural and non-professional families (Strauss, 1951; Uswatte-Aratchi, 1974). It is not clear whether district quotas for admission made a significant overall impact in view of intra-district disparities. The three-tier social composition of science-based professional courses, science courses and arts-based courses (Jayaweera, 1984), however, widened socio-economic and gender inequalities in occupational mobility as seen in the preponderance of arts graduates among the unemployed. The low priority given to English in the school stream and the universities exacerbated socio-economic differentiation in access to employment and avenues of advancement. The mushrooming of international schools in recent years has added a new layer of privilege in education. Through these decades, the vocational education sector has drawn the non-affluent in search of training and employment, but has provided them few avenues of occupational mobility. In an unequal society, it is not surprising that education has facilitated the upward mobility of some individuals and groups and impeded the advancement of others. It has to be noted, however, that educational opportunities were extended in Sri Lanka to more population groups than in most low-income countries.

The experiences of women in different occupations have been documented in various studies. A three-generational study in the late 1980s in seven representative locations examined, inter alia, the educational and occupational mobility patterns of grandmothers, mothers and daughters in families (CENWOR, 1989). Women in low income urban neighbourhoods in plantations were found to be school dropouts and to be engaged in the same low-skill, low-income occupations for three generations. In villages, settlements and among factory workers, a reversal in occupational mobility had taken place. In the generation of the mothers, women with a secondary education had access to teaching jobs and to middle-level occupations in other services. The present generation of women with similar educational attainment were unemployed or in unviable self-employment or low-skill jobs such as in factories, while their spouses were in low-level formal sector jobs. In middle-class and affluent families, the rising educational levels of each generation of women had ensured occupational mobility to prestigious professional jobs within and outside the country while their spouses held managerial jobs at decision making levels. The interface of class and gender in determining educational opportunity and occupational mobility is clearly reflected in these experiences.

Higher education is anxiously sought as an avenue to prestigious and economically rewarding jobs. A study of arts graduates in 1980 found that men and women graduates from low-income families had opted for low-income economic activities in the informal sector as an alternative to unemployment. Several were involved in the same low-income economic activities in which their parents had been engaged for decades (Gunawardena, 1980). A tracer study of women agricultural graduates from the parents to these graduates in terms of education and occupational status. But 46.7 per cent of them, mostly from the rural sector and from less prestigious schools, had been shunted to teaching positions in schools, contrary to their expectations of professional or academic jobs. Gendered perceptions of 'unsuitable jobs' for women were claimed to have influenced recruitment to professional jobs (CENWOR, 1992). A tracer study of women engineers who had graduated from universities also found significant intergenerational mobility in educational levels and in occupation. The majority had moved up from middle-level parental employment, and 96 per cent were married to university-educated engineers, scientists or administrators. They had qualified in a socially constructed area of male excellence, but virtually all the women engineers identified gender-related constraints to access to jobs commensurate with their qualifications and to upward mobility in the engineering profession (Jayaweera and Sanmugam, 1992).

These studies clearly indicate social class and gender differences in the extent and pace of occupational mobility, particularly in recent decades. A bifurcation appears to have emerged. Women from affluent and middle-class family have achieved vertical mobility while other women have been pushed to horizontal mobility in middle-level jobs, in factory work, in domestic science or self-employment. Both men and women from different classes but with the same educational attainments have had different class-based occupational experiences. The exclusion of less privileged young men and women from avenues of upward socio-economic mobility has been the root cause of youth unrest in 1971 and in 1987-89 in the south, and a contributory cause of the ethnic conflict in the north. Concomitantly, men and women with the same educational attainment have reached different levels in the occupational hierarchy as an outcome of prevailing gender role assumptions. Education has therefore assisted in promoting 'selective' mobility in a context of slow growth in the economy and employment, thus reproducing, also, unequal social and gender relations.

Conclusion

The overview of fifty years has broadly explored the multifaceted developments in education and employment that have impinged on the lives of women and their families. The commitment to education and equity on the eve of independence and in the following decades brought social gains to women. However, their experiences were conditioned by the vicissitudes of post-independence history in a political democracy, encompassing shifting priorities in macro-economic policies, globalisation and economic interdependence, fluctuating rates of economc growth, and social and ethnic tensions that erupted into conflict and violence.

The extension of educational opportunities reduced socio-economic and gender inequalities, improved health indicators significantly, reduced family size and raised the 'status' of women. Access to secondary and higher education changed the lives of many women and facilitated their gaining greater physical mobility and control over their lives. Education and employment, or employment by itself, and access to individual incomes were clearly agents of economic empowerment. From a holistic point of view, however, education did not counter the social construction of gender effectively and did not promote national harmony in a multi-ethnic society.

The 'great expectations' from education in the 1950s and 1960s were not fulfilled chiefly as a result of adverse trends in employment after the 1960s. Despite the expansion of the state bureaucracy and professions, the high incidence of unemployment, both overall as well as with respect to secondary school leavers and university graduates after the late 1960s, indicated that the supply of labour exceeded demand in an unstable economy. It was seen that women were more vulnerable to unemployment than men. The demand generated from the 1980s onwards has ranged from business in the market economy to low-skill jobs.

Unemployment has not been solved by policies based on simplistic analyses. It was seen earlier that curriculum reforms, such as the introduction of compulsory crafts, agriculture or pre-vocational subjects and specifically job-oriented courses in universities, and the establishment of specific higher education institutions to develop employable skills, failed in the context of the inability of the economy to absorb the products of such programmes. Education cannot operate in a vacuum, and an expanding economy is more likely to change aspirations than educational reforms.

In a gendered labour market, women in low-income families were unemployed, secondary-educated women were channelled into dead-end jobs in agriculture, industry and overseas domestic labour, and women university graduates applied for clerical jobs or worked in the informal sector, often in low-income economic activities. The glass ceiling prevented many women in the professions and in the administration from reaching the highest levels.

Consequently, the majority of women expanded their economic activities but could not improve their economic status significantly as market demand activated horizontal rather than vertical mobility for two decades. Occupational mobility came to depend on type of education rather than level of education, on access to family resources, and on flawed perceptions of gender roles. Educational gains could not be translated into economic gains for the majority, and the inability of the state to meet rising expectations has created disillusionment and unrest (*Report of the Youth Commission*, 1990) since the late 1960s.

Socio-economic disparities reinforced by education fanned social and political unrest, engulfing the country in unprecedented violence. From the late 1960s, student politics in universities and even in senior secondary schols was caught up in youth unrest, channelled by the revolutionary movement, the Janatha Vimukti Peramuna (People's Liberation Front) (JVP), into open conflict with the state in 1971 and 1987-89. Schools and universities have functioned amidst violence in the north and east in the 1980s and 1990s, and have served as a source of recruitment to the Liberation Tigers of Tamil Eelam (LTTE) movement and its armed forces. Women were involved actively in both movements to a degree not seen in conventional national politics.

Despite positive achievements, education per se cannot ensure radical social changes or economic development. Dichotomous perceptions of economic and social development have nullified the gains expected of education. Fragmented and myopic policy perspectives have aggravated divisive trends and social exclusion. Education reforms were initiated in 1997 on the basis of the recommendations of National Education Commission appointed in 1991. It is hoped that at the end of these fifty years, reforms will make it possible to translate into action the holistic approach to education and human development of the National Education Commission (*First Report of the National Education Commission*, 1992) in a national context of economic transition and social transformation, and within a framework of human rights, social equity and gender equality.

References

Abhayadeva, Chitrangani (1991). Gender and competencies of children at Entry to Primary School, in *Gender and Education*. CENWOR, Colombo.

Alailima, Patricia J. (1992). Education-Employment Linkages in Sri Lanka. *Journal of the Social Sciences*, Vol. 15, pp. 1-46.

—(1997a). Social Policy in Sri Lanka, in W.D. Lakshman (ed.) *Dilemmas of Development*, pp. 127-70. Sri Lanka Association of Economists, Colombo.

—(1997b). *Poverty and Unemployment in Sri Lanka.* Department of National Planning, Colombo.

Annual School Census (various years). Ministry of Education, Statistics Division, Government of Sri Lanka, Colombo.

Ariyabandu, M., and Hiddelege (1995). Structural Adjustment: The Small Producers' Dilemma, *Economic Review,* Vol. 20, Nos 10-11 (People's Bank, Colombo).

Atukorale, P. (1986). The Impact of 1977 Policy Reforms on Domestic Industry. *Upanathu,* Vol. 1, pp. 69-105.

Aturupane, Harsha (1996). *Unemployment among Educated Women in Sri Lanka.* Department of National Planning, Colombo.

Bourdieu, P., and J. Passeron (1990). *Reproduction in Education, Society and Culture* (Theory and Culture Series). Sage Publications, London.

Census of Sri Lanka (various years). Department of Census and Statistics, Government of Sri Lanka, Colombo.

Centre for Women's Research (CENWOR) (1988). *Women in Export Production Villages.* CENWOR, Colombo.

— (1989). *Women's Work and Family Strategies.* CENWOR, Colombo.

— (1992). *Women Graduates in Agriculture.* CENWOR, Colombo.

— (1994). *Export Processing Zones in Sri Lanka: Economic Impact and Social Issues.* International Labour Organisation, Geneva.

Consumer Finances and Socio-Economic Survey (1981-82). Central Bank, Colombo.

De Mel, Gaya (1994). Perceptions of Women Teachers in Selected Teachers' College regarding Gender Issues. Unpublished M.A. thesis, University of Colombo, Colombo.

Demographic and Health Survey (1994). Department of Census and Statistics, Government of Sri Lanka, Colombo.

Dias, Malsiri and Nedra Weerakoon (1995). Migrant Domestic Workers from Sri Lanka: Trends and Issues, In *Facets of Change,* pp. 195-228. CENWOR, Colombo.

First Report of the National Education Commission (1992). Sessional Paper V of 1992, Government Publication Bureau, Colombo.

Goonatilake, Hema (1987). Industrialisation and Women Workers in Sri Lanka, in Noeleen Heyzer (ed.) *Daughters in Industry,* pp. 292-307. Asia and Pacific Development Centre, Kuala Lumpur.

Green, T.L. (1952). Education and Social Needs. *University of Ceylon Review,* Vol. 10, October 1952.

Gunawardena, Chandra (1980). Socio-economic Effectiveness of Higher Education in Sri Lanka—A Study of a Cohort of Arts Graduates, Unpublished Ph.D. thesis, La Trobe, Melbourne, Australia.

— (1994). *Equality of Opportunity at Post School Level in Colombo District.* J.E. Jayasuriya Foundation, unpublished manuscript.

Hettige, S.T. (1991). From Dependent Housewives to Bread Winners, in *Women, Poverty and Family Survival,* pp. 12-26. CENWOR, Colombo.

Household Income and Expenditure Survey (1991). Department of Census and Statistics, Government of Sri Lanka, Colombo.

Jayasuriya, J.E. (1969). *Education in Ceylon Before and After Independence*. Associated Educational Publishers, Colombo.

Jayaweera, Swarna (1976). Vocational Preferences of Secondary School Girls in Sri Lanka. *Modern Ceylon Studies*, Vol. 7, Nos. 1 and 3 (University of Peradeniya).

— (1984). Access to University Education—The Social Composition of University Entrants. *University of Colombo Review*, Vol. 1, No. 4, pp. 6-40.

—(1988). Educational Policies and Change from the Mid-Twentieth Century to 1977. Occasional Paper No. 2, National Institute of Education, Maharagama, Sri Lanka.

—(1991). *Women, Skills Development and Employment*. Institute of Policy Studies, Colombo.

—(1993). Education and Socialisation, in *Shadows and Vistas*, pp. 148-82. CENWOR, Colombo.

—(1995a). Women and Education, in *Facets of Change*, pp. 96-130. CENWOR, Colombo.

—(1995b). Women and Employment, in *Facets of Change*, pp. 156-94. CENWOR, Colombo.

—(1996). *Factors Affecting Women Entrepreneurship in Small and Cottage Industries in Sri Lanka*, ILO-SAAT, New Delhi.

—(1997a). Women, Education and Empowerment in Asia. *Gender and Education*, Vol. 9, No. 4, pp. 411-23.

—(1997b). Higher Education and the Economic and Social Empowerment of Women—The Asian Experience Compared. *British Comparative and International Education Society*, Vol. 27, No. 3, pp. 245-61.

—(1998). *Impact of Structural Adjustment Programmes on the Economic Activities of Women*. ILO, Genewa and CENWOR, Colombo.

Jayaweera, Swarna, and Malsiri (1989). *Subcontracting in Industry: Impact on Women*. Commonwealth Secretariat, London.

Jayaweera, Swarna and S. Rupasinghe (1998). Vocational Preferences of Secondary and School Students—Trends and Issues. Paper presented at the Sixth National Convention on Women's Studies, CENWOR, Colombo.

Jayaweera, Swarna and Thana Sanmugam (1992). *Women Engineers in Sri Lanka*. Sri Lanka Federation of University Women. Colombo.

Jayaweera, Swarna, Malsiri Dias and Nedra Weerakoon (1994). Experience of the Accelerated Mahaweli Development Programme in Sri Lanka, in Noeleen Heyzer and Gita Sen (eds) *Gender, Economic Growth and Poverty*, pp. 202-41. Kali for Women, New Delhi.

Jayaweera, Swarna, S. Rupasinghe and W.S. Perera (1991). Gender Differences in Performance at Secondary School Examinations in Sri Lanka, in *Gender and Education*. CENWOR, Colombo.

Kelly, Terence F., and Carol J. Culler (1990). *Skills Development Policy in Sri Lanka*. Creative Associates International, Washington, D.C.

Kottegoda, Sepali (1991). Women in the Informal Sector. Working Paper No. 2, CENWOR, Colombo.

Kumar, Shanti (1987). The Mahaweli Scheme and Rural Women in Sri Lanka, in Noeleen Heyzer (ed.) *Women Farmers and Rural Changes in Asia*, pp. 220-54. Asia and Pacific Development Centre, Kuala Lumpur.

Labour Force and Socio-Economic Survey (1985-86). Department of Census and Statistics, Government of Sri Lanka, Colombo.

Labour Force Survey (various years). Department of Census and Statistics, Government of Sri Lanka, Colombo.

Lakshman, W.D. (1997). Introduction, in W.D. Lakshman (ed.) *Dilemmas of Development*, pp. 1-27. Sri Lanka Association of Economists, Colombo.

Liyanage, Kamala (1996). Women in Higher Education—Perspectives from the University of Peradeniya. Paper presented at the Fifth National Convention on Women's Studies, March 1996, CENWOR, Colombo.

Macdonald, Madaleine (1980). Socio Cultural Reproduction and Women's Education in Rosemary Deem (ed.) *Schooling for Women's Work*, pp. 13-25. Routledge and Kegan Paul, London.

Marga Institute (1983). University Education and Graduate Employment in Sri Lanka. Marga Institute, Colombo.

Ministry of Education (1972). *Medium Term Programme for the Development of Education*, Government Press, Colombo.

— (various years). *Annual Reports*, Government of Sri Lanka, Colombo.

Ministry of Planning and Economic Affairs (1967). Report of the Planning Committee on Education, Health, Housing and Manpower. Government Press, Colombo.

— (1971). *The Five Year Plan*. Government Press, Colombo.

Rajapakse, Dharshini (1996). *The Great Sandy River: Class and Gender Transformation among Pioneer Settlers in Sri Lanka's Frontier*. Het Sphintanis Publishers, Amsterdam.

Report of the Special Committee on Education (1943). Sessional Paper XXIV of 1943, Government of Sri Lanka, Colombo.

Report of the Youth Commission (1990). Sessional Paper I of 1990, Government of Sri Lanka, Colombo.

Rupasinghe, S. (1988). Students' Perceptions of Their Needs. *Sri Lanka Journal of Social Sciences*, Vol. 11, Nos. 1 and 2.

Rupasinghe, S. (1991). Gender Differences in Achievement at Secondary School Level in Sri Lanka: Apparent or Real? In *Gender and Education*. CENWOR, Colombo.

Socio-Economic Survey (1967-70). Department of Census and Statistics, Government of Sri Lanka, Colombo.

Sri Lanka Federation of University Women (SLFUW) (1980). *Unemployment among Women Arts Graduates.* SLFUW, Colombo.

Strauss, Murray (1951). Family Characteristics and Occupational Choice of University Entrants. *University of Ceylon Review,* Vol. 9, No. 2.

Tertiary and Vocational Education Commission (1992). *Directory of Tertiary and Vocational Training Institutes in Sri Lanka,* Government Press, Colombo.

United Nations Development Programme (UNDP) (1994). *Human Development Report,* UNDP, New York.

University Grants Commission (UGC) (various years). *Statistical Handbook.* Division of Research and Statistics, UGC, Colombo.

University of Colombo (1979). *Status of Women, Sri Lanka.* University of Colombo, Colombo.

Uswatte-Aratchi, G. (1974). University Admissions in Ceylon: Their Economic and Social Background and Employment Expectations. *Modern Asian Studies,* Vol. 8, No. 4, pp. 6-40.

Voice of Women (1983). *Women Workers in the Free Trade Zone.* Voice of Women, Colombo.

Weerasinghe, Rohini (1989). Women Workers in the Katunayake Investment Zone, in *Women and Development,* pp. 306-21. Macmillan, Delhi.

Yapa, L.K. (1995). The Decision Making Process of International Labour Migration with Special Reference to the Sri Lankan Housemaid. Unpublished M.A. thesis, University of Colombo, Colombo.

3

Social Status of Women

In Sri Lanka poor women, especially those who are household heads or old, face enormous hardships and must fight to ensure their family's economic survival. Macro data and micro studies indicate that their quality of life and employment conditions have deteriorated during the last two decades as a result of, among other factors, increased living costs, which pushed women into low-skilled, low-paid jobs. The poorest and most disadvantaged women are those living in low-income households. Strategies to help these women are linked to poverty reduction programs that have already been identified for the poor, however, special emphasis must be given to the needs of women.

The Sri Lankan Constitution seeks to guarantee gender equality as a fundamental right and nondiscriminatory new legislation. It is not possible, however, to challenge earlier legislation that violates women's rights, and the provisions relating to employment are not binding on the private sector, thus a substantial proportion of women are not protected as workers. Sri Lanka ratified the UN Convention on the Elimination of All Forms of Discrimination Against Women (CEDAW) in 1981 and the UN Convention on the Rights of the Child in 1989. A committee of representatives from state agencies and women's organisations formulated a Women's Charter for Sri Lanka, using CEDAW as a model. The Charter was accepted as a state policy in 1993, and women's non-government organisations (NGOs) were successful in lobbying to place it on the political agenda at the 1994 elections in the manifestos of the two major parties.

The Government's National Plan of Action for Women (NPAW) has recommended that this discrimination be eliminated. An aspect of the legal system that tends to conflict with the Constitution and international conventions is the personal law that governs family relations and women's rights within the family in each community-the Sinhalese, Tamils, and Muslims, for example in "matrimonial fault" conditions for divorce under the general law. Uniformity in personal laws appears to be unattainable in the current context of strong ethnic and religious identity.The hundred-year-old Penal Code that treated sexual crimes such as rape as minor offences was amended by Act No. 22 of 1995 after strong lobbying by women's organisations. Stringent punishment is now being imposed for rape and new sections have been introduced in the Penal Code making, for the first time, incest, grave sexual abuse, sexual harassment, and trafficking in women criminal offences. Legislation pertaining to domestic violence has yet to be formulated. Labour legislation conforms to a great extent to international norms established by International Labour Organisation (ILO) conventions.

In recent years, equal remuneration, and extension of maternity leave from six weeks to 84 days for the first two pregnancies have been progressive steps. However, Sri Lanka withdrew in 1984 from the ILO Convention prohibiting right work and has not ratified the Convention regarding Discrimination in respect of Employment and Occupations.

The minimum age of employment is recognised to be 12 years, but young girls below this age are regularly seen to be employed in agricultural labour, family labour, and domestic servants. Regulations regarding the provision of child care services for women workers have never been in operation. The informal sector and domestic service, both areas in which large numbers of women are involved, are outside the ambit of labour legislation.

The enforcement of laws has shortcomings especially in the export processing zones (EPZs), where regulations regarding working hours appear to be violated with impunity. Vulnerability to occupational health hazards and job insecurity are also consequences of weak law enforcement. Legal literacy, counselling, and legal aid programs are available but are very limited in number and in impact. Special women's and children's desks have been opened in 39 police stations but resource constraints have prevented several desks from functioning effectively. Advocacy and monitoring are critical needs in law reform and enforcement. Although universal franchise was introduced almost six decades ago in 1931 and Sri Lanka had the world's first woman Prime Minister in 1960, and has currently a woman Executive President and a woman Prime Minister, the number of women in Parliament and in local councils is abysmally low.

Needless to say the women have been observed to be politically conscious and to participate extensively in elections, but the percentage of women in Parliament has never exceeded 5 per cent as it is now and the percentage is even lower-around 2 per cent in Provincial Councils and Divisional Councils. There have been few women Cabinet Ministers and it was only in the 1994 Parliament that the percentage of Ministers and Deputy Ministers was 16 per cent. There has been only one woman Chief Minister in a Provincial Council, two Mayors of Municipal Councils, and three Chairpersons in over 200 Divisional Councils. Currently, proposals to enforce a quota of 25 per cent for women in Parliament and local assemblies in the new Constitution are discussed. Political parties do not appear to be very sensitive to gender issues or to the need for nominating more women candidates, and women's units in political parties tend to perform a servicing role in consonance with the norm of male leadership. The NPAW recommends wider female participation in politics and the provision of opportunities and training to girls to develop leadership.Even in revolutionary movements such as the "Eelam Tigers" and the "Janatha Vimukthi Peramuna" (People's Liberation Front) in the south, women play a subservient and self-sacrificing role. Indeed the social policies introduced on the eve of political independence in the 1940s promoted free health services that were made increasingly available to women in all economic strata. This island-wide network of health services, especially maternity and child health services established over four decades ago, has contributed significantly to the improvement in the health status of women. There has been very little decline in morbidity. The incidence of diarrhoea, dysentery, respiratory diseases, and malaria is relatively high, and new threats to health and life have increased-hypertension, breast and cervical cancers, suicide, and sexually transmitted diseases including HIV-AIDS.

A continuing problem in recent decades is the incidence of undernutrition and malnutrition. The shift in 1979 in the food subsidy to food stamps that were not indexed to cost of living led to an erosion in their value with inflation and to reduced calorie intake below acceptable levels in low-income families. Acute undernutrition or wasting increased among the under-5 population due to:

(i) protein energy malnutrition,
(ii) iron deficiency,
(iii) iodine deficiency, and
(iv) vitamin A deficiency, to a lesser extent.

Maternal undernutrition has resulted in a high incidence of 20 per cent low birthweight babies, ranging district-wise from 16.1 per cent to 28.3 per cent. While no blatant preference for the son is practised in food allocation within families, food taboos and the still common practice of women eating after other family members could contribute to undernutrition. One of the weaknesses in the approach to women's health at the national levels in Sri Lanka has been the almost exclusive focus on young children and pregnant and lactating mothers without adequate attention to the whole life cycle of women.

The introduction of free primary, secondary, and tertiary education including university education in 1945 and the change in the medium of instruction from English to the local languages, Sinhala and Tamil, in primary education in 1945 and in secondary education in the 1950s, led to a rapid expansion of educational opportunities. Parents no longer had to choose whether to invest in the education of sons or daughters, and the popular perception that education is a major avenue of upward socioeconomic mobility accelerated the equal access of boys and girls, and of men and women to general education.

In the 1990s the ratification of the UN Convention on the Rights of the Child, the Jomtien UN Declaration on "Education for All", the South Asian Association for Regional Cooperation Summits, the provision of further incentives such as school meals and uniforms, and the ongoing educational reforms on the basis of the proposals of the National Education Commission appointed in 1991 have created a more positive climate for educational expansion and change.

Expenditure on education as a percentage of the gross domestic product (GDP), which had declined from 4-5 per cent in the 1960s to 2.3 per cent in 1985, has gradually increased nearly 3 per cent. The distribution of schools reflect the ethnic composition in the country-73 per cent Sinhala, 20 per cent Tamil, and 7 per cent Muslim schools. Around 98 per cent of the school-going population are in state schools and 96.6 per cent of around 10,000 schools, are coeducational.

An island-wide network of schools is available but 22 per cent of schools, and more in some districts, are small impoverished schools. The quality of infrastructure and the learning-teaching environment in many schools has declined over the years due to resource constraints. Only 5 per cent of schools offer science courses at senior secondary level. In 1991, 23.3 per cent of urban schools and only 3.1 per cent of rural schools provided such facilities and 22.9 per cent of urban schools and 45.9 per cent of rural schools were primary or elementary schools. The low priority given to reducing regional disparities in education facilities in the last two decades has resulted in this inequitable distribution of educational opportunities. About 67.3 per cent teachers are women but few hold positions of responsibility as principals except in a minuscule number of girls' schools.

Educational participation rates rose rapidly in response to social demand and gender differences declined sharply by the 1960s. However, there has been only a marginal increase in educational participation in the 1980s- 83.7 per cent boys and 83.6 per cent girls in 1981 and 88.3 per cent and 87.4 per cent, respectively, in 1997 in the 5-14 age groups, and around 40 per cent of the 15-19 age group since the 1970s. There have been more girls than boys in senior secondary grades for two decades-51 per cent in Grades 9-11 and 58 per cent in Grades 12-13 in 1993. Overall around 6-8 per cent of an age cohort do not enter the school system, and around 25 per cent reach Grades 12-13. Dropout rates are higher among boys than among girls except in the plantation sector and among rural Muslims. A high incidence of early school leaving is seen in low-income urban neighbourhoods, settlements, and backward villages and plantations. It is apparent that socioeconomic background rather than gender affects the access of girls to general education.

Gender disparities hardly exist in the population under 45 years of age-the post-free education generations. More women had never been to school than men in 1991, but more women have GCE OL (secondary) and GCE AL (senior secondary) educational attainment than men. Literacy and education have facilitated the utilisation by women of health services and have contributed to improved health indicators and declining family size and population growth rates.

The Government's NPAW recommends that gender role stereotyping in educational materials be eliminated. Higher education is almost synonymous with education in the 11 conventional universities and Open University as alternate opportunities are limited chiefly to the law, accountancy, management, and computer courses, teacher education, and social work. Around 30,000 students are enrolled in universities and an almost equal number in external degrees, and nonuniversity tertiary level institutions including the few new institutions affiliated to overseas institutions-in all, only 3-4 per cent of the relevant age group.

The number of female students has been between 40 and 45 per cent of the total since the end of the 1960s. Faculty-wise distribution indicates that women are well represented in all courses except in engineering where their proportion has stagnated from 12 to 14 per cent since the mid-1970s, in consonance with gender perceptions of "male excellence" in technology. The weakest sector in the educational system is vocational-technical education. Not only are existing facilities inadequate to meet the needs of school leavers, and are uncoordinated and uneven in quality despite the establishment of the Tertiary and Vocational Education Commission in 1991, but there are also very wide gender imbalances in participation in the available opportunities, largely as a consequence of the socialisation process and the gender role assumption of administrators and employers. The Government has recognised this in the NPAW and has proposed advocacy programs and equal access to women in training programs.

In the 31 technical colleges, around 40 per cent of students are women but over 70 per cent of them are enrolled in nontechnical courses. Around 90 per cent of women trainees in the programs of the Vocational Training Authority of the Ministry of Labour, the nontechnical units of the Ministry of Education, the apprenticeship programs of the National Apprenticeship and Industrial Training Authority, and the centres of the National Youth Services Council are enrolled in culturally perceived "feminine" courses such as sewing, dressmaking, home science, and secretarial courses. Training-cum-production centres in rural or local industries have always been gender-differentiated and women are underrepresented in courses in agriculture, fisheries, and construction trades. The private sector is engaged in on-the-job training courses chiefly in semiskilled tasks and in fee-levying courses for the affluent.

International and local NGOs have pioneered non-traditional courses but have limited resources for extensive programs. Women, therefore, have access to a narrow range of skills and tend to be excluded from technology related courses in a country that is seeking more rapid industrialisation and development in information technology.

Educational Reforms

Educational reforms proposed by the National Education Commission have been initiated and compulsory education legislation for the 5–14 age group has been introduced from January 1998. Other programs envisaged are:

i) provision of at least one or two well-equipped senior secondary schools in each administrative division;
ii) improving the quality of education and promoting more creativity in education in schools, teacher education institutions, and universities;
iii) increasing access to English courses, to technology, and to educational and vocational counselling; and
iv) producing adequate vocational education facilities for school leavers and establishing links between universities and training institutions and employers. Women will benefit from reforms pertaining to vocational education.

As economic producers women have been traditionally active in the labour force, although labour force participation rates underestimate their participation, particularly in home-based activities in the informal sector. According to official statistics, the female labour force increased more rapidly than the male labour force since the 1960s and particularly in the 1980s, as a consequence of rising educational levels and economic constraints of families, but decreased temporarily in the early 1990s for reasons that are unclear.

Slow economic growth and consequent decline in the absorptive capacity of the labour market created massive unemployment from the end of the 1960s, particularly of secondary school leavers and university graduates. Women are more vulnerable to unemployment as shown by their unemployment rates, which have been consistently at least double those of men. By the end of 1997 women's unemployment rates were still twice those of men's although the overall level of unemployment had in fact declined.

Paid Employees

The number of women working as paid employees declined during the 1980s and then began to increase in the 1990s again. The reasons for this are not clear. More and more women are becoming own-account and unpaid family labourers. An increase in the number of women who are own-account workers was registered from 1996 to 1997 when the overall percentage rose from 16.9 per cent to 20.5 per cent.

In fisheries, modernisation has affected adversely women's traditional activities such as fish processing and net repair. Plantation women were the earliest women wage earners in Sri Lanka, but they were recruited largely as workers of the family unit in a subordinate position in the male-dominated culture of South India from which they had migrated to meet the labour needs of colonial plantations. These plantations were nationalised in the 1970s.

Women have access to employment opportunities and incomes but they are employed chiefly in semiskilled labour-intensive industries irrespective of their educational level, without opportunities for upgrading skills. Long working hours, exposure to occupational health hazards, vulnerability to job insecurity, inequitable gender division of labour, and gender subordination in the labour market are characteristic features of women's work in Sri Lanka.

The State policy of promoting the concept of "big investor-small producer" in its industrialisation strategy in the 1990s has also led to the proliferation of subcontracting industries, where the majority of producers are women. Women's poverty is also perpetuated by the inequitable distribution of profits among entrepreneurs who reduce production costs by using outworkers, intermediaries who amass profits, and workers paid low piece rate payments and unprotected by labour legislation or trade unions.

In the rural sector, the failure to develop local industries has limited women's access to off-farm employment opportunities. A few "centres of excellence" produce goods for the tourist market but there is a pervasive air of depression in most rural industries. Around half the labour force in professional, semiprofessional, and middle-level employment are women because the education and health services have been their traditional fields of employment. But few women have been able to advance beyond the "glass ceiling" and to reach high-level decision-making positions in the public and private sectors.

The majority of women workers in the services sector are at the bottom of the employment structure in domestic service or manual labour and are outside the purview of labour legislation. However, despite this, the number of female managers has also increased although the number of women employed as professionals has declined. The demand for domestic labour from oil-rich countries in West Asia and East Asia and even Europe drew women from low-income families who were attracted by the relatively high remuneration paid as compared with their local wages or income.

By 1994 these domestic workers accounted for around two thirds of all migrant workers and 78.4 per cent of unskilled migrant workers. Around 68 per cent were between 21 and 35 years and several had young children.

Unlike in earlier years, the Foreign Employment Bureau now attempts to check unscrupulous recruitment practices by agencies, assists migrant women workers with credit and insurance, and provides some pre-employment training. These women make a crucial contribution to foreign exchange revenue and to family income and maintenance. However, the absence of employment contracts and adequate support services results in continuing exploitation of many women by agents and employers, sexual abuse, family dislocation, and children in crisis. Women workers also acquire no new skills to enable them to achieve upward occupational mobility on their return. State policy encourages self-employment as a response to women's unemployment.

Saving Projects

Credit and savings projects patterned after the Grameen Bank model by banks and organisations and social mobilisation introduced initially by the Change Agents program have given women access to credit without collateral on interest guarantee and have strengthened group solidarity and individual self-reliance. The Janashakthi Bank Societies—"banks" organised by women in low-income families in the Hambantota District since 1991—are an example of the credit culture or discipline developed by women operating in small groups. However, most self-employment programs lack critical inputs such as access to technology, vocational skills development, management training, and market information, which are necessary for optimal credit utilisation. Consequently, loan repayment rates are high but there has been little significant increase in incomes and relatively few women have been able to move from low productivity, low-income self-employment to microenterprises. Women are not a homogenous group, but program organisers tend to perceive them as secondary earners with capacity and aptitudes only for *ad hoc* elementary projects.

Patriarchal values still influence gender relations in the Sri Lankan society and economy but women in their central role as mothers and as economic producers have often de facto powers in the family. Studies have indicated that education, employment, and access to an independent income over which women have control have empowered women both in the family and in society.

For instance, women wage agricultural or factory labourers have more "power" than women whose economic contribution is subsumed in family income. Dual-worker families appear to have a more egalitarian relationship. There has even been a role reversal in some families in which women are primary income earners. Studies have shown that joint decision-making by spouses in household matters and the welfare of children is more prevalent than is apt to be presumed. The exception is the plantation labour community who in their enclaves have clearly unequal relationships in which men have even claimed access officially to their spouses' wages.

Gender ideologies that impact adversely on women are still predominant in Sri Lanka. Women continue to be seen by many policymakers and administrators as "dependent wives" or "supplementary earners" to be used as a labour reserve. The inequitable gender division of labour within households has changed very little and despite the extension of women's economic roles, household work is seen as "women's work"—a norm that some women tend to internalise. The education process does not seem to have empowered women adequately to challenge existing sociocultural practices by promoting the equality of women and men or to respond adequately to changes in the external environment. Increasing awareness of women's rights can be expected to contribute to the erosion of negative sociocultural values about women.

While Sri Lankan women enjoy high status compared to the rest of South Asia, gender issues have yet to be mainstreamed into the national or local planning process and tend to receive scant attention in national plans as seen in the sporadic reference to women's issues in mainstream development planning in the annual Public Investment Program, which operates as a five-year rolling plan. Improvements in Sri Lanka's social indicators such as high literacy, increased life expectancy, and a low fertility rate were achieved through universal application of social policy that did not discriminate against women but, at the same time, did not seek to actively promote women's issues.

The most significant achievement has been the formulation of a Women's Charter for Sri Lanka by representatives of the Ministry of Women's Affairs (MWA) and other key ministries, as well as women's organisations who have been lobbying over the years on critical issues pertaining to women.

The Charter is an adaptation of CEDAW to local needs and has seven sections— Civil and Political Rights, Rights within the Family, Right to Health, Right to Education and Training, Economic Rights, Social Discrimination, and Gender-Based Violence. The Charter was accepted as a national policy by the Government in March 1993, and a national committee was appointed in 1994 of 15 women and men from state agencies and NGOs, representing diverse areas of interest to oversee the implementation of its Charter.

Women's organisations lobbied on the eve of the 1994 general elections for more visibility of the Charter at the national level and were successful in obtaining a commitment to the Charter from the two major political parties. However, the Charter has no legal validity as it is as yet only a policy document reflecting aspirations and intentions, and the ethnic conflict appears to have relegated its implementation to a lower level of priority.

The National Committee has neither been equipped with resources to facilitate the implementation of its Charter nor does it have qualified personnel to undertake its functions as a referral channel for women victims of violations of human rights. The term of the first Committee expired in August 1997 and a new committee has been appointed.

The NPAW was prepared in 1995 by MWA, the National Committee for Women, and representatives of women's organisations, but it has not yet been incorporated in national or sectoral programs although sectoral activity plans have been prepared. This NPAW identified eight areas of critical concern:

Organisation

i) violence against women, women and human rights and women and armed conflict;
ii) political participation and decision-making;
iii) health;
iv) education and training;
v) economic activities and poverty;
vi) media and communication;
vii) environment; and
viii) institutional strengthening and support.

In 1998, MWA prepared a three-year development plan and a project has been developed with support from the United Nations Development Programme (UNDP) for strengthening the MWA. Meanwhile, national and district programs have been generally "gender blind" while claiming to be "gender neutral."

The Accelerated Mahaweli Women's Program saw women chiefly as farmers' wives, and women's cheap labour has been utilised in industrialisation and in meeting the demands of the international labour market. National policies have not been examined at the stage of formulation or implementation for their impact on women. Meanwhile, women make a crucial contribution to the economy, but have been incorporated in the global market on unequal terms without commensurate benefits and under poor working conditions. The majority of participants in state-sponsored self-employment programs are women but such programs are concentrated in low-skill, low-productivity, low-income economic activities without adequate inputs to improve skills, technology, and market information.

Legal reforms have not been fully responsive to the needs of women, although recent amendments to the Penal Code are expected to reduce the incidence of gender-based violence. Most importantly, women appear to have problems in access to the highest levels in decision-making in the public and private sectors.Gender concerns are not taken into account in the work of policy-oriented state institutions such as the National Development Council, the Human Resources Development Council, the Institute of Policy Studies, the Council for Agricultural Research Policy, and the Industries Commission, or in major state research institutions such as the Ceylon Institute of Scientific and Industrial Research and the National Aquatic Research Agency. With the exception of the Foreign Employment Bureau, the Ministry of Labour has not been concerned strongly with the working conditions of women and its Women and Children's Unit has been understaffed.

The national machinery for women's affairs has functioned as a compartmentalised entity in the public sector and has not been able to mainstream gender issues or even the NPAW in Sri Lanka's national plans. The Women's Bureau was, over the years, part of a larger ministry with more prestigious functions such as health and subsequently, transport.

A separate MWA was created in 1997 and it is hoped that

it will not be marginalised as a women's domain. The National Committee for Women created in 1993 is a policy advisory body. There is as yet no mechanism that effectively links the national machinery with the Department of National Planning. MWA however faces a major problem in promoting the implementation of programs island-wide as women's affairs is not a devolved subject under the 1989 Amendment to the Constitution. Provincial Councils include women's issues in their mandates but no provincial ministries for women exist. There are no official links between MWA and provincial ministries and there is ambiguity in their relationship.

The Women's Bureau operated in the past as a "project unit." It has implemented projects over the years particularly in the Integrated Rural Development Programs (IRDP), but these have been ad hoc women's projects that have operated outside the main IRDP sectoral programs. In the late 1980s, it promoted the organisation of Women's Societies in communities, but evaluation studies reported that they had not been successful in empowering women at the grassroots level. In the 1990s it has implemented programs with a broader perspective such as in legal literacy, counselling, and establishing women's and children's desks in police stations, but they have been hampered by limited resources.

State Agency

The only other women-specific state agency is the Farm Women's Agricultural Extension Program of the Department of Agriculture, which has a limited mandate in improving home gardens and has therefore little scope for increasing women's productivity and incomes in the agriculture sector. NGOs have been active since the early twentieth century in welfare-oriented programs. Local women's organisations such as the Lanka Mahila Samithi, the Sri Lanka Federation of University Women, and the Sri Lanka Women's Conference, which are affiliates of international organisations, have been active since the 1930s and 1940s. It is during the UN Decade for Women, however, that they have extended their activities from delivery of services, community development, and self-employment enterprise development to research, advocacy, and activism.

In fact, the most visible development since the Beijing Conference has been the organisation of women at all levels, from the grass roots upwards in groups, although there is no strong women's movement in Sri Lanka. NGO lobbying on the Charter on the eve of the general elections in 1994 has been effective on issues such as gender-based violence culminating, for instance, in amendments to the hundred-year-old Penal Code. NGOs, particularly women's organisations, have been engaged in recent years in gender sensitisation at all levels, from policymakers to large communities.

Both the Women's Charter and the NPAW have been the outcome of State-NGO collaboration. Consciousness has been created among women of the critical issues in the Beijing Platform for Action by the NGO Forum, which was established initially to assist the country's participation at the Beijing Conference.NGOs and women's organisations often have their own special focus, for example, rural women, rural development, university women, social mobilisation for collective action, credit, entrepreneurship, legal reform, research,. advocacy, training and activism, domestic violence, family health and rehabilitation, environment, and media. NGO consortia at national or district levels have developed in recent years to promote solidarity. Also active in the field and with greater resources than local organisations who are donor-dependent, are international NGOs such as World University Service, Swiss Contact, CARE, Humanist Institute for Co-operation with Developing Countries (HIVOS), For ut vikling (FORUT), Oxford Famine Relief (OXFAM), CEBEMO, Netherlands Organisation for International Development Cooperation (NOVIB), Plan International, Intermediate Technology Development Group, and the International Council on Research on Women. Much still remains to be done, however, by both external funding agencies and NGOs to increase the incomes of poor women and to facilitate their exit from poverty.

Sri Lanka's civil conflict has not been well documented from a gender perspective despite women's roles and the impacts of this conflict on them. As migrant workers, Sri Lankan women make tremendous contributions to the economy but the social consequences of this phenomenon are less well understood. In Sri Lanka poor women, especially those who are household heads or old, face enormous hardships and must struggle to ensure their family's economic survival. Macro data and micro studies indicate that their quality of life and employment conditions have deteriorated during the last two decades as a result of, among other factors, increased living costs, which pushed women into low-skilled, low-paid jobs. Indeed in the NPAW, the Government acknowledged that "Women have faced continuing unequal access to economic policies followed by the governments over the last two decades with an increase in the number of women in poverty with little state support for them to withstand the adverse impact of such development policies". Women who need to support themselves and their families as a consequence of the death, physical incapacitation, or unemployment of their spouses, divorce, or separation, or who are unmarried mothers or single women who are not parents but who bear the main burden of supporting their families are a part of the process of "feminisation of poverty" if they do not have adequate resources to cope with changes or economic constraints. Such women tend also to be disadvantaged by low educational status, have limited or no access to land, or are victims of gender inequality in wages in employment.

Low Income Families

Women in low-income families bear the increasing burden of maintaining families in the context of escalating costs of living, declining real incomes, and reduced state support. The most vulnerable are the unemployed, the unviable self-employed, landless labourers, small farmers, workers in small enterprises, petty traders, and domestic and construction workers.

Women who have not been economically active have been rendered destitute by the loss of male breadwinners, and have had to seek avenues of income generation for family survival. Many have been displaced from their homes and face psychological trauma. They have shown great courage in developing coping strategies but they need assistance to acquire economic resources and to undergo counselling.

In Sri Lanka pro-poor policies date from the 1940s with free education and health services and subsidised food. The erosion of some of these benefits in the 1980s led to the introduction of national poverty reduction programs, the

Janasaviya in 1989 and Samurdhi in 1995, and to other programs such as the World Bank-funded National Development Trust Fund (NDTF) in 1991, implemented in a context of social unrest created by hardships. Recent evaluations of these and other programs, particularly self-employment programs for women in low-income families indicate that they have not increased income levels significantly and that most participants are still trapped in a poverty syndrome. Poverty reduction programs are temporary measures to protect the poor. They cannot counter macro policies that create or perpetuate poverty. Macro policies need to accelerate economic growth, increasing at the same time the access of women to productive activities and assets, skills training, employment, and credit, to challenge gender role stereotypes, and to provide or promote support services such as subsidised day care, insurance policies for all ages, homes for the aged, and rehabilitation of war victims.

Since 1983, Sri Lanka has been engulfed in civil conflict burgeoning largely from youth unrest and ethnic conflict that has been a life-threatening and traumatic experience for women. Conflict and violence have been located mainly in two regions. These conflicts have had social and economic impacts on women and led to an increase in the number of female-headed households.

In the south, youth unrest unleashed an intensive period of violence by the Janatha Vimukthi Peramuna, with counter-violence by the State between 1987 and 1991. The violence took the form of assassinations, disappearances, and torture. Few women were reported to be killed but some were detained and tortured, raped in custody, or disappeared. The survivors of this violence were chiefly women and children who, despite the cessation of violence six years ago, still bear the scars of their experiences.

Women widowed by the conflict lost family assets such as land through the negative attitudes of kinsfolk and officials and had no access to free legal aid to secure their rights. Widows who belonged largely to the age group 20–40 years were vulnerable to sexual harassment and violence at the hands of men in the community as well as by officials. The psychological effects of torture, disappearances of spouses and children, family disruption, and reduction to destitution have created trauma and psychosomatic disorders with hardly any access to counselling services or to assistance in developing appropriate coping strategies.

In the north and east, the war has continued unabated for over a decade. Women have been victims of rape by military personnel (both Indian and Sri Lankan) and have consequently faced social ostracisation vis-a-vis traditional cultural norms. Some young women have been "militarised" by enlistment in the Eelam Tiger cadres in a syndrome of glorification of violence and have been sacrificed as suicide bombers and "martyrs." The Liberation Tigers for Tamil Eelam has established a women's wing that comprises approximately 3,000 female fighters. There is a separate training camp for women with its own leadership structure. Most recent recruits tend to be young (in their teens), fresh out of school, and not as educated as the male recruits.

As Refugee-Widows

Large numbers of women are now household heads. Many have been widowed by loss of husbands through death or abduction, thus leading to an increase in the number of female-headed households. The majority of them have been confronted with problems of adjustment to new situations of displacement, as refugees overseas or internally. The internally displaced belong to all three ethnic groups—Tamil, Muslim, and Sinhalese—and women in these families have borne the brunt of an arduous life in refugee camps and resettlements or return to heavily war-damaged homes. Despite the state rehabilitation program of assistance to displaced families, sanitary and health conditions have been substandard due to limited resources and sometimes because of mismanagement. Women face constraints in child care and in the education of their children, and lack access to economically productive activities. Overarching all these tribulations are the psychological effects of violence, particularly anxiety, depression, and trauma. As in the south, counselling services are minuscule and have been left to voluntary organisations. There are no reliable estimates of families affected by violence in the north, east, and south. What is clear, however, is that women in affected families are meeting challenges and constraints with courage but have inadequate support with respect to material and even basic needs, legal aid, and psychological counselling.

A new trend in the economic activities of Sri Lankan women in the last two decades has been their migration overseas in large numbers for employment. A confluence of factors at the end of the 1970s precipitated this movement. The economic hardships of low-income families in a context of rising living costs caused by the implementation of structural adjustment programs since 1977 and the continuing high incidence of unemployment pushed many women to respond to the increasing demand for domestic labour in recently oil-rich West Asia, in relatively affluent countries such as Singapore and Hong Kong, China, and even in western Europe. Market liberalisation and consequent relaxation of travel and foreign exchange restrictions facilitated the process. The State even promoted such migration with a view to reducing unemployment and balance-of-payments problems. The dimensions of such migration are significant, expanding from a thin trickle in the mid-1970s to a large outflow in the 1980s and 1990s. The percentage of women among the migrant workers was only 0.4 per cent in 1976.

Gender inequalities are apparent in the migration of labour. In 1979, 84.9 per cent of professionals, 84 per cent of middle-level workers, and 98.2 per cent of skilled workers were men and 77 per cent of unskilled workers were women. By 1992, 94 per cent of the total female labour outflow were domestic workers or housemaids, at the bottom level of the process in terms of skills, remuneration, and prestige. It is also interesting to note that Sri Lanka was until recently the only country in South Asia to "permit' women to seek such employment overseas. In Sri Lanka, too, migrant women workers also included large numbers of the most conservative community, the Muslims, partly because they had preferential access to Arab countries in the "Middle East" or West Asia. Around 60 per cent of women migrant workers are employed in Saudi Arabia and Kuwait, another 30 per cent in other Arab countries, and 10 per cent in all other destinations.

Access to child care services is minuscule, compelling them to entrust the welfare of young children to their extended family—chiefly to their husband, grandmother, or even to a neighbour in some instances. In their workplace they are often exploited by employers, working long hours without adequate sleep, confined to houses, and several have been vulnerable to sexual abuse and physical violence, without legal protection.

Without adequate guidance regarding bank facilities or investment their remittances have been sometimes misused by spouses and their savings misappropriated. Lack of adequate information prevents generalisation from these experiences. Studies have found that large numbers have had positive experiences and have contributed significantly to family resources and welfare such as in acquisition of land, housing improvements, and education of children, in addition to visible changes in consumption lifestyles. As in other developing countries, development policies and programs in Sri Lanka have had a differential impact on women and men. This is clearly a consequence of economic and social structures that reflect both the gender inequality as well as the gender role assumptions of policymakers, planners, and administrators who develop ostensibly "gender neutral" policies. Sri Lankan women have made a crucial contribution to their country's development process in domestic and plantation agriculture, in industry, and in services. At the national level, industrialisation has depended to a significant extent on the labour of women. At the household level, family survival and maintenance in low-income families depended on the labour inputs of women in these families.

Domestic Labour

Women have responded to the demand for overseas domestic labour and have sought active participation in self-employment programs that have proliferated in the last two decades. There has been insufficient recognition by development planners of the nexus between Sri Lankan women's traditional role and their other economic and social roles. The dichotomy between these roles in planning and implementation has led to the development of programs that focus on women's roles or maximise their labour inputs for economic development with poor returns. Sri Lanka possesses a unique and well-developed system of social safety nets and distributive policies that help spread the fruits of growth relatively evenly. The Government remains committed to continue support for these programs during the strategy period, although more focused or targeted interventions may be required in consideration of fiscal constraints. This will be essential in reaching women and the poor.

The status of Sri Lankan women is at a higher level than other countries in the region. Sri Lankan women outlive men, enjoy high human development, and are recognised as equals under the country's Constitution. However, despite the advances made by women, numerous inequities remain that prevent women from being equal partners in Sri Lanka's economic and social development. Accordingly, the main goal of the gender strategy for Sri Lanka should be to ensure that the benefits of economic growth and poverty reduction accrue to women. In particular, efforts must be made to reduce women's unemployment, which is double that of men, by increasing women's access to employment and/or productive assets. Lastly, the emerging issue of Sri Lanka's aging population is especially pertinent because women are starting to outlive men and there is real concern that the number of poor, elderly women will increase in the short to medium term.

Despite the pioneering role of Sri Lanka in the appointment of women to positions of political leadership, the percentage of women in senior administrative posts remains below 10 per cent. The orientation of the current education and training systems tends to perpetuate the employment of women in low-paying jobs and fails to recognise the opportunity and potential of educating women to be an engine of change towards the planned modern economy. Women also remain disadvantaged in areas such as divorce settlement, land-titling, and custody of children and though protected by labour legislation in the formal sector, remain vulnerable to economic exploitation in the larger, informal sector where most are employed. A less visible but widespread problem affects the increasing number of women working as overseas domestic workers. The promotion of the development of small-scale self-employment schemes for women, especially rural women already working in agriculture or women living in urban poor areas, may be a good approach to improving their income. Such activities could serve as a "springboard" to larger micro-enterprises. All Bank-financed microfinance initiatives should make credit for poor women a high priority. Special emphasis should be placed on access to credit for women victims of the civil conflict, plantation workers, returning migrant workers, and poor women. Vocational training, especially in nontraditional areas, should be given to women pursuing self-employment to be financed by credit.

At the national level of policy and institutional reforms, there is clearly a need to "mainstream" gender issues into the planning process and to ensure gender sensitivity in formulating policy directions. Unfortunately, even the provisions of high profile instruments such as UN conventions and the Women's Charter of Sri Lanka have not yet been integrated into national policies and plans. Incorporating a gender perspective in policy reforms is therefore imperative to economic development, gender equity, and human resource development in Sri Lanka.

In Private Sector

The private sector is already dominant in the manufacturing sector, and the garment industry, the main contributor to exports, has been virtually "feminised." Studies have shown that women have been used as low-cost dispensable labour in low-skill/low-wage employment, and unless there is more rapid transfer of technology and upgrading of skills, significant human resources will be underutilised and women denied upward occupational mobility and hence the opportunity to improve their status in the Sri Lankan economy. Currently it is chiefly NGOs and women's organisations who have taken action to reduce gender imbalances in enrolment in vocational and technical education, to diversify training and thereby provide employment opportunities for women, and to provide vocational information and counselling in collaboration with the private sector operating as a catalyst of change. Such initiatives can be replicated and extended through national policy and action, again in collaboration with the private sector, so that women are not disadvantaged in access to skills and resources.

Projects in the area of self-employment and credit in the context of human resource development also highlight several gender issues. Access to microcredit without inputs in skills training, technology, and market information have confined women to production for the low-income consumers' market and perpetuated their low economic status and poverty. Underlying the negative experiences of the past two decades is inequality in access to skills and services and gendered perceptions of the peripheral role of women in development.

The interface between poverty and gender, and the need to protect vulnerable groups through macro economic and social policies, must be clearly recognised. The increasing population of ageing women caused by relatively higher female life expectancy, and the lack of support for such women in low-income families, in particular, creates a new vulnerable group.The active participation of women in forestry and water resources projects not only as users and carriers, but also as managers. A number of specific issues concerning women can be identified in some of the sectors where the NGOs should be active include:

i) *Human resource development:* Training opportunities for women need to be diversified so that they will not be displaced or marginalised in an increasingly technologically sophisticated economy. Traditionally, women tend to be excluded from many new sectors, a result of the educational system and the socialisation process. Imbalances in technical training programs should be reduced and better vocational counselling made available to girls.

ii) *Policy and institutional reforms:* In the agriculture sector very few rural women have opportunities for off-farm employment. It is important to recognise that rural women are not a homogeneous group and may have different capabilities depending on their educational levels. For example, women with a secondary school education can work in areas such as food production, which utilise relatively sophisticated technology. In so-called "traditional" rural industries, such as coir and pottery, rural women are marginalised by the lack of access to new designs, technology, and skills and therefore, markets.

iii) *Infrastructure improvement*: The impact on and involvement of women is often not recognised in infrastructure projects. In the water sector, for example, women's participation in projects could be built in by training them in the maintenance of new facilities. In transport sector projects, women's needs and demands need to be assessed and potential benefits, as well as adverse impacts, determined.

iv) *Mitigation of the environmental and social impacts* associated with the national economic and social transition. The specific environmental and social impacts on women need to be included in all aspects of program design. As concerns social safety nets, the situation of the growing number of Sri Lankan women living in poverty must be considered as a present and future reality.

At the macro level MWA and the Women's Bureau, and since 1993, the National Committee on Women, are the focal points for women's issues. These components of the national machinery for women's affairs are relatively isolated from mainstream national planning. Collaboration with them is necessary for focusing on gender issues.

At the policy level the most important link is with the Department of National Planning of the Ministry of Finance and Planning, which is responsible for the preparation of the Public Investment Program and for approval and supervision of donor-assisted programs. The critical role of the department in integrating gender in national planning is hardly recognised and gender issues receive relatively low priority in its own perception. The most effective mechanism for institutional support of gender-related planning perspectives would be the establishment of a gender unit within the Department of National Planning with representation from the state national machinery for women's affairs, other relevant ministries, NGOs and women's organisations, and the private sector.

The unit could monitor plans and implementation activities for their impact on women. Despite suggestions by women's institutions and organisations and official sources, the unit has yet to achieve reality.It is currently envisaged that a gender steering committee could examine programs at the planning stage and monitor their implementation. Technical inputs are also necessary on gender policy analysis and gender audit to ensure that programs meet women's needs and aspirations and national development goals.

Peace Processes

Peace processes consist of a complex range of informal and formal activities. Informal activities include peace marches and protests, inter-group dialogue, the promotion of inter-cultural tolerance and understanding and the empowerment of ordinary citizens in economic, social, cultural and political spheres. These activities are conducted by a range of actors, such as United Nations entities, international, regional, national and local organizations, and grassroots organizations, including peace groups, women's groups, religious organizations and individuals.

Formal peace processes generally include early warning, preventive diplomacy, conflict prevention, peacemaking, peace-building and global disarmament. Activities include, inter alia, conflict resolution, peace negotiations, reconciliation, reconstruction of infrastructure and the provision of humanitarian aid. These activities are conducted by political leaders, the military, international organizations, such as the United Nations, regional and subregional organizations, such as the African Union (AU) (formerly the Organization for African Unity (OAU)), the Organization for Security and Co-operation in Europe (OSCE), the Organization of American States (OAS), the Economic Community of West African States (ECOWAS), as well as governmental, non-governmental and humanitarian organizations.

The participation of women and girls and the inclusion of gender perspectives in both formal and informal peace processes are crucial in the establishment of sustainable peace. Women cannot voice their concerns if they are not consulted by fact-finding missions or if they are not involved in peace negotiations.

Involvement of Women and Girls in Informal Peace Processes

At the global level, women have long been active in peace and disarmament issues. Individually and in groups, women have lobbied for the goal of disarmament. During the First World

War, nearly 1,200 women from warring and neutral countries came together to protest against the conflict, and formed the Women's International League for Peace and Freedom.

(WILPF), an organization that continues to advocate internationally for disarmament and human rights. Since then, women around the world have continued to pursue the goal of disarmament, including the total elimination of weapons of mass destruction, strengthened controls over the production and sale of conventional arms, the control of missiles, the need to reduce military expenditures and arms exports. For example, organized efforts by women—prompted by the discovery of strontium in mother's milk and other radioactive hazards from the fall out from atmospheric nuclear tests -contributed to the conclusion of the Partial Test Ban Treaty in 1963. In the 1980s, a global women's peace movement spread across Europe, the United States of America, Canada and Australia with women's peace camps, established in at least 11 countries. In the Pacific, women organized against nuclear testing, and Japanese women set up a peace camp at the base of Mount Fuji. Women's groups in Africa advocated for peace and reconstruction. Peace tents were a regular feature of the United Nations World Conferences on Women in Mexico, Copenhagen, Nairobi and Beijing.

The interest of women and girls in becoming involved in peace processes often stems from their experiences of armed conflict, whether primarily as victims or as armed participants. However, even those women and girls who voluntarily serve as combatants are normally excluded from the male-dominated political groups that make decisions during conflict and in peace processes. Women and girls in conflict areas are aware of the potential for transformation and reform in periods of peacemaking and often work intensively to be part of this process. It is important, however, not to generalize about "women" as not all women work for peace.

Involvement in peace processes can inspire or confirm in women an awareness of the political dimensions of conflicts and of their own political position. Women have identified working for peace as a unique opportunity to become organized, an experience that has proved useful in other aspects of postwar reconstruction. Women's peace movements often focus on the shared social experiences of women, thus producing greater solidarity across lines of division and making it harder to cast the enemy as an ethnic and dehumanized other, which is often a tactic of wartime propaganda. These opportunities for solidarity have been successfully utilized in Burundi, Cyprus, the former Yugoslavia and Sri Lanka.

Active involvement in informal or formal peace processes is a challenge for most local actors. It requires specific skills and access to resources and institutional support, which are difficult to access in conflict situations.

Women and girls face additional constraints. Prevailing assumptions about their appropriate roles in a society, particularly in relation to decision-making, and stereotypical assumptions about their areas of expertise, have been used to exclude them from informal and formal peace processes. At the Burundi peace talks, for example, some male delegates questioned the presence of women, seeing their wish to be involved as interference in the process in which the men represented them. In Guatemala, some men and women saw women's political mobilization as a direct threat to their culture and traditions. In Cyprus, the activities of local women activists were disapproved of, and women were told to stay at home and care for their children.

Local peace organizations may be resistant to the involvement of women. Male-dominated groups - even those devoted to peace - can reproduce assumptions about appropriate and inappropriate roles of women in society. In some cases, women may be invited to join existing peace groups, but can then be denied access to decision-making positions within the organizations, and relegated to 'housekeeping' functions.

The concerns these groups have about their children give them a social legitimacy and a linkage with women from different sides of the conflict. Their identity as mothers sometimes, though not always, offers a degree of protection from official oppression. The National Cooperation of Guatemalan Widows, for example, continues to campaign against the conscription of young men for a number of reasons, including the mothers' economic dependence on their sons. In

Colombia, the mothers, wives and relatives of soldiers and policemen who were being held by the guerrillas have worked with both governmental agencies and guerilla groups to reach humanitarian agreements and, on occasion, have worked for the exchange of prisoners.

It is often assumed that women and girls are not associated with violence during armed conflict, and as such they have enjoyed opportunities to press for peace that were not available to their male counterparts who are seen as the planners, instigators and combatants. In some cases, women and girls have encountered fewer difficulties than men and boys in expressing their concerns about a conflict. For example, a women's march in Sierra Leone, in May 2000, set the stage for a march of parliamentarians and civil society organizations a few days later. Local observers noted that had it not been for the women's march demonstrating that peaceful expressions against the conflict were possible, the latter would have been impossible without inciting a violent reaction.

Women had been organizing networks of their local groups when the conflict broke out. They continued to organize in their own communities and to use their influence as intermediaries to the warring factions to keep a dialogue going across the conflict lines. They held peace marches, reconciliation ceremonies, prayer meetings, petitioned and led a protest against soldiers who were preventing the delivery of humanitarian aid. In 1991, they were able to create a "peace area" from which armed men were excluded.

The opportunity to attend various national and international conferences gave impetus to the organizing activities of the women. The peace conference organized by the Papua New Guinea Government in 1994, the Fourth World Conference on Women in 1995, conferences subsequently facilitated by church groups and others held in Australia and New Zealand, gave the women an opportunity to discuss lasting solutions to the crisis in Bougainville. In a statement on peace at the signing of the Lincóln Agreement in January 1998, women insisted on being parties to all stages of the political process. As the signing of the final agreement drew closer, a Women's Summit, sponsored by the New Zealand Government, was held. Women set out their visions and proposed guide lines for the Government's responsibilities for women's affairs. Women stated their interest in greater participation in the new government and in political education to that end.

Women are frequently active in reconciliation efforts. A Rwandan women's organization, the Women's Consultative Committee, is comprised of 95 separate associations. Of the 2,055 members, 60 per cent are widows of genocide victims and the other members are married to alleged killers who are in prison.

Women have also used the media as part of peace processes, or to educate the public about armed conflict generally and its impact on women, adolescent girls, and girl children. In Croatia, the women's human rights and peace group B.a.B.e secured space for articles regarding peace and human rights for women in leading weekly magazines. In El Salvador, the radio programme "Buenos Tiempos Mujer", provided a space for dialogue between opposing groups to address violence in the family and society. In Guatemala, the publication of Rigoberta Menchu's autobiography, "I, Rigoberta", and the ensuing publicity campaign attracted international attention to the conflict between indigenous people and the military Government. In Burundi, the Centre for Women uses a series of media technologies to encourage and carry out inter-societal dialogue among women and their communities in an effort to strengthen women's work to resolve conflict and build peace. While a significant part of the organizing that women do in support of peace is related to health and reproductive services, the scope of these activities often extends to other areas that include advocacy and training in women's rights. The Medica Women's Therapy Centre, for example, which was established in Bosnia and Herzegovina in April 1993 to respond to women and children's psychological, gynecological and social needs that resulted from male abuse during the war, now also works on women's rights in the post-conflict era.

Women have also been involved in regional and international peace efforts. The Women's Peacemaker Programme of the International Fellowship of Reconciliation provides regional consultations that bring together women from different sides of conflicts for dialogue to deepen their understanding of conflict resolution and peace. The African

Women's Committee on Peace and Development, launched in 1999, and Femmes Africa Solidarite have focused on promoting conflict resolution in a number of African countries. Similarly, the Mano River Women's Peace Network brings together women from Guinea, Liberia and Sierra Leone. Women in Black, a women's peace network, that started in Israel, has inspired similar peace acclivities around the world, for example, in Cyprus and the former Yugoslavia.

The tactic in all cases remains the same: women - usually from both sides of a conflict - stand together in silent vigil as a way to proclaim to State and military leaders "you are not doing this in my name". Another organization is Jerusalem Link comprising women from Israel and Palestine working for peace. Its representatives addressed Security Council members in an Arria Formula meeting in 2002.

Early Warning, Conflict Prevention and Preventive Diplomacy

Although the primary responsibility for conflict prevention rests with national Governments, civil society also plays an important role. The role of the United Nations and the international community is to support national efforts for conflict prevention and assist in building national capacity in this field. Despite the importance of these processes, there has been little attention to women's participation and gender differences and inequalities in these processes.

Understanding the gender norms and customs of a society may prove useful in early-warning. At the beginning of a conflict, there is often a marked increase in militarism. There may be a corresponding increase in patriarchal values with intensification of nationalism that identifies men as the protectors of the nation and women as the bearers of the culture of the nation. The suspension of or restriction on women's enjoyment of their human rights often accompanies an increase in nationalism. There may be restrictions on inter-ethnic marriages or increased pro-natalism policies directed at women of one group.

Indicators of impending conflict may include increased activity by women in food preparation. Farmers of both sexes, but especially women, may switch to planting short-cycle crops if a prolonged conflict is anticipated. Women may also become involved in the production of weapons, especially traditional ones, for purposes of defence or attack. A detailed understanding of the society, the roles that women and men play, together with customs and norms associated with both male and female behaviour, is necessary to develop a comprehensive array of early-warning indicators of conflict for specific locales.

Conflict prevention requires a variety of approaches, including measures aimed at building mutual confidence, reducing perceptions of threat, eliminating the risk of surprise attack, discouraging competitive arms accumulation and creating an enabling environment for agreements on arms limitation and reduction, as well as on military expenditures. It encompasses both short-term and long-term political, diplomatic, humanitarian, human rights, developmental, institutional and other measures taken by the international community in cooperation with national and regional actors.

The Secretary-General has observed that an essential element of conflict prevention is the strengthening of the rule of law, and within that the protection of women's human rights achieved through a focus on gender equality in constitutional, legislative, judicial and electoral reform. The Secretary- General has recognized that to be effective preventive action must be initiated at the earliest possible stage of a conflict. One of its main aims is to address the deep-rooted socioeconomic, cultural, environmental, institutional and other structural causes that underlie the immediate political symptoms of a conflict, and thus reinforce sustainable and equitable development activities.

Preventive diplomacy is a process closely identified with conflict prevention. It aims to prevent disputes from arising, limit the escalation of existing disputes, and minimize the spread of conflict. Preventive diplomacy is performed by the Secretary-General personally, the Security Council or the General Assembly, or senior staff of the Secretariat, programmes and specialized agencies, and regional organizations in cooperation with the United Nations.

Fact-finding is facilitated by soliciting information from all sectors of society, including women's groups and networks as well as individual women and girls. The appointment of more women as Special Representatives, Special Envoys and regional directors in peace missions may facilitate networking with local women or women's groups. Currently, assessment missions focus almost exclusively on the activities of political parties and other formal political actors. Women are largely ignored because they may not be considered as serious political actors and are under-represented in this sphere. Discussions with women and girls and women's organizations would convey more details how conflict or emerging conflict affects people on the ground and provide information about the concerns that women may have. In the past two years the Security Council has made a point of meeting with women's groups during some of its assessment missions, such as in the Democratic Republic of the Congo, Kosovo and Sierra Leone.

Information provided by women is only useful if formal actors pay attention to what they are saying. Women report that the information they provide is frequently dismissed. In Liberia, for example, on several occasions, women reported a series of unusual movements of men and supplies on border waterways at night. The integrity of a woman Minister and the women informants was questioned and the information, which later proved to be accurate.

Article 41 of the Charter of the United Nations provides that sanctions are one of the instruments the Security Council may use "to apply measures not involving the use of armed force in order to maintain or restore international peace and security". The increased use by the Security Council of this instrument has brought to light a number of difficulties, including unintended effects on vulnerable groups in the target country. Sanctions can contribute to the suffering and death of civilians, particularly children; complicate the work of humanitarian agencies; conflict with development objectives; and do long-term damage to the productive capacity of the target country. Government, the target of the sanctions, tend to be the least affected.

It is the most vulnerable groups, such as the elderly, children and the poor, who suffer as economies are destabilized, livelihoods destroyed, food and medical supplies reduced and electricity cut, affecting water, sanitation and health care infrastructure.

There has been little analysis of sanctions from a gender perspective, but studies on the Persian Gulf War and the sanctions imposed on Iraq indicate that, due to the war, women increasingly became heads of households and primary income-earners. Whereas prior to the war and sanctions, households spent 50 per cent of their income on food, in the aftermath most were spending nearly all their income on food for their families. As food prices increased sharply, many households suffered from malnutrition.

Women and children throughout Iraq could obtain only two-thirds of their daily caloric needs. The workloads of urban women and adolescent girls increased as, with the destruction of infrastructure, they had to travel further to find food and water. Treatable diseases were left untreated due to shortage of medical supplies or electricity to preserve medicines. These factors resulted in 30 times more civilians dying in the aftermath of the war than during the war.

The Security Council and the Secretary-General have called for efforts to fine-tune sanctions and measure their effects with a view to maximizing their political impact and minimizing their unintended negative consequences on civilians. Data disaggregated by sex and age is critical to ensure an adequate understanding of the gender-specific consequences of sanctions.

Peace Negotiations

Formal peace negotiations aim at achieving a settlement between the protagonists in a conflict, which are usually Governments, political parties, opposition groups, armies, warlords or militias. Most negotiation processes exclude a significant number of actors, including women, who fall outside these official groups but who are equally affected by the conflict and are essential for building lasting peace.

Women are under-represented in formal peace negotiations, whether as local participants representing warring factions, or as representatives of international authorities overseeing or mediating deliberations and institutions invited to the negotiating table. In addition, central issues of concern to women, including their participation in post-conflict political, social, civil, economic and judicial structures, do not always reach the negotiating table, in part because of the exclusion of women from the formal peace negotiations. Women not only call for issues specific to themselves but raise issues that affect society as a whole, such as land reform, access to loans and capacity-building. All actors committed to equality and non-discrimination—whether male or female—should have the responsibility and capacity to ensure that peace agreements incorporate gender equality issues.

Some women's groups, such as the Liberian Women's Initiative and the Northern Ireland Women's Coalition, have had success in including their proposals for peace and reconciliation in formal peace negotiations and plans. In Burundi, as a result of extensive advocacy, women were brought into the peace process, but only as observers because of the strong opposition from Burundian men. Yet, even as observers they were able to unite across ethnic, political and class backgrounds to develop a clear agenda, and almost all of their jointly-made recommendations were included in the Burundi Peace Agreement. In Sierra Leone, women's groups actively participated in successive public consultations that preceded the signing of the Lomé Peace Accord in 1999.

In South Africa, women agreed across party lines that each party should have one-third women within the negotiating team for the formal constitutional process. This resulted in important gains for women. The South African Constitution includes a comprehensive Bill of Rights with provisions which prohibit discrimination on the basis of gender, sex, marital status or pregnancy; the right of women to make decisions about reproduction and control over their bodies; property rights; the right to health care, including reproductive health care; the right to education; and the right to enjoy and practice their own cultural and religious beliefs.

The opportunities for the involvement of women in formal peace negotiations and their capacity for effective participation are often dependent on their political mobilization prior to the peace process itself, as evidenced by the examples of Guatemala, Israel and Palestine, where women and adolescent girls were mobilized politically before the start of the formal peace process. At the same time, however, women and adolescent girls who have traditionally been excluded from decision-making and peace processes can become more actively involved if they receive support from local and international actors.

Social Status

In Sri Lanka, there are several lifestyles and behaviour in which women play important role. It is impossible to say, when describing any one group of Sri Lankas: "This is the lifestyle of the Sri Lankan." But one can talk about the values they share. Women share major part in social and cultural activities. In a Sri Lankan family, women play important part.

Shared Values. They pride in their close-knit families. Often it is an extended family where a young family unit lives under the same roof with aunts, uncles, grand-parents and even great-grandparents.

Another shared quality among Sri Lankans is the respect they show old people. The aged are looked after and made to feel wanted. There are homes for elders, of course, but residents in them are usually unfortunate people with no relatives. Old people with family are seldom left to live alone. Children grow up with the idea that it is their duty to care for their parents. Buddhism, a major religion in Sri Lanka, stresses this.

Children are doted upon. Babies are hardly ever allowed to cry. Several years ago, children of the rich were looked after by *ayahs* (nannies). The situation has changed. Today, young working mothers often interrupt their careers to look after their young children and there is a growing preference among men for non-working wives. Young mothers have a lot of help in caring for their children as there is often no lack of relatives to lend a hand.

Respect. Sri Lankans respect their elders and betters. Thus, parents, monks, nuns, priests padres and schoolteachers are respected. On the first day of school a pupil may greet his or her teacher with a sheaf of betel leaves and go down on knees with palms together. This form of salutation is made at other formal occasions, for example when greeting one's parents at the New Year or inviting relatives to a family wedding.

Hospitality. Women maintain the whole affairs of the house. Homes are orderly, clean and generally peaceful which are kept by the female members. However, poor, they are places of sharing and caring. Sri Lankans are rennowed for their hospitality. Visitors dropping in are invariably invited to stay for a meal; foreign guests are treated with special graciousness.

Impetuosity. Sri Lankans are mostly impetuous. Bets taken during parliamentary elections range from shaving one's head to giving away all one's possessions. A party can start any time, anywhere. Travelling on a train, one is apt to suddenly hear the latest popular Hindi song blaring from a tape recorder and see young people dancing in the car.

Love of Water. Streams, rivers, *wewa* (irrigation tanks), beaches and swimming pools are always crowded. The Sri Lankan is an avid bather, probably because the country is tropical and clear, cool water is plentiful. Cleanliness is godliness to most.

Birth Through Childhood

A pregnant mother is given special consideration. The country may be overpopulated, the government may promote family planning, but to any family a new baby is never unwelcome. A fuss is made over appeasing a pregnant woman's craving for exotic or unusual food. If she is working, her co-workers will ply her with pickles, chutneys (spicy fruit preserve) and raw fruits. Her mother, grandmother or mother-in-law will supervise her meals.

The baby is usually delivered in a hospital or a nursing home. Even villages have their own maternity homes. There was a time when the birth took place in the parental home with a midwife in attendance. Infant mortality was high then. It is not the custom in Sri Lanka to throw a baby shower, but soon after a child is born visitors bring the baby gifts.

First Rice Meal and Lesson. Both Tamils and Sinhalese make a ritual of the first time the baby, around eight months old, is given boiled rice. Hindus feed the baby the first mouthful of milk rice in the *kovil* (Hindu temple).

The Sinhalese lay a mat with dishes of *kiributh* (milk rice), bananas, traditional sweets, a book and a piece of jewellery and the baby is allowed to crawl and take its pick. If it reaches for the book everyone knows they are in presence of one destined to be a scholar or an intellectual. If the item of jewellery is picked, the baby shows promise of wealth and good business. If an item of food is grabbed, it is feared the baby will become a layabout!

At about the age of two the child has its first lesson, which is given at an auspicious hour by a learned relative, the temple monk or the principal of the local school.

Growing Up

A Sinhalese or Tamil girl who reaches puberty may celebrate the occasion with her family to mark her coming of age and eligibility for marriage. Many families now ignore the rituals that are part of the celebration.

In traditional homes, the Tamils keep the young girl in seclusion for about 16 days. The Sinhalese too forbid normal activity and it is considered bad luck for the girl to look upon a male, even her brother. At the auspicious time the girl is bathed by a *dhoby* (washerwoman) who pours water on her from a clay pot and then dashes it on the ground. the *dhoby* takes away the jewellery and clothes the girl was wearing when she started her first menstruation. The teenager receives gifts, often jewellery or cash.

There are no special ceremonies for the boys, unless they are Moslem. Moslem boys are circumcized when they are in their early teens.

Marriage

The single state is abhorred and for many Sri Lankan women, spinsterhood is still a fate to be avoided. Teen marriages were once common, but now marriages take place later for economic reasons.

Around 60 per cent of marriages are arranged. This was once the work of a black-coated marriage broker, the *magul kapuwa,* who visited the parents of eligible young people, helping them to "fix" their son or daughter. The *magul kapuwa* is an extinct species, replaced by the marriage proposal column in the Sunday newspapers, aunts, friends, colleagues or parents.

The go-betweens propose, check credentials and investigate the morals of candidates for marriage. Dowries are settled discreetly. The groom likes his bride to bring a dowry but is reluctant to ask for it, so it is left to the good graces of the bride's parents and their concern to endow her with property, cash, jewellery and a house. A Tamil custom allows a man to use part of the dowry he gets to settle his own sister in marriage.

Weddings are celebrated lavishly: a village wedding may last days while the urban rich patronize the big hotels. More people, however, are now choosing to invite only their closest relatives and friends to their home. The traditional custom is for the bridal couple to go to the groom's family home after the celebration in the bride's home. Her immediate family visit her the next day. Most honeymooning couples return to a homecoming party at the groom's family home.

The Ceremony. Tamils get married in the temple or if the wedding is in a hotel, a priest performs the ceremony before the guests. Moslems celebrate in the evening in the bride's home or in a hotel in Arabian Nights splendor. Burghers get married in church and may have a reception after the ceremony. Many Christian Sinhalese follow this practice.

An astrologer decides the auspicious time for every step of the Sinhalese Buddhist ceremony. The couple gets married in a *poruwa,* a house-like decorated structure, and the bride's maternal uncle guides the rituals. The little fingers of the couple are tied with gold thread and water is poured over the knot from a silver urn to symbolize sharing. A bevy of girls sings *jayamangala gatha*—songs of wishes and celebration.

Brides are exotically dressed in rich silks embroidered with gold thread. A Kandyan bride wears the traditional seven *padakkam* (pendants), graded in size and length of chain, starting with a choker and ending with a chain that reaches her knees. The jewellery she wears are heirlooms and her family may fall into debt to deck her with all the traditional pieces.

Horoscopes, the Ancient Consultant

A horoscope is cast by an astrologer who takes the time of birth as the basis for prediction. The time of birth determines the zodiac sign, as well as the group to which a person belongs: *deva, manussa* or *raksha* (goldy, human or devilish).

Horoscopes come in the form of a chart on a sheet of paper or as an *ola* scroll made of a cured piece of talipot palm leaf. Good and bad periods of a person's life are listed.

When a marriage is proposed, the horoscopes of both the man and the women are compared as the very first step. If more than half of 20 "conditions" are favourable the union can go through with no disastrous results.

Horoscopes are read by an astrologer at various junctures of a person's life: at puberty, whenever an important decision has to be made, an examination sat, a job taken, or a house built. Horoscopes do help in this way; at least decision-making is guided!

Horoscopes and Ayurvedic Medicine

Is a horoscope important to someone who is ill? It is, when the patient needs to consult an Ayurvedic doctor.

Folk medicine, or the use of herbal and traditional cures, is a thriving practice in Sri Lanka. So important is this traditional 2,500-year practice that there are five times as many doctors practising what the Sri Lankans and Indians call Ayurvedic medicine as there are the kind we are more familiar with, trained in Western medicine. There is even a government ministry responsible for Ayurvedic medicine.

An Ayurvedic cure treats the whole patient, not just the ailment! Even the person's horoscope and temperament are relevant. Herbs, roots and spices are taken as medicine. A tea of ginger and coriander, for example, may be prescribed for the common cold.

It is commonly held among Sri Lankans that when Western drugs fail, it is time to resort to Ayurvedic cures. Many Sri Lankans believe that both Western and Ayurvedic medicines can be used simultaneously. This is why pharmacies stock both Western drugs and Ayurvedic herbs. The World Health Organisation acknowledges that both branches of medicine can learn much from each other.

Death and Funerals

Buddhists and Hindus cremate their dead; Christians and Moslems bury theirs. But now even Christians are opting for cremation.

When wood was cheaper a wood pyre of special kinds of timber was built. Gas crematoriums in the big cities make funerals more convenient. Yet, funerals in Sri Lanka are expensive. Except for Moslems who bury their dead within 24 hours, Sri Lankans have the body embalmed and keep it in the house or sometimes in a funeral parlor so that relatives and friends can pay their last respects. In villages funerals are social events.

For reasons of economy, however, funerals are becoming simpler with the exception of state funerals for political and religious persons of high rank. Many non-Moslems now hold a funeral within a day of a person's death, and some stipulate that their bodies be given to a medical faculty, thus saying their families the expense of even a coffin.

Buddhists observe last rites for the dead called the *pansakula.* Monks are invited to the home where the body lies, or to the cemetery. They chant a verse in Pali which says that all things are transient; they decay and pass away. A sermon is preached to comfort the mourners who give 20 yards of a white cloth to the temple.

The nearest relatives pour water from a jug into a bowl so that it brims over, signifying the transference of merit to the dead. The greater the merit, the better the chance of rebirth in a good place as a human being. Two nephews of the dead person circle the pyre or crematorium thrice before the cremation. The day after the cremation, the ashes of the body are collected in a clay urn and later buried.

Dane (alms) are given to the temple on the seventh day after the day of death. Three months later and on every anniversary of the death, monks are invited home for almsgiving. This is believed to confer merit on the dead person and also on the living, who by this act of giving lessen their craving for material things.

Christians hold a church service, either in church or in the cemetery. Handfuls of soil are thrown on the lowered coffin by those present, signifying "ashes to ashes, dust to dust."

Moslems carry their dead to the cemetery in a covered wicker stretcher and bury their dead without a coffin. The few Zoroastrians who live in Sri Lanka leave their dead to be devoured by vultures in a section of the cemetery set apart for this.

4

Discrimination Against Women

Sri Lanka was a developing country, currently experiencing severe economic constraints resulting primarily from the long civil unrest in the country, which, besides draining the country's human and capital resources, also militated against its human development efforts. One third of the total population of Sri Lanka lived below the poverty line, with Government welfare support, and that, despite this, Sri Lanka had sustained positive social indicators, particularly with regard to education and health. According to the 2001 Human Development Report, the Human Development Index for Sri Lanka had risen to 81, while the country's Gender Development Index was 70

There is an improvement in the literacy rate of women had improved, thereby narrowing the literacy gap between women and men, as had women's educational achievements. Progress was also seen in relation to the increase of women's participation in the labour force. Women had penetrated into a variety of new fields hitherto dominated by men. Women's contributions to the country's foreign exchange earnings through employment overseas — in the Export Processing Zones and the plantation sector — had received recognition, and rural women had been mobilized into economic activity through special savings, credit and skills development programmes.

In 1994, a woman was elected executive President of the country. Sri Lanka continued to focus on: improving the law and order situation to address violence against women; eliminating gender stereotyping; introducing special care programmes for ageing women; introducing programmes for the improvement of the nutritional status of mothers;

implementing educational programmes to prevent the spread of HIV/AIDS among women; encouraging women to take up non-traditional vocations; and empowering women migrant workers and those employed in the Export Promotion Zones. In addition, Sri Lanka continued to focus on providing humanitarian assistance to the families affected by the conflict, creating an enabling environment to motivate women to assume political leadership, engendering legislation and stepping up efforts in gender mainstreaming.

The Government had taken several measures to establish administrative mechanisms with proactive mandates in order to prevent abuse and harassment of persons affected by armed conflict, particularly women and children. The Government was adopting a multi-pronged approach when dealing with those internally displaced as a result of the conflict. Plans had been formulated and programmes implemented with respect to humanitarian assistance and compensation, for building temporary shelters and for dealing with resettlement and relocation. Violence against women and human rights violations committed by the security or police personnel were not condoned. Sri Lanka submitted regular reports to the human rights machinery of the United Nations and was preparing to sign the Optional Protocol to the Convention.

Over the past years, the country's national machinery had been vested with various powers and functions. The new Government, established in December 2001, had directed that every programme should contain a gender component and that the gender impact of every programme should be assessed. It was expected that this commitment would provide the leverage for new initiatives for gender mainstreaming across the entirety of the government machinery and this would facilitate the implementation of the components of the National Plan of Action for Women. The 2002 National Plan of Action for Women highlighted all priority areas of intervention, including the need to address the inadequate participation of women in power-sharing and decision-making processes. The political climate of the recent past was perceived as having created an environment that was detrimental to women's political participation and that, with a change in the political culture, it was hoped that women would be empowered to become partners in implementing values of good governance. The representative also stated that the Government expected the national legislation giving statutory recognition to the National Commission on Women to be enacted shortly.

The Government was working in cooperation with non-governmental organizations and with the support of the donor community. However, in its efforts to honour its obligations under the Convention, the Government was faced with difficulties stemming from both the internal conflict and the external pressures arising from global uncertainties. Sri Lanka hoped the current initiatives towards securing a resolution to its internal conflict would be successful in order that the ensuing peace would bring benefits to Sri Lankan women.

The educational achievements and improved literacy rate of women, as well as the curriculum reforms and teacher training programmes to eliminate gender role stereotypes. The easy access to family planning for women and men and the well-developed maternal and child health care system, which has contributed to a decline in maternal mortality. Sri Lankans welcomes the very active and lively participation of women's organizations in monitoring and implementing the Convention and Beijing Platform for Action.

Implementation of the Beijing Platform for Action - Sri Lanka

The critical areas of concern identified in the Platform for Action were among those reviewd on the eve of the Beijing World Conference. Two initiatives were taken immediately after the Conference. The Ministry of the Women's Affairs and the National Committee on Women, together with representatives of relevant line Ministries and women's organizations formulated a "National Plan of Action for Women in Sri Lanka - Towards Gender Equality" in late 1995 and 1996. This Plan was discussed with a broad group of participants comprising representatives of line Ministries and a large number of NGOs and women's organizations from all parts of the country, approved by the Ministry, published and re-appraised in 1998. Regrettably, this Plan has not been translated systematically into action nor incorporated in National plans, including the Six-Year Plan developed by the Government in 1998.

Nevertheless, some of action proposals have been and are being implemented by state agencies and women's organizations as components of their programmes.

A special session on the girl-child was not considered necessary as her concerns are incorporated in the proposals and the girl-child is not seen to be specially disadvantaged in Sri Lanka.

The NGO Forum for Women has implemented an ESCAP-supported programme to popularise the BPFA. Activities comprised media-focused workshops, posters and a Handbook/Guide to Action. Subsequently, the NGO Forum has initiated a media campaign on seven of the critical issues which includes newspaper advertisements,posters and TV spots.

The NGO Forum for Women organised also a meeting of these community based organisations to discuss the National Plan for Action for Women in order to mobilise them to implement programmes within their capacities.

In 1994, female and male literacy rates of the population over 10 years were 87.9% and 92.5%, respectively. Age-specific participation rates were 89.5% for girls and 89.4% for boys in the 5 -14 age group; 55.3% for girls and 53.4% for boys in the 15 -19 age group; and 4.6% and 4.7%, respectively in the 20 - 24 age group. Gender disparities in enrolments in schools have been minimal for over three decades, and 58% of the enrolment in senior secondary grades and around 45% of students enrolled in Universities have been girls/women since the early 1970's.

Yet universal primary education has not been achieved and a significant proportion of the population do not have access to secondary education in Grades 12-13 and to tertiary education. Levels of basic educational competencies have declined with the reduction in public social sector expenditure as a consequence of structural adjustment programmes. Educational reforms proposed by the National Education Commission and introduced gradually since 1997 have addressed some of these issues.

Compulsary education regulations for the 5 -14 age group were introduced in January 1998 and it now remains to pursue effectively steps to ensure that children in economically disadvantaged communities in low income urban neighborhoods, remote rural locations and plantations who comprise the out-of-school population, are brought within the ambit of the educational system - the formal school system and in this period of transition, functional literacy centres.

The inequitable distribution of senior secondary schools providing science education has been a major concern over the years in the context of the goal of "science and technology for all". The programme initiated to establish or upgrade at least one well-equipped senior secondary school in each local Division is intended to fill this lacuna and needs to be accelerated to equalise educational opportunities. The lack of adequate and relevant alternative opportunities to university education in the tertiary education sector remains a problem that needs to be addressed in the context of the demand for tertiary level education and the high incidence of unemployment.

Overall expenditure on education needs to be increased to safeguard the gains of the past, to universalise primary education, to increase access to secondary and tertiary education and to improve the quality of education.

Under the on going curriculum reforms, efforts are being made to improve the level of competencies, to develop the whole personality of the child, to promote creativity and values such as human righrs, citizenship, and national harmony and to develop a wholesome orientation to the 'world of work'.

Women's studies courses are found in only two of the twelve universities and even these have yet to be incorporated in mainstream curricula. The challenge now is to ensure that the current curriculum reforms in schools and universities including the proposed counselling programmes, promote the concept of equal partnerhsip of girls and boys, and women and men, and gender equality in the economy, polity and society.

The school can provide only an orientation to the world of work and current university reforms are expected to promote linkages with potential employers in order to reduce the incidence of graduate unemployment, to which women are more vulnerable than men.

The Tertiary and Secondary Vocational Sector has, however, a direct link with the labour market. In the past this sector has seen ad hoc development with mininal liaison with unemployment agencies and it has not expanded adequately to meet the needs of school leavers. Wide gender imbalances exist in enrolment, with women concentrated in traditional "feminine" courses linked to their perceived servicing and nurturing roles, resulting in limiting women to a narrow range of skills in an economy that is changing in response to technological advancement in increasing industrialisation. It is important, therefore, that the ongoing reforms address this issue purposefully from the perspectives of both national human resources development and gender equality.

Education is widely perceived in employment terms as a "feminised" sector in Sri Lanka but studies indicate that the "glass ceiling" appears to operate as strongly as in other sectors to limit the upward mobility of women to the highest decision-making position. In 1998, 68.3% of teachers, and 25.5 and of Principals of schools were women.

Women were virtually invisible in the highest positions in the educational administration at the central, provincial and divisional levels. In the Universities, 45% of students, 33.6% of academic staff and 11.3% of Professors are women. But the first woman Vice-Chancellor of a University was appointed only this week. While some women are reluctant to assume responsibility through time constraints caused by their multiple roles or through low self-esteem, the highest management level appears to be seen yet as an area of "male excellence".

As in education, decades of progressive health policies, provision or matenal and child health services and later, primary health care facilities in communities have resulted in positive health indicators such as 74 years female life expectancy and 70 years male life expectancy, a maternal mortality rate of 0.4/1,000 and an infant mortality rate of 15/1000. Both female mortality and female infant mortality rates are lower than male rates. Total fertility is 2.2 and the annual population growth rate has declined to 1.2%. Nevertheless, district-wise disparities still prevail with high mortality rates in low income urban neighborhoods and the plantations, and specific programmes are necessary in these locations.

While survival may not be a major issue, the incidence of morbidity has not declined appreciably over the years. Poor environmental sanitation and inadequate access to safe drinking water result in high prevalence of dysentery and malaria in several districts. Low nutritional levels caused by poverty and the reduction in food subsidies since the 1980s affect the health of women and children, particularly with respect to protein-energy malnutrition, iron deficiency and iodine deficiency. The incidence of around 20% low birth weight babies is generally associated with maternal under-nutrition. Women suffer as both victims and carers in the increasing incidence of S.T.D. and HIV/AIDS.

While the mother-child syndrome over the years has limited perceptions of the health needs of women, the new approach to reproductive health should focus on the whole life cycle of women and direct more attention to the health needs of adolescent girls, including information on sexuality, the occupational health needs of women workers, geriatric care for ageing women in the context of the changing population structure, and the disabled and victims of substance abuse.

Role in Economic Development

While the contribution of women to economic development has been belatedly recognised, and there is growing awareness that women domestic and plantation agriculture, in burgeoning garment industries and in overseas domestic employment are helping to "hold up the economy", it is not at all clear that their working conditions or opportunities for advancement have improved significantly.

Macro-economic policies stemming from market liberalisation and structural adjustment have opened new employment avenues for women in export-oriented industries and in entrepreneurship activities. But there is evidence from the collapse of local industries and their continuing depressed status and the travails of women in the urban and informal sector in an incessant search for a livelihood for family survival, that macro-economic policies, including the withdrawal of the State have resulted in the social exclusion of large numbers of women in urban and rural poverty groups from the benefits of "development".

It appears that macro-ecoomic policies are biased against the micro-scale sector in employment, in comparison with the incentives and support offered to large-scale export oriented industries. It appears also from the experiences of self-employment programmes over recent decades that women have a high participation rate in such programmes, have relatively easier access to credit in recent years, have been mobilised and are often very articulate in expressing their needs, but a lack of adequate access to technology, vocational and management skills and market information have prevented them from increasing their income significantly and consequently they tend to remain below or around the "poverty line".

While a minority of women from families with resources have become successful entreprenuers and have penetrated export markets, the large majority of self-employed women remain enmeshed in poverty, in low skill, low income economic activities.

Sri Lanka has introduced poverty alleviation programmes and the National programme, Samurdhi, implemented since 1995, is intended to support entrepreneur development, but any poverty alleviation programme is likely to fail in an inhospitable macro-economic policy environment. Evaluation studies indicate that an immediate need for women workers in the formal and informal sectors is increasing access to technology and technical skills that can contribute to developing their potential and generating satisfactory incomes.

While women have participated in large numbers in export oriented industries, the demand is chiefly for low-cost, semi-skilled labour. Consequently, these women, the majority with a secondary education, have limited opportunities for upward occupational mobility. Their problems of long working hours, and vulnerability to occupational health hazards and job insecurity have yet to be resolved.

Much more remains to be done through bilateral agreements to ensure protection and adequate returns during employment, and to promote employment through investment in enterprises after return. It is important to note also that while the current international trend is towards deregulation with respect to labour legislation, the real need is for women (and men) in sub-contracting industries and inother home-based economic activities to be brought within the ambit of labour laws.

The shrinking of the public sector with increasing privatisation has reduced traditional employment opportunities in the services sector. While unemployment rates have declined since 1995, the unemployment rate of women continues to be double that of men - 15.5% and 7.7%, respectively, in 1997. Overall, the gender specific demands in the labour markets have tended to accelerate a shift for many women from vertical to horizontal occupational mobility. There are no constraints to women in Sri Lanka reaching the height of political power as President or Prime Minister. Below this level, however, women's representation in legislative bodies and in politics and in decision-making positions in the public and private sector is very poor. Only 5% of Members of Parliament and 2% - 3% of members of Local Government Councils are women.

Although currently around 12% of Ministers are women, few women head local government bodies. Reasons for low participation are complex. The multiple roles and time constraints of women, socio-cultural norms of male leadership and the prevailing climate of violence limit the number of women who come forward to be candidates for election. Political parties and Trade Unions which nurture leadership are seen to be gender insensitive in their choice of officials or candidates. A recent proposal that 25% of candidates in local elections should be women has not seen successful fruition although local elections are scheduled next week.

The "glass ceiling" operates effectively in the public and private sectors. There is only one women Secretary in a Cabinet Ministry - the Ministry of Women's Affairs. A few women hold key positions but the majority are concentrated at the "additional", "deputy" and "assistant" levels.

Violence, Human Rights and Armed Conflict

Since the Vienna World Conference on Human Rights, there is greater awareness among policy makers and the general public that women's rights are human rights and that gender-based violence needs to be eliminated. A major achievement has been the amendment of the hundred year-old Penal Code in 1995/96 to increase penalties for rape and to make incest, sexual harassment and grave sexual abuse punishable offenses. More publicity is given now to these sexual offenses, particularly as a result of lobbying by women's organisations.

Prevention of child abuse is being given priority attention currently. Domestic violence legislation has, however, yet to be formulated and tends to be hidden under a facade of privacy. The new Constitution that is being drafted needs to strengthen women's rights as fundamental rights. Measures to protect the employment rights of workers outside the public sector and to prevent gender discrimination under Personal Laws need to be introduced as they are currently not provided by the Constitution.

The armed conflict that engulfed the South in the late 1980's and the North, East and neighbouring districts since the early 1980's, has created unprecedented problems. Violations of human rights including the sexual abuse of women in conflict areas are no longer overlooked and both legal action and administrative measures are being taken currently. Nevertheless, cases of disappearances still occur. Women have been victims of violence both directly and as widows, members of refugees and internally displaced families, often as female heads of households in difficult circumstances.

Programmes have been implemented to provide financial and other forms of assistance. But relieving economic deprivation and the psychological trauma of violence are major tasks that need to be addressed by rehabilitation programmes.

While women's organisations campaign for gender sensitive media programmes and attempt to use the media for corrective action, there has been no action at policy level to prevent the distortion of the image of women by media agencies. Electronic communication, and particularly Internet, has increased the volume of pornographic material that exacerbate the situation.

The environmental lobby is extremely strong in Sri Lanka, focusing attention on the environmental hazards of development schemes. A large number of Environmental Impact Assessments have been carried out but the evidence is that none of them have incorporated gender concerns in their criteria or assessment.

The National Committee on Women appointed under the Women's Charter to oversee its implementation has been virtually resourceless and powerless since its inception in 1993. An Act of Parliament formulated to convert it to a National Commission with greater powers was formulated in 1994 but has yet to be introduced or discussed. The absence of adequate gender disaggregated data has been a constraint to more gender sensitive planning, implementation and monitoring of programmes.

In 1997/98, a Commonwealth Secretariat initiative in "Engendering the National Budget", has generated both interest and data. An ESCAP supported programme has strengthened the capacity and sensitivity of the Department of Census and Statistics to produce gender disaggregated data. Preparations are afoot for Census 2001 - a process that requires gender senstive interventions.

A noteworthy feature in recent years has been the increased activity of women's organizations at all levels after the stimulus of the Beijing Conference. They have become in particular an articulate lobby for action to eliminate violence against women. Regrettably, these organisations tend to cooperate outside mainstream programmes and their activities are bedevilled by lack of adequate resources.

Women and Peace in Sri Lanka

The ethnic conflict in Sri Lanka is one of the world's forgotten wars. It has dragged on for over 15 years, causing the deaths of tens of thousands of people and the destruction of precious natural resources. It has also created tens of thousands of refugees and internally displaced people.

The conflict has seen the long-term engagement of the security forces of the Sri Lankan government with members of armed Tamil militant groups, as well as brutal massacres, ethnic riots and large-scale attacks on civilian populations living away from conflict zones with bombings happening in public places and in public transport, for example.

The root causes of the conflict in Sri Lanka is embedded in the majoritarian democratic system that Sri Lanka inherited from the British after it gained independence in 1948. The most critical issues around which the conflict has grown include discrimination against the Tamils—the largest minority group who constitute a little over 18 percent of the population—in state-sponsored development in Tamil areas; discrimination in terms of access to public sector employment and education; and the denial of the right to use the Tamil language in official and procedural matters.

Since 1948, tensions between successive Sinhala-dominated governments and representatives of the Tamils have led to the creation of various solutions for sharing power and control over resources. However, these offers have never formed the basis of any serious attempts to resolve the conflict. Over the years of conflict, there have been several waves of movements of people out of the northern and eastern parts of the island, where the majority of Tamils have lived historically.

Hundreds of thousands of Sri Lankans—most of them Tamils—have fled from the island to other countries around the world. Many of them live in exile and seek asylum in the receiving country. While the economic and social condition of many of these exiles is not to be envied, their circumstances are still somewhat better than those who stayed behind. During this period, the conflict has caused the displacement of tens of thousands of Sri Lankans. Each time a situation occurs where people from a particular area are displaced, they move into welfare centres set up by the state in schools, places of worship and other public buildings. They are deprived of their means of livelihood and their dependence on the munificence of the state and of humanitarian agencies robs them of their dignity.

The traditional occupations of the people of these areas have been farming (mostly paddy agriculture), fishing (in the sea and in freshwater reservoirs), and gathering firewood, cane, honey and other natural produce from the forests. All of these means of livelihood are restricted due to the ongoing conflict. The seas are the sites of battles between the Sri Lankan Navy and the Liberation Tigers of Tamil Eelam (LTTE).

Security forces determine the hours when fishermen may go out to fish and the places where they may fish. Often, there are reports of the hazards faced by fishermen in this situation. They are caught in the crossfire between the two contending parties. Sometimes, the LTTE abducts the fishermen and destroy their boats; sometimes, the Navy mistakes the fishermen for the LTTE and shoots them on the beach or at sea.

Farmers face similar problems. In the dry zone, the paddy fields are located outside the village, and there are large extents of paddy land in areas that, for example, constitute the border between the eastern and northern provinces. Thus, it is prohibited to go to these areas. Sometimes, after petitioning the army, farmers are allowed to go to work on their paddy fields under military surveillance. There have been occasions when the LTTE attacked the army at such a moment, and farmers have either died or been abducted in the ensuing melee. Entry into the forests, most of which are in areas under LTTE control, is prohibited.

The situation of women within this context of ongoing conflict is always fraught with dangers and hazards. In the case of Sri Lanka, because of the nature of the conflict, we also need to be able to deconstruct the term "woman" into the separate ethnic, religious and linguistic communities that are involved in the conflict in order to decipher the totality of a woman's experience. The shared experience of all women living in areas directly caught in the conflict in the north and east of the island is that of being deprived of their right to life and livelihood. Most of the women in these communities who are poor and face many economic hardships work outside their homes, in their own fields and in the fields of others to augment their family's income. In the east, for example, women traditionally weave mats and baskets out of cane and a particular kind of reed that grows along the edges of bodies of fresh water. The conflict has taken away the possibility to do this kind of work from women, since their sources of raw material had become inaccessible due to the conflict. Incomes have also dropped drastically, and many of the women who are not displaced complain of even more severe hardships than before. The fact that the men too are deprived of their livelihood leads to a great deal of frustration, and this often results in violence against the women and children in the home.

Sri Lanka has been governed under the Emergency Regulations and the Prevention of Terrorism Act for almost all of the past 20 years. The situation has heightened mistrust against the Tamil people who are often detained "on suspicion." Over the past years, there have also been instances when the army has retaliated for an LTTE attack on their cadre through indiscriminate shooting in villages. In such situations, women and children are among the dead. In addition, the military in the north and east has been known to abduct and kill suspicious young men and women.

Sexual abuse and violence against women by members of the armed forces have been one of the main issues on which there has been a great deal of campaigning by women's groups throughout Sri Lanka. The most notorious of these cases and one of the few that went to trial was that of the rape and murder of 16-year old schoolgirl Krishanthy Kumarasamy in Jaffna in 1997.

In addition, women are urged to reproduce to replace the population decimated by the conflict. This conservatism leads to the imposition of dress codes for women, restrictions on women's mobility, and reinforcement of women's traditional roles within the home and the family. This reaffirmation of traditional roles for women is also reflected in the media, in the cinema, and in television serials. The issue of violence against women, especially in the context of armed conflict, is further complicated in the Sri Lankan case by the fact that we both have a woman Prime Minister and a woman President.

There are many assumptions that this fact in itself should make a difference in the situation. Unfortunately, this is not so. Once these women became leaders and powerbrokers, as has been the case in other countries, they became agents of particular groups and party interests rather than promoters of women's interests. Although President Kumaratunga came to power in 1994 with the understanding that she would negotiate a settlement of the conflict, she has been unable to do so and the war has taken a heavier toll on lives in the five years that she has been in power than in the previous 10 years.

Another Suicide Squad in LTTE

Another critical feature of the conflict in Sri Lanka has been the increasing participation of women on both sides in the actual conflict as soldiers. In the early years, women recruited into the Sri Lankan security forces were always in auxiliary positions. However, this began to change in the 1990s, and in recent years women members of the security forces have been involved in action on the battlefront. The LTTE too has its own women fighters and a squad of women suicide killers as well.

The assassination of Indian Prime Minister Rajiv Gandhi by a woman suicide killer of the LTTE in 1991 brought them to the attention of the international media, and challenged many existing assumptions about the role of women in war. In addition to being directly involved in the conflict, Sri Lankan women have also been active in lobbying and campaigning for an end to the war, for respect of the rights of all communities but especially of the rights of minority communities, and for a peaceful and negotiated settlement to the ethnic conflict.

In 1983, shortly before the anti-Tamil riots of July that year, a group of women's organisations from different parts of the country came together as the Women's Action Committee (WAC). Their principal slogan was the acceptance of the principle of self-determination and calling for an end to the war and a repeal of repressive legislation.

In each celebration of the International Women's Day from 1983 to 1987, there was always a Tamil woman speaker and the banner on the screen behind the speakers always read: "Respect the right to self-determination of the Tamil people." The leaflets of the organisation always made reference to the conflict and made a call for peace. In WAC's activities, the conflict and women's role within it as peace-builders in particular has a major focus. WAC consists of Sinhala and Tamil women, and reached out to other organisations in solidarity and in collaboration on a wide range of actions and activities against the war.

In 1986, at a time when most of the men refused to come out in fear of a retaliatory attack, arrest or indefinite detention, it was Tamil women in Jaffna who challenged the authorities. They called themselves the Mothers' Front and marched in the first public demonstration in Jaffna for many years, demanding that the authorities tell them about the whereabouts of over 100 young men and boys who had been arrested by the army.

In the south, there was an organisation called Women for Peace, which engaged in many public education campaigns for peace and ethnic harmony. In 1990, when there was a major repression of a southern-based insurgency by the state, and tens of thousands of young men disappeared, Sinhala women in the south of the country also organised themselves as a Mothers' Front, demanding justice and acknowledgement of the whereabouts of their family members. It is perhaps a measure of the power and success of both groups that their call was co-opted by mainstream political parties.

In the elections of 1994, members of the Mothers' Front featured prominently on opposition platforms, and the President identified herself as one of them (since her father and her husband had both been victims of political assassinations). In 1990, a broad network of women's groups called Mothers and Daughters also came into prominence, organising a multi-religious meeting at a time when all public demonstrations were banned.

In more recent years, other groups have emerged such as the Women's Coalition for Peace, the Muslim Women's Research and Action Front, the Sri Lanka Women's NGO Forum and the North-East Forum for Women, all of which have a considerable focus on peace and democracy in their work. The most interesting feature of the work carried on by some of these groups has been attempting to engage in peace-building at the community level, especially in areas of the north and east as well as in the plantation communities where there are large numbers of Tamil women. The basis for this work is the understanding that even if the two warring factions were to sign a peace agreement, there would be a great deal of work remaining to be done to bring together the different communities that have been driven apart by the violence and mistrust in the past 15 years.

Ethnic Conflict and its Impact

In the Eastern province for example, where there have been Sinhala, Muslim and Tamil villages co-existing side by side for centuries, the ethnic conflict has divided them and separated them in a very far-reaching manner. In each of the villages, there are bitter experiences of being attacked by the other group, of seeing their families brutally murdered, their homes being burned down, their fields looted and destroyed. In this context, one cannot simply expect that the past would be forgotten and the villagers would go back to living side by side as they did previously. The hostilities run too deep for that.

Faced with this dilemma, several of the women's groups representing different language and ethnic communities have come together to work at community-building exercises with women and children from different villages and different communities. Exchange visits and shared workshops in creativity are some of the strategies and methods being used to bring women together so they can talk about their experiences, share the bitterness and pain, and discuss ways and means of creating some sense of community among themselves.

— Increase the participation of women in conflict resolution at decision-making levels and protect women living under foreign occupation or in situations of armed and other conflicts.
— Reduce excessive military expenditure and control the availability of armaments.
— Promote non-violent forms of conflict resolution and reduce the incidence of human rights abuse in conflict situations.
— Promote women's contribution to fostering a culture of peace.
— Provide protection, assistance and training to refugee women, internally displaced women, and other displaced women in need of international protection.
— Provide assistance to women of the colonies and non-self governing territories.

The process of working for gender sensitivity in the statute of the International Criminal Court also provided another space in which those who share similar concerns regarding armed conflict could come together to draw on their own experiences to evolve a definition of rape and other forms of sexual violence that would be acceptable to the international community. Based on the experience of working with women victims of violence and abuse, women were also able to bring their particular concerns regarding testimonies and witness protection to the discussions on the statute.

Many women's groups all over the world are going to review the Beijing Platform for Action in 2000. In the Section on Armed Conflict, it seems that little has happened that could change the situation of women in conflict situations, or encourage the international community to include more women in peace-building and peace negotiating activities. However, from the point of view of women deeply involved in this issue, it seems that much more clarity has developed regarding the concerns that need to be highlighted and focused on in the coming years.

The denial of civil and political rights to refugees and displaced persons, the lack of protection of the reproductive and sexual rights of refugee and displaced women, the continued use of "tradition" to justify various forms of aggression and violence against women, the continuation of forced prostitution and the sexual slavery of women in conflict situations, the inadequate representation of women in conflict-resolution activities at the decision-making levels and the failure of both state and non-state actors to adhere to the norms of international humanitarian law with regard to the treatment of civilians in conflict have now been highlighted as key issues to be focused on in the coming years.

Gender Profile: Sri Lanka (August 2001)

Patriarchal values influence gender relations in the Sri Lankan society, but women, in their central role as mothers and economic producers, often have *de facto* powers in the family. Studies indicate that education, employment and access to an independent income over which they have control have empowered women both in the family and in society. The last factor, access to an independent income and control of the resources it generates, appears to be the most critical (Asian Development Bank [AsDB]).

Compared to the rest of South Asia, Sri Lankan women are well-off, enjoy a high life expectancy (74 years), are nearly all literate, and have access to economic opportunities (AsDB). Within the family, they are less vulnerable to discrimination and oppression than other women in the South Asian region.

Preference for male children is not so evident, extreme cases of male dominance are absent, and the purdah refers to the isolation of women which sometimes includes the mandatory wearing of a veil and, by extension, the separation of men's and women's roles in society, along with restrictions to the participation of women outside of the domestic sphere (social activities, employment, education, etc.). is not practiced (ESCAP).

The Constitution provides for freedom of speech and expression; however, in practice, the Government restricts these rights, often using national security grounds permitted by law.

During 2000, the Government limited access to information for domestic and foreign media and continues to censor news relating to the military and security situation.

Traditional concepts concerning the way economies operate offer little well-defined guidance when it comes to promoting women's empowerment or finding solutions towards a better economic justice between the sexes. [...]

Women have to defend their right to paid work in the face of familial and community opposition, their right to better working conditions in the face of global competitive pressures, and their right to a better sharing out of and to an adequate support for unpaid care giving in the face of economic appraisals that do not take into account the costs and benefits of this type of work.

According to official statistics, the female labor force has increased more rapidly than the male labor force since the 1960s and particularly in the 1980s, as a consequence of rising educational levels and economic constraints of families, but has decreased temporarily in the early 1990s for reasons that are unclear.

In 1999, 35% of employed adults (15 years and over) were women. Despite the entry of a few women in new employment sectors, most of them were concentrated in the domestic sphere, plantations, local traditional industries, assembly-lines of the modern sector's industries, sub-sectors of the education and health industries, and domestic services.

Women in the Work Environment

The quality of employment for women has deteriorated since the end of the 1970s. There has been a tendency to push women off stable employment in the formal sector toward marginal economic activities and unprofitable self-employment, while the percentage of unpaid family workers that had declined to 6.5% in 1981 rose to over 20% in the 1980s and the 1990s.

Women's share of administrative and managerial positions has increased from 13 to 18% from the mid 1980s to the mid 1990s, but it is still low. Also, this indicator tends to over-estimate women's decision-making power because these occupations cover a range level of responsibility, while women tend to be concentrated in the lower levels of responsibility.

State policy encourages self-employment as a response to women's unemployment. Women have been major participants in these programs but have generally enjoyed only minimal economic returns. Women operating in small groups develop a credit culture and a discipline of savings.

However, most self-employment programs lack critical inputs such as access to technology, vocational skills development, management training and market information, which are necessary for optimal credit utilization. Consequently, loan payment rates are high, but there has been little significant increase in income, and relatively few women have been able to move from low productivity, low-income self-employment to micro-enterprises.

Long working hours, exposure to occupational health hazards, vulnerability to job insecurity, inequitable gender division of labor, and gender subordination in the labor market are characteristic features of women's work.

Most permanent full-time workers are covered by laws that prohibit them from working regularly more than 45 hours per week. Workers also receive a 14-day annual leave, 14 to 21 days of medical leave, and approximately 20 local holidays each year. The Government respects the constitutional right of workers to establish unions. Any seven workers may form a union, adopt a charter, elect a leader and publicize their views. Overall, over 800,000 union members, 650,000 are women.

Most large unions are affiliated with political parties and play a prominent role in the political process, though the major union in the public sector is politically independent. Several laws protect the safety and health of industrial workers. However, the Ministry of Labor's small staff of inspectors is inadequate to enforce compliance with the laws. Health and safety regulation does not meet international standards.

Around 1997, women's wages were 90% of men's wages in industry and services, and 85% in manufacturing. Maternity leave is available for permanent and casual workers. Women are allowed 84 days, paid in full by employers. There are laws governing sexual molestation and sexual harassment in the workplace.

Living Conditions of Women

The percentage of deliveries attended by skilled health staff in 1995-98 was 94%, according to the latest data available . The maternal mortality ratio was 60 per 100,000 live births for 1990/1998, according to the latest data available . It is estimated that a woman will have an average of 2,1 children throughout her life.

It has not been adequately recognized that domestic violence can be life-threatening for women and that women affected or displaced by violence and conflict situations in the country need intensive counseling and access to basic health services. Unequal power relations have been most resistant to change. This is reflected in male control of female sexuality as in incidences of rape, incest and sexual harassment, and in domestic violence.

Amendments to the Penal Code introduced in 1995 specifically address sexual abuse and exploitation and have modified rape laws to create a more equitable burden and to make punishment more stringent. Since 1983, Sri Lanka is engaged in a civil ethnic conflict in the Northern and Eastern provinces that has resulted in a life-threatening and traumatic experience for women. Survivors of this violence are chiefly women and children who, despite the cessation of violence six years ago in 1993, still bear the scars of this experience.

Living Conditions of Children

The Government is committed to protecting the welfare and rights of children, but is constrained by a lack of resources. The approximate number of children who die within one year of birth, per 1000 children alive (infant mortality rate), is slightly higher for boys (19) than for girls (16).

The average rate of vaccination for main diseases (BCG, DPT3, Measles, Polio3) is 98%, and 100% of routine EPI vaccines are financed by the government. While no blatant preference for male children is practiced in food allocation within families, food taboos and the still common practice of women eating after other family members could contribute to malnutrition of girls· The government created the National Child Protection Authority (NCPA) in 1998.

The minimum age of employment is recognized to be 14, although the law allows the employment of younger children by their parents or guardians in limited agricultural work. In January 2000, Parliament repealed a regulation allowing domestic employment of children as young as 12. Persons under the age of 16 may not be employed in any public enterprise in which life or limb is endangered. Regular employment of children occurs mainly in the informal sector and in family enterprises such as family farms, crafts, small trade establishments, restaurants and repairs shops. Children are also involved in the manufacture of coconut fiber products, bricks, fishing, tobacco wrapping, street trading, and farming. Government inspections are unable to eliminate these forms of child labor.

The introduction of free primary, secondary, and tertiary education, including university education, in 1945 and the change in the medium of instruction from English to the local languages in primary education in 1945 and in secondary education in the 1950s, led to a rapid increase of educational opportunities. Parents no longer had to choose whether to invest in the education of sons or daughters, and the popular perception that education is a major avenue of upward socioeconomic mobility accelerated equal access to general education for boys and girls, and for men and women.

In 1997, the estimated adult illiteracy rate for the total population was 6% for men and 12.2% for women. In 2000, the rate was 5.6% for men and 11% for women, an improvement. UNESCO defines an illiterate person as someone who, while understanding the situation, cannot read or write a short, simple statement on his or her everyday life.

According to UNESCO, the gross enrolment rate is the total enrolment in primary and secondary education, regardless of age, divided by the population of the age group which officially corresponds to primary or secondary schooling (the ratios include the number of children who repeat a school year). The gross enrolment ratio for tertiary education, regardless of age, is expressed as percentage of the population in the five-year age group following on from secondary-school leaving age.

The social composition of the university student population ceased to be elitist by the end of the 1960s, and since then around 70% of the students have been from the rural sector and less than 35% are from the upper- and middle- class families. The number of female students has been between 40-45% of the total since the end of 1960s

Consequent upon the continuously rising participation of women in the education system, there has been a steady increase in the level of their educational attainment as measured in terms of the proportion of women completing particular educational level or cycles, as well as in terms of overall literacy rates (ESCAP).

Women in Politics

Women have been observed to be politically conscious and to participate extensively in elections, but the percentage of women in Parliament has never exceeded 5%, as it is now, and the percentage is even lower - around 2%-in Provincial councils and Divisional councils. Between 1995 and 1999, the percentage of parliamentary seats in single or lower chamber occupied by women was steady at 5. In 2000, the number of seats occupied by women also reached nearly 5 (4, 9).

Between 1994 and 1998, the number of women in decision-making positions in government has increased slightly, but their numbers remained largely insignificant in 1998, with only 13% of women at the ministerial level and 5% at the sub-ministerial level.

The Constitution of Sri Lanka seeks to guarantee gender equality as a fundamental right and nondiscriminatory new legislation. A committee of representatives from state agencies and women's organizations has formulated a Women's Charter for Sri Lanka, using CEDAW as a model. The Charter was accepted as a state policy in 1993, but the provisions of the UN Convention and the Charter, however, lack legal validity, as steps have not yet been taken to incorporate these rights to the national legal system.

The National Plan of Action for Women in Sri Lanka was prepared in 1995 by the Ministry of Women's Affairs (MWA), the National Committee for Women, and representatives of women's organizations, but has not yet been incorporated to national or sectoral programs, although sectoral activity plans have been prepared. In 1998, the Ministry of Women's Affairs prepared a three-year development plan for the Ministry, and a project was developed with support from the United Nation's Development Program to strengthen the Ministry.

Four international conferences on gender issues were held between 1975 and 1995. The last one took place in Beijing in 1995 and gathered more than 47,000 representatives from various countries and non-governmental organizations (NGOs).

Participants unanimously adopted the Beijing Declaration and the Platform for Action that was in essence an agenda for women's empowerment.

Sri Lanka has signed the United Nations Convention on the Elimination of All Forms of Discrimination Against Women (CEDAW) in 1981. Following the Fourth World Conference on Women in Beijing, Sri Lanka has not presented to the United Nations Secretariat its plan to implement the Platform for Action.

In 1984, Sri Lanka withdrew from the ILO Convention prohibiting night work and has not ratified the convention on Discrimination and Respect of Employment and Occupations.

Health Situation

The immunization coverage of children against six diseases is high and sustained at above 90 percent. Tetanus toxoid immunization of pregnant women is nearly 80 percent. Sri Lanka is now poised for launching new vaccination initiatives. The total fertility rate in Sri Lanka has progressively decreased over the years. According to the latest Demographic Health Survey it is 2.3 in 1993, as against 2.8 in 1987 and 3.4 in 1974, which leads to population growth rate of one percent.

The coverage of MCH/FP services continue to improve and more emphasis is now on the quality of care. The coverage of four selected key elements of MCH services are: Percentage of pregnant women attended by trained personnel during pregnancy - 98%; Percentage of deliveries attended by trained personnel - 95%; percentage of infants attended by trained personnel - 98; and Percentage of married women of childbearing age use family planning - 66.1.

National Committee on Women

The National Committee on Women is a Presidential Committee appointed in terms of the Women's Charter of Sri Lanka, which was adopted by the Government in 1993 for the purpose of implementing the provisions of the Charter. The members of the Committee are persons competent in several areas which are of particular concern to women, such as law, health, economic development, education, science and technology, and the environment, as well as persons who have distinguished themselves in voluntary organisations or in the sphere of women's activities.

The Women's Charter is a 'Bill of Rights' for women. The State adopted the Women's Charter and established the

National Committee on Women on recognising that discrimination against women is a reality in Sri Lanka despite the country's constitutional guarantee of non-discrimination on the grounds, inter alia, of sex, and despite Sri Lanka's ratification of international instruments against such discrimination, such as the Convention on the Elimination of All Forms of Discrimination Against Women (CEDAW). It is important to note that the Committee is "on" women and not "of" women, and that men also serve on it.

The Committee shall consist of 15 members as follows and the general structure is as follows:

- Two members each appointed by the President of Sri Lanka from amongst persons of standing in the community who have distinguished themselves in the fields of:
    - Law
    - Health
    - Economic development Education
    - Science and Technology
    - Environment
- Two members appointed by the President of Sri Lanka from amongst persons who have distinguished themselves in the work of women's Voluntary Organizations or in the sphere of women's activities;
- An Executive Director appointed by the President of Sri Lanka who shall be of a rank not less than Class I of the All Island State Services or of like or equal rank in the non-government sector, having experience in the work related to women and development. The Executive Director shall also be a member and a full-time official of the Committee.
- The Chairperson of the Committee shall be appointed by the President of Sri Lanka from amongst the 14 members appointed under paragraphs (1) and (2) of this sub-section.
- There shall be a Secretary to the Committee who shall be a full- time official also appointed by the President of Sri Lanka.
- The Chairperson and the other members of the Committee shall hold office for a period of 4 years and shall be eligible for re-appointment for one consecutive period.
- Subject to the approval of the President of Sri Lanka the Minister may appoint a suitable person to fill any vacancy

occurring among the members and any person so appointed shall hold office for the unexpired period of the term of office of the member whom she/he succeeds.

— The quorum for any meeting of the Committee shall be 7 members.

— The Committee shall meet as often as may be necessary and at least once in every two months.

— Any member may resign her/his office by a letter addressed to the Minister.

— The Committee may act notwithstanding any vacancy among the members thereof.

— The Committee shall have a permanent office and a Secretariat with full-time staff functioning under the Executive Director .

The functions of the Committee shall be as follows:

- to entertain and scrutinise complaints of gender discrimination and channel such complaints where appropriate to the relevant administrative authorities and concerned persons or bodies for necessary action;
- to refer complaints of violation of the provisions contained in this Charter to governmental and non-governmental organization for redress, legal aid and / or mediation services;
- to monitor such action and require annual reports of progress from relevant administrative authorities and make these reports widely available within the country;
- to evaluate the impact of allegislative and development policies on the rights and responsibilities of women as contained in this Charter;
- to help to realise the objectives of the Charter through the encouragement of relevant research and to make recommendations for reforms based on such research; and
- to advise the Minister (responsible for the Status of Women) on such matters relating to the Status of Women as the Minister may refer to the Committee for its consideration, or as the Committee may deem appropriate.

In the 1970s, women's issues focused on discrimination in political and economic benefits and an equitable development process for women of the Third World. The major international convention which dealt with women's rights, The Convention on the Elimination of All Forms of Discrimination Against Women (CEDAW), which came into force in 1979, adopted the "non- discrimination" model; women's rights were violated only if women were denied the same benefits as men. Though there were sections on custom and traditional practices, the Convention was silent on the issue of violence against women.

At the World Conference celebrating the Women's Decade in Nairobi in 1985, the problem of violence against women was raised but in a marginal manner, as an afterthought to the other provisions dealing with discrimination, health, economic, and social issues.

There are in effect three approaches to the issue of violence against women (Omvedt). The radical feminist approach locates the discussion in an understanding of patriarchy. According to this approach, violence is intrinsic in the relationship between men and women and manifests itself in sexuality as well as in the social and political institutions of society. This leads to a focus on problems of domestic violence, and rape as a manifestation of the initial inequality in the relationship between the sexes. Violence is, therefore, pervasive and inherent in women's daily interaction with men.

Socialist feminism approaches the question of violence against women in a fundamentally different way. Violence is seen as a part of the social and economic forces which operate in society, forces which make women one of many victims. The struggle against violence is, therefore, not a struggle against men and male domination alone, but against systems of exploitation which disempower women.

Violence is a result of economic exploitation and only secondarily a function of the male-female relationship. Third world socialist feminists see female workers in certain industries as being victims of violence. There is also a concern with the commodification of women as sexual objects in prostitution and the international trafficking of women.

Eco-feminism also deals with violence against women in a significantly different way. It sees relationships between women and nature, between subsistence production in which certain women engage, and violent accumulation in which certain men engage, and the state.

The human rights paradigm, on the other hand, privileges a certain type of human personality, namely, the free, independent woman as an individual endowed with rights and rational agency. The core concept of the human rights approach centres around the issue of empowerment. Violence against women involves the use of force or the threat of the use of force to prevent the necessary empowerment of women within society.

In addition, violence was initially seen as an act of private individuals, and the human rights model was not structured to hold states accountable for the acts of private citizens. But in recent times, there has been a growing understanding that state responsibility includes the duty to prevent the rights of individuals from being violated by private actors, whether they be individuals or corporations. The emergence of state responsibility for violence in society has been one of the most important contributions of the women's movement to the issue of human rights.

The human rights approach to violence, therefore, is based on the rights of individuals to be free and independent without being threatened by the use of force. If force is not strictly construed to mean only the actual use of physical force, the mandate is a broad one. It implies the right to investigate all forms of action which disempower women because of the fear of violence, whether that fear is instilled by the State, by actors in the community or by members of the family. This broad approach appears to have been adopted by the General Assembly in its Declaration on the Elimination of Violence Against Women.

Violence and economic exploitation refers to aspects of a woman's life which are related to her labour. This includes labour in sweat shops as well as prostitution and trafficking. It also includes violence against women as bonded labour or agricultural workers. Finally, violence and culture refers to cultural practices devised by different societies, such as female circumcision.

One may also categorize violence in terms of women's relationships to men and society. Women are subject to violence because of being female. In this capacity, they are subject to rape, female circumcision, genital mutilation, and female infanticide. These relate again to the construction of female sexuality. A woman is also subject to violence because of her relationship to a man. These include domestic violence, dowry murder, sati

Finally, a woman is subject to violence because of the social group to which she belongs. In times of war, riots or ethnic and caste violence, a woman may be raped or brutalized as a means of humiliating the community to which she belongs.

In recent times, violence has been categorized by the location of the violence: violence in the family, in the community, and by the state. The UN Declaration on the Elimination of Violence Against Women categorizes violence in this manner, and recent social science writing has also accepted this categorization.

The General Assembly Declaration on the Elimination of Violence Against Women defines violence as:

> any act of gender-based violence that results in or is likely to result in physical, sexual or psychological harm or suffering to women, including threats of such acts, coercion or arbitrary deprivation ofliberty whether occurring in public or private life.

This definition appears to envision individual victims at the receiving end of individual acts of violence. Women from the Third World would want to expand the interpretation of this section for a broader reading of violence.

Causes of Violence Against Women

A large majority of women writers appear to link violence against women with a lack of economic independence. Levinson studied 90 societies and found wife-beating to be prevalent in 75 (Levinson). The four cultural factors that are strong predictors for wife abuse are sexual economic inequality, a pattern of using violence for conflict resolution, male authority and decision- making in the home, and divorce restrictions I for women.

Women's economic dependence disempowers them and makes them not only susceptible to violence, but also unable to challenge and fight against violence. Linked to the notion of economic dependency are other sorts of legal, political, and social dependency which make it difficult for women to assert their independence when confronted with violence.

Legal systems which do not permit women to divorce, for example, or which do not support women when they are in a situation of violence aggravate the problem. Women are expected to remain in situations where violence is being used against them and, therefore, the nature and extent of the violence increases. An undemocratic society which uses the military as the tool of repression is likely to have a great deal of violence directed against women.

Violence against women is also the result of a society which wants to control the expression of female sexuality. Violence is often directed against women to ensure that she is "chaste" and virtuous. It is argued that this is to ensure that the children she gives birth to are the children of the correct father and, therefore, the lawful heirs to his property. Allegations of adultery were the major reason for wife beating in Papua New Guinea.

Sexual harassment of free trade zone workers is often excused by the fact that they dress "provocatively." And, of course, it is always a defence for rape and harassment that the woman in her demeanor " asked for it." The fear of violence is an important part of women's reality and it conditions women's behaviour in many aspects of their day to day lives.

Male alcoholism is also one of the major reasons for violence in the family, along with a woman's refusal to perform her "wifely duties", a euphemism for sexual intercourse. Although social workers have to take these causes into consideration, it is imperative that the legal system not recognize any of these excuses for violence as legitimate.

The Role of the State in the Violence

In the past, strict judicial interpretations of international law only held the state responsible for its own actions, for example, in relation to women in custody or detention, and during armed conflict. Domestic violence, rape, and sexual harassment, for example, were not seen as state action but only as the acts of individuals. This narrow interpretation has been recently challenged.

A state which tolerates violence against women at the community and family level, and which does not take effective measures to prevent this violence or hold accountable those who are responsible for the violence, is as guilty as the individual perpetrators.

Until recently, there was no real set of international legal standards which relate to violence against women. The approach during the early stages was to make violence an aspect of discrimination and, therefore, central in spirit to CEDAW. Violence against women was seen to violate articles 2, 3, 5, 6, 11, 12, and 16 of CEDAW. These articles deal specifically with prohibition of discrimination by public and private actors, the obligation to ensure full development and advancement of women, the need to eliminate traditional practices which discriminate against women, the need to eliminate trafficking in women, and the need to promote employment, health, and equality in the family. Though none of the provisions deal directly with the issue of violence, it was argued that eliminating the problem of violence is part of the elimination of discrimination.

The Committee in charge of implementing the CEDAW stated clearly in General Recommendation that violence is a form of discrimination. The attempt to stretch the Convention to include violence has been somewhat successful, but more specific international standards are necessary. Those standards have been clearly spelled out in the UN Declaration on the Elimination of Violence Against Women passed by the General Assembly in December 1993.

The preamble to the Declaration locates the problem of violence against women in unequal power and women's structural subordination. It also identifies particularly vulnerable groups of women who are at the receiving end of violence. These include minority women, indigenous groups, refugee women, migrant women, women living in rural or remote communities, destitute women, women in detention, female children, women with disabilities, elderly women, and women in situations of armed conflict.

The Declaration defines violence broadly to include physical, sexual, and psychological violence. It is categorized according to whether it occurs in the family, in the community, or by the state. Under each category, the type of violence which is prevalent is enumerated. In the family, these include: battering, sexual abuse of female children, dowry-related violence, marital rape, female genital mutilation, traditional practices which are harmful to women, non- spousal violence, and violence relating to exploitation.

Other specific state obligations outlined in Article 4 of the Declaration include the ratification of CEDAW, the exercise of due diligence in preventing and investigating violence against women, in accordance with national legislation, and the punishment of acts of violence by the state or by private persons. There are specific directives for developing legal and administrative mechanisms to ensure effective justice for victims of violence and to ensure that there is support and rehabilitation for women victims of violence.

The Declaration recommends training judicial and police officials, reforming educational curricula, promoting research in this area, and engaging in full reporting of the problem of violence against women to international human rights mechanisms. The Declaration sees the international community as an essential actor in the process of eliminating violence against women. UN agencies are responsible for promoting awareness of the issues in their program, collecting data on the problem, periodically analyzing the trends, formulating guidelines and manuals on the issue, and cooperating with NGOs in addressing the issue.

The UN Declaration is not a binding document, but it sets out international standards in a clear and comprehensive manner. The Declaration should be an integral part of the mandate of the Special Rapporteur on Violence Against Women and provide her with guidance in her work.

Violence in the community raises different issues. Although the Declaration states that states should not invoke cultural or religious factors as an excuse for condoning violence against women, these identities are extremely powerful, especially in the Third World. A purely legalistic approach to these issues will not suffice and, in fact, may raise the argument that the Declaration is a "western" draft not related to the situation in the East or other parts of the Third World. If international action can link with NGOs in putting forward an argument that violence against women is never a part of an essentialist national " culture," only a man- made practice which distorts that culture, then the likelihood of making an impact in these societies is greater.

Violence by the state also raises particular issues. In repressive states, the problem of women in custody and detention is significant. In this context, the thrust to make the state answerable for violence against women is part of the general struggle for human rights and democratization. In pursuing these issues, it is important to work with NGOs and other groups who are interested in the general problems of democracy and human rights. The women's issue cannot be seen in isolation. State responsibility for the general violence in society directed against women is, perhaps, the most important principle to emerge in this context. The assertion of this principle is, perhaps, the primary vehicle for making it clear to government that it is responsible if effective action is not taken to prevent, investigate, and to punish acts of violence directed against women.

Trafficking in Women

Trafficking in women is an issue affecting countries within Asia as well as other parts of the world. Women and children are trafficked for prostitution and other forms of sexual exploitation, such as sex tourism and pornography. Female domestic workers, beggars and workers on construction sites face other forms of exploitation, and some are trafficked as mail order brides. ESCAP points out in its paper, "Trafficking-Regional and International Mechanisms, Initiatives and Prospects: An Overview," that the increasing use of new information technologies, in particular the Internet, presents a new dimension to the problem.

A Convention to prevent trafficking of women and children was drafted by a group of experts in New Delhi in June 1988 and was accepted by the Council of Ministers at the SAARC summit in Colombo in 1998, and is open for signature at the next summit to be held in Kathmandu. It will fulfil a long-felt need to counteract a vicious phenomenon with transnational implications that had been on the increase in the Asian region.

The globalization process and the advent of open economies have severed traditional socio-economic relations, making women and children more vulnerable. In this situation, they have become a commodity to be sold in the "World Market". Traditional attitudes towards women and girl children, as well as poverty and the caste system of some countries, are some of the factors that contribute to this unfortunate state. Discriminatory laws, denial of property rights and certain religious taboos have created negative conditions that militate against them. A woman or a girl child is seen in this context as a burden to the family.

Poverty and economic deprivation are behind this problem, and the victims are lured by promises of greener pastures, often promises of marriage and employment. They are duped, coerced, abducted, and, in some cases sold, thus becoming victims of this organized crime. There are cases of kidnapping as well. These victims cannot escape their slave-like conditions even if they wanted to, unless disease, old age or death overtakes them. They often lack legal protection, and accurate statistics relating to this problem at the national, regional and international levels are inadequate.

However, many countries have now undertaken research on trafficking and are compiling information on all aspects of the issue. It is clear that the problem has increased, especially in Asia, and continues to increase. Asia is considered the world centre for this trade.

The UN Convention for the Suppression of the Trafficking in Persons and the Exploitation or the Prostitution of Others of 1949 is the earliest international standard on this subject. It defines trafficking within the context of prostitution in the following terms: "any person who procures, entices or leads away for the purpose of prostitution another person, even with the consent of the other person: (2) exploits the prostitution of another person, even with the consent of the other person." This definition was further expanded by Article 6 of the Convention for the Elimination of all forms of Discrimination Against Women (CEDAW) in 1979 to include other forms of exploitation, such as the deception of migrant women and false or mail order marriages, all other forms of sexual exploitation, sex tourism and forced domestic labour recruited from developing to developed countries.

Sri Lanka has a natural advantage as an island with respect to the phenomenon of large scale cross-border trafficking of women and children: it simply cannot occur. However, many young women have fallen prey within the country to so-called job agents who lure unemployed rural girls to the city. These women may eventually become trapped in a cultural environment that stigmatises victims of rape or abuse.

In the late 1980s, the trafficking of children from Sri Lanka for adoption by Westerners came to light. This racket was carried on by some Sri Lankans who exploited the facility provided by the Department of Immigration and Emigration to attach the names of children to the passports of their parents. The adoption of babies in Sri Lanka, a "commercial enterprise" in the seventies and eighties, gave rise to baby farms and the cross-border trafficking of babies for adoption by foreigners. Stringent law enforcement has, fortunately, curbed this form of abuse.

Approximately 45,000 women from Sri Lanka work in West Asia. The run away rate is high, as ILO standards and labour protection legislation are absent. These women face the risks of ending up in brothels or working as domestic slaves. Bonded labour is also a reality when women depend on the recruiter for their tickets. When these women reach their destination, they are forced to surrender their passports and other important documents to prevent them from running away; these conditions are tantamount to forced labour. There have been 343 death reported through consular channels, and over 7000 cases of reported harassment from 1993 to 1995. There are many who are stranded abroad and large numbers are reported to have sought refuge in Sri Lankan missions abroad.

A study on the socio-economic dimensions of HIV / AIDS, carried out in 1996, revealed a total of approximately 12,000 sex workers in the country. A study by Professor Ratnapala estimated their numbers to be about 20,000. Police reports indicate that 646 women were arrested under the Vagrant's Ordinance in 1985, -and the number had risen to 2210 in 1993. In 1985, there were 20 women convicted of soliciting-a figure which rose to 276 in 1993. The total number thus rose from 1586 in 1986 to 2517 in 1993. However, there is no information available on how many of these women were trafficked for the sex trade. Trafficking, therefore, does not surface as a cause for concern.

The sex trade is mainly concentrated in Colombo, in several provincial towns, and in the tourist area in the coastal belt. Sri Lanka is known to receive women and girls through trafficking from East European countries and Thailand.

However, it is the sexual exploitation of children, especially in the coastal areas-a repercussion of tourism-which is a cause for concern. It is estimated that approximately 30,000 children are victims of sexual abuse, but this number may not be accurate. German magazines like Spartecus advertise Sri Lanka along with Thailand and the Philippines as prime destinations for paedophiles.

Efforts by the FPASL in implementing the ICPD Programme of Action

THE Family Planning Association of Sri Lanka pioneered family planning in the country in 1953, and has since been the main NGO contributor to Sri Lanka's National Family Planning Programme. Since the ICPD Programme of Action was agreed, the Association has developed activities to move away from exclusive family planning to a wider programme of reproductive health.

- Co-operation with other NGOs avoids duplication of activities and links programmes and services.
- Through its advocacy work, the Association works to eliminate unsafe abortion.
- By organizing workshops, young people are given opportunities to interact and discuss their sexual and reproductive needs, and what can be done to meet the identified needs in the future.
- By working in refugee camps, the Association tries to secure at least some reproductive rights of the marginalized group of involuntarily displaced persons.
- Community-based education and advocacy campaigns strive to improve gender equity and women's empowerment.

To develop and strengthen existing NGOs, the concept of *Mother NGO* emerged. The *Mother NGO* should ideally help build the capacity of community-based organizations and help integrate reproductive health activities into existing programmes. The community-based organizations that have until now been involved with Mother NGOs in Sri Lanka have most often been involved in specialized activities such as sports, cultural programmes, agricultural and farming, youth work, or helping women with income-generation activities.

The FPASL has been recognized by the EC/ UNFPA as a Mother NGO and has in this way secured funding to help 30 organizations with the development of their management capacity and infrastructure. Funds to initiate reproductive health activities are also available for most of the organizations. A further 25 organizations are working with the three other key national family planning NGOs, now also termed *Mother NGOs*.

The project has worked extremely well - all the organizations linked to *Mother NGOs* have introduced reproductive health activities along with their work in their communities. Activities include educational programmes, clinics providing specialized medical services, referral of family planning acceptors to government clinics, and at times the distribution of contraceptives through community-based outlets.

The Sri Lankan Association held five workshops around the country for youth leaders where the recommendations of the ICPD Youth Caucus were discussed. The unmet needs of youth in Sri Lanka were discussed and possible ways of meeting these needs were explored. Young men and women from community-level organizations participated in the workshops, which were conducted by selected youth organizations.

The workshops included lectures on subjects related to the needs of young people and discussions on the findings of different research studies on knowledge, attitude and behaviour of Sri Lankan youth. The participants had plenty of opportunities to discuss and make recommendations on how some of their needs could be addressed in future years.

The participants agreed that the print media should be encouraged to provide correct information related to sexual and reproductive health, that the electronic media, especially TV, should conduct educational programmes aimed specifically at adolescents and that more resources should be made available for national youth organizations to strengthen their work.

Today there are at least three radio-stations that produce live radio programmes where young people can ask questions over the telephone on sexual health issues. The answers do not only benefit the individual caller, but all the listeners.

Also, almost all the weekly newspapers, which are aimed at young people, today carry feature articles and special pages to answer questions on reproductive health issues. The Association has also conducted training activities for a group of young journalists with great success. Following the training, feature articles on sexual health have appeared in several journals and newspapers.

During a seminar for youth journalists held recently, a representative from one of the radio-stations organized a live question-answer session during the seminar. As an immediate outcome more than 15 articles related to reproductive health were published in different weekly newspapers.

The abortion business is doing well in Sri Lanka. The business thrives on the illegality of the procedure and the resulting lack of choice for the consumer - the woman seeking an abortion. Because of the illegality, prices are high while quality and safety are left uncontrolled. Although abortion is illegal in Sri Lanka, except in cases where the woman's life is in danger, the procedure takes place 750 times every day in the country according to the UNFPA.

That means that for every birth taking place in Sri Lanka an abortion is performed. A woman can easily obtain a safe abortion if she has the money to pay for it. Depending on the amount of money available, she can have it done in a state-of-the-art hospital in a foreign country or in a plush clinic in Colombo. But the poor have to settle on a back-street clinic where the hygiene is highly questionable. As with many other health issues around the world, the poor pay a relatively high price for very little value.

In the case of abortion, the poor do not receive proper medical care, but are instead subjected to health risks - including complications from which they may die. It is not rare for women leaving the abortion clinic to become infected by reproductive tract infections, or to have had their reproductive organs seriously damaged. Everyone agrees - something must be done. Both married and unmarried women, from rural and urban areas, seek abortion services. They each have their reason for wanting to terminate the pregnancy.

Family Planning

While the Family Planning Association in Sri Lanka is not promoting abortion as a family planning method, it is advocating for the prevention of unsafe abortions. The Association has worked with the media in trying to get the attention of government officials and other influential leaders. They want the government to consider appropriate action to prevent unsafe abortions and to consider legalizing it, at least in cases of contraceptive failure and sexual abuse, such as rape and incest. To date, the government has responded to the request from foreign non-governmental organizations and the Family Planning Association to look into the issue of unsafe abortions.

Although there is a high contraceptive prevalence rate in Sri Lanka (about seven in ten couples use contraception), this includes many couples relying on natural methods such as 'withdrawal' before ejaculation and sex during the 'safe period'. In addition to the family planning services, which the Association has provided since 1954, an emergency contraceptive pill is now made available from retail outlets. The Association has begun an educational programme for General Medical Practitioners and Pharmacists on the use of this pill and is seeking their support to prescribe the pill for those who need it to prevent unwanted pregnancy.

In promoting the pill, the Association started a telephone hotline. During the first six months more than 5,000 people called to get information. The Association also launched a campaign with posters, leaflets and newspaper advertisements to promote the use of the new pill. Hundreds of makeshift dwellings - homes to thousands of people - depict the human misery that an armed conflict has caused. Those who work with the people will tell you that "You cannot possibly understand unless you are a victim" of the traumatic experience of being forced to leave your home. But this is what people had to do when a conflict between two groups at war could no longer 'accommodate' a group of people in the middle of the 'war-zone'. Hundreds of families, mostly Muslims, have migrated from different conflict zones only to find space in refugee camps with few basic facilities.

The absence of facilities such as adequate sanitation and health care makes not only epidemics common, but also increases the infant and maternal mortality rates. The Family Planning Association in Sri Lanka has initiated a project covering 15,000 of the displaced persons. The initiative made possible by the Netherlands Trust Fund, aims to strengthen community participation in improving sexual and reproductive health.

Currently, the Association is supporting 24 Health Committees at the camp level. The committees comprise both camp leaders and official health staff and this set up is part of the strategy to facilitate links between community and government. It is hoped that the government will increasingly take responsibility for providing the communities with health care infrastructure. With the help of 410 volunteers, family planning advice and health education including vital information on nutrition and sanitation is provided.

Community-based contraceptive distributors ensure that family planning methods are readily available. The Association hopes that the mix of health officials, local leaders, and the commitment of volunteers will ensure that the communities will gain increasing access to sexual and reproductive health care.

Mahila Shanti

Commenting on a community meeting, a teacher of Dodangaslanda Mahavidaylaya school said: "We have no objections to women gaining their rightful place in the society. Our religion and our culture have never undermined them, but what we fear is that too much freedom, and unrestricted emancipation might lead to the destruction of our traditional family set-up, we don't like to see our families break up."

The teacher was listening in at a community meeting where the Family Planning Association of Sri Lanka provided information on gender equity and women's rights. Although part of the goal of the Association's community meetings is to open up for discussions, this goal rarely needs input. Debates usually follow whether the Association's facilitator stays or leaves.

Since 1997, the Association has held community meetings and participated in discussions in 25 communities around Sri

Lanka on gender and women's issues. Attitudinal change takes a long time. Judging from initial reactions, it is not impossible to change people's perception of social roles and responsibilities. As the teacher went on to say, "... If, as you say, women's equity and empowerment is aimed at enhancing their knowledge, skills, and capabilities, then we are sure families will have a better and brighter future."

The reality is, unfortunately, that many women are subjected to domestic violence, often both physical and psychological. The baseline-survey for the Mahila Shanti project indicated that the majority of people felt that women should be treated equally. However, once the volunteers had established personal contacts and were let in on 'family secrets', they found that both physical and psychological violence and abuse were taking place.

Over 300 trained volunteers, under the leadership of grassroot committees, have facilitated seminars, group meetings, debates, and home-discussions in communities. The events centre on women's status in Sri Lankan society. Women's and men's access to, and control over resources are explored in group-discussions. On a few occasions, issues of domestic violence have been raised. The project is still in its initial stages. So far, rapport has been established in some of the communities, but most of the volunteers are convinced that it is just a matter of time before the process accelerates.

In many developing countries, women still do not have access to good antenatal care or adequate nutrition during pregnancy. Only about half of all deliveries are assisted by a skilled birth attendant (a doctor, midwife, nurse or community worker with midwifery training) — one of the key requisites for safe motherhood. Every year, 60 million births take place in which the mother is helped by a family member or an untrained traditional birth attendant — or gives birth alone.

The problem is often compounded by poor follow-up care for both mother and baby and by a lack of family planning services to ensure that any future births are well spaced. WHO estimates that providing this minimum level of care — the so-called Mother-Baby Package — would cost about US$ 3 per person each year in low-income countries.

Disregard of Human Rights

In the midst of this casual disregard for the human rights and well-being of millions of women in developing countries, Sri Lanka is one country that stands out for its long-term commitment to safe motherhood. Infection rates have been reduced and the maternal mortality ratio is one of the lowest in the developing world at 60 per 100 000 live births. Since 1990, the number of maternal deaths has been halved from 520 to 250 in 1998.

Today, over 96% of deliveries in Sri Lanka are attended by a skilled birth attendant and over 90% take place in a health facility — with a referral system in place to ensure transport to one of 45 hospitals if complications occur. All first pregnancies and high-risk pregnancies are referred to health facilities with obstetricians. And a network of community midwives provides antenatal care for about 75% of women throughout their pregnancy.

Yet Sri Lanka is not a rich country. In 1998, its GDP was only US$ 802 per capita and more than a third of the population were estimated to be living below the national poverty line. By comparison, in Côte d'Ivoire, with a slightly higher GDP of US$ 823, maternal mortality ratios are ten times higher. Sri Lanka's success in preventing maternal deaths has been achieved against a backdrop of government commitment to improving education and health care. Over 93% of people today have access to basic health care.

Another driving force today is the education and relatively high status of women. Adult literacy rates among women are 88% and girls have access to free education up to university level. As a result, there has been an increase in the age of marriage — to 25 in 1993 — and women are better able to take advantage of family planning and maternal health services.

However, continuing efforts will be needed to reach the small percentage of women in Sri Lanka who still do not have access to good maternal health care. Of the 5% of women who give birth at home, not all have access to a skilled birth attendant. And maternal death ratios are far higher in the north of the country due to the ongoing civil conflict and poor living conditions. Elsewhere, unsafe abortions account for an estimated 5%-9% of maternal deaths each year.

The Plight of Sri Lankan Women

The women of Sri Lanka bring in most of the country's much-needed foreign exchange, they have yet to receive adequate legal protection against violence and other social threats confronting them. 'Women have entered the public arena in a big way, (but) there's been no corresponding protection to go along with that phenomenon' she observes. 'Right now there's no law against sexual harassment. It is a very common factor wherever women are'.

Today, the Government acknowledge and even boasts that garments and foreign employment of Sri Lankans are the two biggest foreign exchange earners for the country. It has overtaken traditional commodity exports like tea, rubber and coconuts in the last decade. The truth of the matter is that it is women who create most of this income for Sri Lanka.

Their pitiful work conditions in both these areas seem to be nobody's concern agree many social welfare analysts here. Sri Lanka earned Rs.76.6 billion (about US$1.5 billion) in 1994 from garment exports .produced mainly in the Free Trade Zones (FTZ) in the country - which made up 48% of its export income. Out of the 100,000 jobs created in the FTZs in recent years, 80% have gone to women. There are 500,000 migrant workers, mainly in the Middle-East, who contributed Rs.35 billion (US$ 0.7 billion) to the national coffers in 1994 - over 50% of them are women, working as maids.

In March last year alone, 11 deaths were reported from the Middle-East, the Sri Lankan embassies and local non-governmental welfare agencies get at an average 400 complaints a month about physical and verbal abuse, and there are some 300 Sri Lankans in the United Arab Emirates (UAE) prisons.

On 13 April 1995, when most Sri Lankans were celebrating the national new year, a young Sri Lankan maid, Sithi Unisa, faced a firing squad in the UAE. The Foreign Ministry in Colombo learnt about her death only four days later. The family knew about it through a telephone message delivered to a nearby temple from another maid in the UAE. Another maid who had returned home from UAE told Unisa's family, that she had been executed for a murder she had never committed. An infant child had died after falling off the hands of her mother, but the mistress blamed the maid for the death. This is typical of many cases which come to light at regular intervals regarding Sri Lankan maids overseas.

Helen Perera,the President of the Rural Womens' Front (RWF), which is discouraging women from leaving their villages for jobs abroad argues that the Government is not opposed to Sri Lankan women going overseas to work because of the foreign exchange the national coffers receive as a result.

Recently Sri Lankans were shocked by a dramatic increase in the reported cases of incest. According to Dr Tilak Hettiarachchi, senior lecturer in Psychology at the University of Colombo, this has mainly happened in homes where the wife is out in the Middle-East and the man is left alone with the children. 'When money starts coming in, the man gives up his job and starts consuming alcohol and sleeping with his daughter. The worse thing is, men even justify their actions,' says Dr Hettiarachi. 'In many cases these men have said that since their wives are away, they need to be satisfied sexually and this they get from their daughter.'

Many women social workers here have mixed feelings about the increased job creation for women under Sri Lanka's economic liberalisation policies since 1977. The FTZs which have been at the hub of Sri Lanka's economic liberalisation policies have created more jobs for women than men.

Most of the women who work in these are young girls who have been protected in the villagers and are now on their own in these zones. To attract foreign investors, Sri Lanka has completely done away with the law, which previously prohibited women from working night-shifts. Thus, some women finish their shifts late at night or early in the morning and get exposed to many dangerous situations on their way back home.

The studies done by the Colombo University have found that the FTZs have been the preying grounds for pimps from brothels in Colombo and the tourist centres on the coast, where they befriend unsuspecting village girls. They are gradually transformed from being girl friends to sex workers.

Sri Lanka's Gender Development Statistics

Around 22% of all households in Sri Lanka are female-headed. Many of these women have been thrust into the role of breadwinner with little knowledge of income-earning methods and few coping skills. Moreover, the word withawi (for widow) has connotations of a deplorable and pitiable condition. Social isolation are poverty are inevitable for these women, many of whom are widowed at a young age.

Although the percentage of Sri Lankan women entering universities increased from 42% in 1989 to 52% in 1999 (bearing in mind that only 1% of the population has access to university education), women are still under-represented in many disciplines, and tend to find employment at the bottom of the employment pyramid. When they do find work, it is usually in low-status, low-skilled and low-paying jobs in peasant and plantation agriculture. In addition to this, the female unemployment rate, at 22%, is double that of men in Sri Lanka.

Furthermore, a majority of jobs available to women are in the unorganised and informal sectors, which are outside the purview of labour regulations. An example of this is the growing number of women engaged in the garment industry, who are prone to suffer physical disabilities directly linked to long hours of hard labour.

This same fate awaits the women who represent around 76% of the unskilled migrant labour force working in oil-rich countries and South-East Asian countries. Reports in local newspapers highlight tales of woe where many of these women have suffered untold hardships, including beatings, torture and even death, due to lack of cross-border employment agreements and regulatory practices between national governments.

Besides garment workers and migrant workers, the largest proportion of women in the informal sector is engaged in cultivation. A growing threat to the livelihood security of these women is the increasing mechanisation of agriculture.

As a result, the female whose sense of self-worth was linked to her ability to contribute to the productive process now finds herself left out, and her contribution deemed worthless. This reduces her value within the family and community, and must be considered by governments and

NGOs [non-governmental organisations] that may opt to promote mechanisation of agriculture as a means of 'development'. Discriminatory practices over land inheritance and custody battles further contribute to the decline in self-worth among women in Sri Lanka. In such cases, males are often given preferential treatment. This despite constitutionally guaranteed laws that grant women equal rights with men.

As for the political empowerment of women, it bears mention that both the president and prime minister of Sri Lanka are women. However, this does not necessarily indicate a high political profile for the average woman, nor does it represent the involvement of women in policy-planning and decision-making at higher levels. A survey found that women in Sri Lanka do not aspire to be active in politics, which is amply demonstrated by the fact that few women opt for political careers, and fewer still are elected to Parliament at the regional and provincial levels.

All of these factors indicate that there is a hidden dimension to the image presented in printed statistics - a dimension rarely highlighted and only dimly visible to the observer. Within this context it would be only correct to say that, despite impressive human development indicators, Sri Lanka still has a long way to go in fully utilising the skills and talents of its female citizens to move the country's development and peace processes forward.

Women's Property and Inheritance Rights

Bangladesh, Cambodia, Nepal, and Sri Lanka were selected as target countries to receive grants to support activities in two areas. The two areas are: (1) activities that advocate, report on, or seek to inform women and/or governmental officials (executive branch or parliamentarians) and judicial and legal professionals of women's property and inheritance rights; and (2) activities that focus on a consolidated effort or approach among the NGO and government community to address issues of property and inheritance rights in a targeted country.

The Office of Women in Development has awarded small grants to the following NGOs in Sri Lanka through the Office's Small Grants Program.

In the 1980s, the Vehilihini Development Centre (VDC)-based in southeastern Moneragala District, the second largest district in the country-conducted a study of 610 families living on land grants, of which two-thirds were women-headed households. The findings of the study indicated that of the women-headed households, almost 90% had a problem with the provisions of the Land Development Ordinance (LDO) established by the British in 1935.

One provision under the land ordinance-which is considered General Law, one of four different legal systems affecting succession of property-states that the land is given to the head of the household (recognized as the husband) and upon his death, the wife will get life interest, which means she can use the property, but cannot transfer or sell it. Further, single women have not been considered eligible to receive land.

This grant allows VDC to identify provisions of the land ordinance that discriminate against women. Following identification of these discriminatory provisions, three different groups from the community participated in awareness-raising workshops. The first group comprised 120 women activists and volunteers from throughout the district who attended a three-day workshop. Following this workshop, all 120 women met with their community groups to further build awareness. Second, local government officials, such as Government Administrators and Land Revenue Office Officials, received training to enable them to better enforce the Land Development Ordinance. Third, VDC provided sessions to 40 unmarried adolescent girls who are completing their secondary education in order to mobilize their support for amending this act.

Over 750 women's property and inheritance cases have been collected and are available in Sinhala. VDC has also been working with other Sri Lankan NGOs and lawyers to prepare draft amendments. More than 800 women travelled to Colombo on March 8 as part of the annual celebration of International Women's Day to deliver a petition to the Land Ministry to amend the outdated act.

They run a shelter in Colombo and have a hotline, which is now connected to the General Hospital, enabling their social workers and volunteers to provide immediate counseling in emergency situations. This grant is supporting WIN to fulfill a number of objectives: to conduct research on discriminatory customary practices, especially under the Kandyan and Muslim

Law; take action on five cases brought forward through activities conducted; conduct awareness-raising programs through community-based organizations, with the target of raising awareness among 5,000 people; and mobilize support from policymakers for changing discriminatory provisions under Kandyan and Muslim Law. Nine one-day awareness-raising workshops have been organized by WIN, which include a panel of lawyers discussing General Law, Muslim Law, and Kandyan Law and addressing up to 100 participants' questions about property issues. Two workshops have targeted government officials, including police.

5

Women's Participation in Government

Sri Lanka is considered to be one of the most densely populated countries in the world. In 1991 the density was 292 persons per square kilometre and according to estimates it will exceed 310 by the year 2005. The population is concentrated mostly in the western and central parts of the country. However, migration of the rural population to the urban areas has been slower than in most developing countries. An increase of the urban population from 15 percent of the total population in 1946 to 22.5 percent in 1971 was witnessed. The shift has been contained thereafter.

Implementation of large scale colonization schemes in rural areas, location of industries and other projects in remote areas, increased land prices and higher cost of living in urban areas have contributed to this trend. Sri Lanka has a liberalized, market oriented economy brought about through structural reforms and a privatization programme.

Average Depreciation of Rupee Against Dollar

The gross domestic product (GDP) of the country for 1999 was Rs.1111 billion at current market prices. This indicated a per capita income of US$ 829 on the basis of an estimated midyear population of 19 million people. The rate of growth of the GDP in real terms in 1999 was 4.3 percent and this growth is considered to be satisfactory, although the long run annual average growth rate was around 5 percent, in view of the current security difficulties faced by the country.

The annual average depreciation of the rupee against the dollar in 1999 was 8.2 percent. The unemployment rate has continued to decline as a result of growth of employment in the private sector. Nevertheless, during the first three quarters of 1999 unemployment stood at 8.8 percent of the labour force. Sri

Lanka has achieved much in the sphere of the health of the population during the last fifty years. The present high levels have been reached through an island-wide network of medical institutions and public health programs. All aspects of the health needs of the people are met free by the public health services provided by the government. There has also been a steady increase in the provision of health services by the private sector since the latter part of the 1980s.

In Sri Lanka all students are provided with free education including education at university level. This scheme was introduced in 1945. Prior to it what existed was a dual system of fee levying English schools and non-fee levying Sinhala and Tamil schools. As the government paid more attention to English education then, the schools in rural areas, which were always vernacular schools, were neglected.

After independence in 1948, several policy reforms were introduced by the government, with a view to ensure better enrolment levels and improve the quality of education. A free midday meal programme was in existence at the time and issue of free school books and free school uniforms was introduced in 1980 and 1993 respectively.

Improvement of schemes for the recruitment of teachers, provision of pre-service training to teacher-recruits, in-service training and restructuring of curricula have been some of the measures taken to better the quality of education. Facilities provided for education have shown a large increase during the last 50 years. The number of government schools, which stood at 3091 in 1948 increased to 10280 in 1996. The number of teachers increased sixfold, from 32704 to 195203 during this period. Where the university education is concerned, the number of students increased from 1611 to 33948 and the number of teachers from 121 to 2747 between 1947 and 1996. The expenditure on public education, as a percentage of the GNP, for the years 1993-96 averaged 3.4.

Women in National Level

A few high positions at decision-making level are held by women. Mrs. Chandrika Bandaranaike Kumaratunga is the Executive President of the country. She was first elected to this office in 1994 and was re-elected for a second term in 1999. She also holds the portfolio of Finance. Mrs. Sirimavo R.D.

Bandaranaike became the Prime Minister of the country in 1960 and was the first woman Prime Minister in the world. She held this position on several occasions for a total period of 18 years and resigned recently. Two other women also hold ministerial positions and the number of female Deputy Ministers is three. Their subjects include women's affairs, social services, health, trade and food.

The total number of women members in the Parliament at present is 11 elected and 1 nominated. Though the proportion is not very significant, over the years there has been an increase in the number of women entering Parliament.

A notable feature is that a majority of them are from rural and semi-urban areas of the country. Entry, to Parliament, of politicians from rural areas was a shift that started with the Parliamentary Elections of 1956, but the change was slow in the case of women.

Table 1
Women's Representation at Sub-National and Urban Local Levels
Position as at 30.6.2000

Type of Council	*No. of Councils*	*No. of Repres-entatives*			*Females as a % of Total*
		Female	*Male*	*Total*	
Provincial Councils	7	15	364	379	4.0
Municipal Councils	14	7	294	301	2.3
Urban Councils	37	5	358	363	1.4

Since the setting up of the Provincial Councils (by the 13 th Amendment to the Constitution in 1987 and by an Act of Parliament in 1988) three elections have been held in 1989, 1993 and 1999. In the short history of the Provincial Council system, two women have held the position of Chief Minister. As shown in Table 1, of a total of 379 representatives in Provincial Councils as at 30.6.2000, only 15 were females. This is a mere 4 percent of the total.

The overall proportion of women in higher positions does not compare well with the proportion of women undergoing university education, which is about 40 percent of the student population in universities.

Factors such as difficulties in obtaining domestic help, responsibilities of bringing up children intervening during the period crucial for career development activities and cultural values which restrict the mobility of women have been recognized as constraining women from reaching higher levels in administration, although a large number of women are employed in the private sector and in the lower levels of the public service.

However, in recent times women have occupied some high positions such as Commissioner General of Inland Revenue, Director General of External Resources, Director General of National Planning, Post Master General, Director General of the Bribery Commission, Judge of the Court of Appeal and Judge of the Supreme Court among a few others.

Women's Participation in Urban Local Government

In Sri Lanka there are no laws that promote women's participation in urban local government. However, the Constitution stipulates, that no person shall be discriminated on the grounds of sex. It also provides that special provision may be made by law, subordinate legislation or executive action, for the advancement of women, children or disabled persons.

A study undertaken by the Centre for Women's Research-Sri Lanka, (CENWOR) has identified, "gender inequality in family relations caused by male dominance and resulting in physical immobility as well as an unequal gender division of labour within the household and consequent time constraints to participation in activities outside the home" as constraints. Women's responsibilities towards the family and caring for children take up much of their time. Another constraint that has been identified in the study is the "gender role assumptions that allocate political and community affairs to men and exclude women from what are perceived to be unsuitable activities for women".

Opportunities

The question of provision of opportunities to women for participation in the affairs of the society received the attention of the Commission of Inquiry on Local Government Reforms appointed by the President in 1998. The Commission, in order to ensure women's participation in local governance has recommended creation of forums for dialogue between youth and women's sections of the society on the one hand and elected members of councils on the other, compulsory inclusion of competent persons and representatives of youth and women in various committees and provision of opportunities for youth, women and special sections of the people to contest at elections freely and without any restrictions, as it is difficult to provide for their compulsory representation. The Commission has further recommended that representatives elected to local authorities should work with women's organizations and allow for women's contribution to local government.

Fluctuations of the total number of people casting the vote at different elections, as a percentage of the total number of registered voters has been mainly due to factors peculiar to the relevant periods, such as security problems which affect both the female and the m ale voter. These high levels of voting have been due to political conciousness of the people (though, no doubt, awareness and their perceptions as to what encompasses political activity are of varying degrees). Thus, a need for special efforts to increase the participation of women in voting itself does not seem to exist.

With regard to the other elements of participation, as stated earlier, efforts undertaken by different organizations have been minimal. In the case of political parties in the country, they have their women's wings and the membership is given a basic political education by the party. But these programmes do not aim particularly to increase women's participation in local politics or elections. It is also to be noted that efforts in this respect by NGOs, are not totally absent. A few, in some parts of the country have launched programmes to increase female participation in all aspects of political activity and have also taken up issues such as prevention of violence at elections.

Elections

In activities connected with educating the voters and providing information to them, it is the political parties and some of the advocacy groups that become active, although at election times only. These exercises also do not target women alone but are directed at the entire electorate.

Elections in the country generally are keenly contested and election campaigns are intensive ones. Large numbers of election meetings and house-to-house campaigns are held by political parties and their candidates. Press advertisements and radio and television time are made use of to disseminate information to voters. Advocacy groups mainly use the printed media and pamphlets.

Programmes undertaken by urban local government institutions to encourage women to participate in governance or to obtain their views for purposes of planning and development too have not been of sufficient magnitude. Only in the case of a very few local authorities have efforts been made to set up women's organizations and only for specific sectors such as environment.

Programmes of government agencies and other organizations to sensitize urban local governments A small number of NGOs, and a federation of trade unions of local government employees have had a few programmes to sensitize urban local governments with regard to special concerns and needs of women.

However, a fair amount of work is being done in this area particularly by government officials and government agencies involved in local government , and in general administration, namely the Provincial Commissioners of Local Government, the Sri Lanka Institute of Local Governance and the Management Development and Training Units of the Provincial Councils.

It is also to be noted that there is a Ministry of Women's Affairs headed by a woman Minister. The mission of this Ministry is to work towards advancement of women through initiating, formulating and monitoring policies, projects and programmes to facilitate mainstreaming of gender equity, ensuring human and fundamental rights with the coordination of public and private sectors, international agencies and NGOs. At sub-national level too, in the Provincial Councils, women's affairs is a function assigned to a Provincial Minister.

Sex-disegregated data is used only in an ad hoc manner by urban local government institutions in the country for policy and programme formulation and not routinely and consistently. They are utilized only for projects that address issues mainly concerning women.

Laws that mandate a quota for women's representation There are no laws that mandate a quota for women's representation in Urban Local Government. In this connection it is interesting to note that the Commission of Inquiry on Local Government Reforms, state that proposals were made before the Commission that while continuing the provisions for youth representation in local authority elections, there should be provision for women's representation too. The Commission (while recommending that election of representatives to local bodies be held on the basis of the ward system) states that women and youth as categories of voters need not have a fixed percentage of candidates or representatives and that they should be free to contest in any desired numbers.

The Commission also notes that any attempt to accommodate a proportion under the ward system would be detrimental to democratic ideals and that if the voters so decided it should be possible for these categories to have even 100 percent representation. Initiatives to recruit or encourage women to stand in Urban Local Government Elections Initiatives taken by political parties, non-governmental organizations, women's organizations and other civil society organizations to encourage women to stand in urban local government have been very few. These exercises do not seem to have had much impact.

Special measures taken by the Government to recruit women to civil/administrative service of Urban Local Government and its decision - making positions. Appointments to positions at higher levels in the civil/ administrative service of urban local government are mainly made from the Sri Lanka Administrative Service. In the case of some Urban Councils, due to special circumstances, the posts of Secretary (which post is comparable to the post of Municipal Commissioner with regard to the duties involved) are filled with senior officers from outside the Sri Lanka Administrative Service.

At present there are no barriers for women to enter the Sri Lanka Administrative Service. This service was thrown open to women too in 1963 with the stipulation that the female intake would be limited to 20 percent of the recruits. Later the quota was changed and in 1981 it stood at 25 percent. In 1982 the quota was done away with altogether. In an environment where both sexes have equal access and opportunities for education and employment special initiatives to recruit women to specified cadres would not seem quite necessary.

Special Programmes

There are several special programmes implemented by the government for training of women elected to Urban Local Government Institutions as well as women officials attached to them.

However, most of these programmes are conducted for both females and males and not targeted for women alone. Political parties, non-government organizations and other civil society organizations do not appear to have undertaken this activity.

An important step taken by the Government in this regard is the establishment of a separate institute - Sri Lanka Institute of Local Governance - as a statutory body by an Act of Parliament in 1999. This institute has been set up as the main arm of the government for training of elected members and officials of local government institutions as well as of the Provincial Councils. Among its functions specified in the Act are the following:

To provide training to the members and officers and servants of Provincial Councils and local authorities with a view to equipping them to perform their official duties efficiently and effectively.

To conduct workshops and training courses on Provincial and Local Government Management. To assist in the building up of a cadre of competent provincial and local government officers and personnel in the country with a view to ensuring good governance.

The institute commenced functioning in 1999 itself and it has already completed much of the work relating to preparatory activities such as formulation of training modules. During the first six months of 2000 it has held several training programmes in a number of subject areas. Prior to the setting up of the institute, this work was carried out from the centre through a division in the Ministry of Provincial Councils and Local Government named the Local Government Management Unit and the institute is virtually the successor to this unit. The functions of the unit were more or less similar to those of the new institute in respect of training and during the past years quite a significant amount of work had been done by it.

The Provincial Commissioners of Local Government who function at sub-national level too conduct training for both elected members and officials. In addition, a Management Development and Training Unit functions in each of the Provincial Councils. These units are managed by the Deputy Chief Secretaries of the Provincial Councils. The training given by these units, however, is for officials serving in the Provinces and those attached to local government authorities and not for elected members. During the first six months of 2000 these units and the Provincial Commissioners of Local Government had conducted 131 programmes in different subject areas.

Associations of women elected to, and in civil/administrative service of, Urban Local Government. Women elected to, and in the civil/administrative service of, urban local government have not formed associations and forums to exchange ideas, to support each other, for lobbying etc.

Coupled with this is the view expressed by four of the respondents that the society considers politics as territory not suitable for women or that they are dissuaded by their elders from participating in political activity. Male dominance and the tendency for the society to focus criticism on the activities of women more, than on the activities of men were also cited. Vulnerability of women to imputations made by opponents which harm the character, intimidation and political violence were the other factors considered to be preventing females from embarking on political activity.

In order to remedy this situation, the respondents felt that what was needed was gender sensitization, to educate the society, the women and the males. They considered it necessary to conduct programmes aimed at the society and the males to make them aware of the dual role of women in the society and of the need for women to enter the field of politics, to give equal status to women and to change the traditional role entrusted to women within the family and the household.

They also thought it necessary to bring about political awareness among women through similar educational programmes.

The officials interviewed did not consider that barriers existed for women to prevent them from entering service in the area of urban local government. This obviously is owing to the equal opportunities that both sexes have in the field of education and employment. Contribution from family to enter urban local government Encouragement given by family members and also by others seem to have facilitated a majority of the elected representatives to enter local politics. Of the 9 elected representatives 5 had been either actively encouraged to enter urban local government by a parent, husband or some other member of the family or been inspired by a relative or a close associate.

These relatives and associates had been holding elected office at local level or been active supporters of the political parties they were affiliated to. Of the other 4, 2 had been encouraged by politicians who held positions at national level. At the other end of the scale was one respondent who stated that her immediate family members showed displeasure at her being away from home at unusual times attending to political and social work.

However, once in office, 3 of the elected women faced difficulties or discrimination from their colleagues. These appear to have stemmed from the traditional perception that women are "weak", resulting in male dominance. These difficulties that they had to face had come in the form of arrogance, rough behaviour or intentional disregard on the part of male colleagues. One other respondent had found that her family members were unhappy when she was away at unusual hours attending to her work. None of the 9 women officials had faced any discrimination after appointment to their positions.

Transformative Role of Women in Urban Local Government

A majority of the respondents - all the 9 elected representatives and 7 of the 9 officials - felt that lack of awareness, both among women and in the society in general, prevented women from participating in political activity at all levels and also in the affairs of the society. They perceived that this lack of awareness was in relation to the place due to women in the society and in the political process and the potential that women had for rendering service to the community through political activities.

These respondents thought that conducting awareness programmes should be a major strategy to remedy this situation and that action in that direction was a responsibility cast upon women leaders in the society. Such programmes should take the form of seminars and group discussions and should be designed to bring about attitudinal changes that would release women from the traditional and conventional roles that have been assigned to them, bring about equitable division of work in the household, create political awareness in women and make them and the society in general conscious of their potential for political work.

Several other steps were also identified as necessary measures for achieving gender equity. These included advocacy to highlight gender issues, formation of women's groups for collective action, assisting women to acquire skills of articulating their views and identification of individual women with capability and dedication for community work and introducing them to various levels in the political establishment.

Evidently the concerns of the elected representatives interviewed were more in matters that affected the people in their daily lives and they preferred to concentrate more on action programmes that directly impacted on physical well-being and the social status of the members of the community. The officials, while emphasizing the need for such an approach were naturally concerned, unlike the elected representatives, on the regulatory functions of their local authorities.

In translating their views to action in the aspect of upliftment of the conditions of women in their localities they had undertaken diverse activities and contributed to it in various ways. Several of them had organized women's groups or organizations as forums to discuss and air women's problems, to safeguard women's rights or to assist them to venture into income earning activities. Programmes on training of skills had been implemented and the beneficiaries had been provided with other necessary assistance to embark on economic activities.

For the benefit of the general population in their areas, their approach had led them to initiate or actively support public utility services such as provision of water, sanitary facilities, housing and drainage, and community services such as provision of libraries and playgrounds.

Labour Camps

Organization of labour camps, implementation of health programmes for women and children and action on conservation of environment had been some of the other areas. In all these activities what is apparent was that promotion of organized participation and facilitation of the participation of vulnerable groups had been attempted. Thirteen of the 18 respondents were of the view that their work in the positions they hold had resulted in changes in their local government institutions for the better in certain aspects. Several of them felt that they had been able to make the administration of their institutions more efficient and that it had resulted in the services being made available to the people more expeditiously than before. Three of the respondents stated that their contribution had enabled the respective local authorities to obtain the participation of the people, specially women, in carrying out their functions while two stated that their institutions paid attention to environmental matters more.

In the case of elected representatives who were interviewed, the nature of their responsibilities as they saw them and the changes that they thought had occurred due to their being in urban local government were indicative of the degree of their sense of sensitivity to the needs of the people. Almost all of them thought that their main responsibility was to attend to the daily needs, of their constituents, relating to public utility services and community services. Two of the representatives whose local authority areas had problems peculiar to their localities, sea erosion and periodical floods, gave priority to resettlement of the victims of such disasters and provision of their basic needs.

Many of the respondents also felt that their contribution to local governance had made the administration in their local government institutions more efficient which meant that these institutions had gained capacity to attend to the needs of the people within a reasonable time.

Most of the respondents believed that women are more concerned than men about aspects such as health, cleanliness, water, sanitation, housing conditions of the public and the environment and that it was due to the influence of the nature of work that they usually have to attend in their homes in bringing up children and managing the household. They, therefore, felt that increasing the number of women in local governance could cause the local government institutions to become more responsive and effective and that it would, in turn, have a positive effect on the status of women in general. Organizations that are active or could potentially become active in promoting, training or supporting the participation of women in urban local government in Sri Lanka.

Employment Opportunities

In Srilanka, high percentage of females enrolled in secondary and tertiary education, women have not been able to capitalize upon their educational gains to access economic opportunities as readily as men. The percentage of women in the formal adult labour force in 1995 was 36 percent, representing only a 9 percent increase in twenty years, and unemployment rates for women were double that of men in 1992.

Women are employed in all the sections, but as in many other countries, they dominate the lower paying jobs. Tea-pickers, are of the lowest-paid, re mostly women. About 80 per cent of the factory workers in the trade zones are young single women who live in nearly boarding houses.

With the exception of accounting jobs, women tend to be concentrated in culturally demarcated "feminine" occupations-generally lower paying jobs as household domestic, clerical, or semiskilled factory workers. Sri Lanka's need to redress these gender imbalances grows more urgent as its social and economic activities become increasingly complex and technology-dependent.

Although vocational training is equally available to men and women, gender differences in the types of training received by women is a barrier to equity in employment. Relatively few women are enrolled in technical courses that are seen as belonging to the domain of males, such as engineering or carpentry and woodwork.

Similarly, the majority of women students in technical colleges take secretarial, commerce, and home economics courses, which may not prepare them adequately for employment in a changing economy.

On-the-job training opportunities for women in private industry are primarily in semiskilled occupations where the wages are low and the possibilities for professional advancement slim. The nongovernmental training sector has tended to concentrate on income-generating projects requiring minimal training, although a few have pioneered nontraditional employment for women.

In response to the lack of vocational training information available to girls and women, the Centre for Women's Research (CENWOR) in Colombo designed and conducted a pilot intervention from 1986 to 1988 aimed at increasing the participation of females in nontraditional programs.

CENWOR, established in 1984 by a group of women's studies professionals, conducts action-oriented studies and programs that improve the status of Sri Lankan women.

The long-term objective of the CENWOR study was to facilitate access by women and girls to a wide range of vocational skills and employment opportunities. Specific objectives were to:

— Substantially increase the access of female students and their parents to vocational training information; Expand the knowledge base for advocacy and counselling;
— Motivate women to enrol in nontraditional training programs leading to remunerative employment in a modernizing economy;
— Promote more positive attitudes among policymakers, administrators, educators, and trainers about including women in all training programs and economic activities according to their aspirations.

The project was implemented in six contiguous subdivisions in four administrative districts, selected through the Ministry of

Education because of industrial growth occurring in their areas. Field visits to these selected pilot locations and discussion with school authorities and female students, administrators of training institutions, and employers indicated an almost total lack of knowledge about the subject of vocational/career choices for girls leaving school.

Further, virtually no materials existed that were specifically intended to provide vocational training information to girls and women. CENWOR's approach involved: preparing, producing, and disseminating information and motivational materials; designing and conducting school workshops; establishing links with relevant ministries and state training agencies; and using the media to disseminate pertinent messages.

Steering Committee

The project appointed a Steering Committee comprising, among others, representatives from the Tertiary and Vocational Education Commission, Ministry of Education, Ministry of Women's Affairs, Ministry of Agriculture, Department of Labour, the National Apprentice and Industrial Training Authority, and the Federation of Chambers of Industry and Commerce. The Steering Committee stimulated support for the project objectives among policymakers and brought it visibility in the state training sector.

Despite some initial delays, high quality materials were produced in three languages (Sinhala, Tamil, and English). At the post-project evaluation session, they were assessed to be attractive, informative, and thought provoking. Some of the materials were as follows:

— A cartoon, "Shanthi's World," was produced for girls finishing secondary school and on the threshold of making important decisions regarding employment and/or further education. Noting that it doesn't have to be only "a man's world," the cartoon encourages these girls to diversify their vocational aspirations by considering nontraditional occupations and discusses the importance of preparing for economic change (10,000 of each were distributed).

— "New Visions-a Handbook on Training Opportunities" was produced to provide detailed vocational information for girls in 24 vocational areas, the market's projected employment opportunities, as well as possibilities for self-employment- including availability of loans for start-up costs and estimated amounts (3,500 of these were distributed). A short pamphlet for employers, "A Technologically Advanced Society Needs Trained Women," highlights the advantages and availability of skilled female workers and their potential to improve the productivity of enterprises if given the opportunity (3,500 were distributed).

— Media materials that were produced included 30,000 posters with photographs and captions pertaining to five nontraditional trades and a set of slides of women engaged in training for nontraditional employment. A video, "Meeting Challenges," shows women being trained or in post-training employment in nontraditional sectors such as lathe work, welding, masonry, boat and motor repair, and computers.

In total, 15 workshops were conducted for over 450 participants. The basic approach involved: an introduction about the need for gender equity in access to vocational training; a discussion of changing attitudes; a presentation by a nontraditional female role model; and viewing of the aforementioned video as a basis for discussion. These experiences are being used in the development of a training manual for future workshops.

Of the 87 percent of senior girls who completed evaluations, almost all claimed that they had changed their perceptions regarding vocational training, and as many expressed their interest and intention to pursue vocational training because of its usefulness in providing access to employment opportunities, or as an avenue to higher status in society. However, only 63.3 percent of the students reported that they understood the relevance of gender equality in training and employment opportunities as a value. Additionally, the school principals-all men- were largely indifferent to the purpose of the workshops.

The National Youth Services Council (NYSC) requested that CENWOR conduct more workshops, which Swisscontact funded in 10 more schools in the Kalutara district. CENWOR workshops have also had a multiplier effect among collaborating NGOs, who have subsequently conducted their own workshops.

Advocacy with Key Ministries and Agencies Advocacy meetings with decisionmakers on the need to increase the vocational training access of girls and women were successful in educating officials about gender equality. They resulted in the opening of all NYSC training programs to women, who had previously been limited to "female-oriented" courses. CENWOR was also asked by the Secretary of the Ministry of Vocational Training to present critical gender issues to a team from the Asian Development Bank preparing a proposal to support a national program in vocational training. Other advocacy activities included:

— A presentation to the Secretary of the Ministry of Education. The Secretary, impressed by the materials, instructed his field staff to use them and asked CENWOR to advise the Non-Formal Education Division and to provide input into the training of 300 teachers/school counsellors in the state's School Counselling Program.
— A presentation to the Central Council of the Federation of Chambers of Industry and Commerce, the apex body of employers. Initially, some reservations about women's economic participation were evident, but the employers' organizations eventually endorsed the objective of increasing women's access to middie-and high-level technical jobs, and promised their cooperation.

The establishment of links with three international NGOs engaged in the field of vocational training and enterprise development- World University Service of Canada, German Agency for Technical Cooperation (GTZ), and Swisscontact. These NGOs and the three local collaborating NGOs with island-wide networks met and agreed to distribute materials and conduct programs in more than half of the districts in the country.

The project tapped an unmet need for information on vocational opportunities available to girls and women, particularly in rural areas, and the materials and workshops developed for this purpose were very well received. The cost of reproducing the written materials was CENWOR's greatest obstacle to a wider dissemination. Given an adequate budget, the state and other NGOs can quite easily replicate CENWOR's pilot efforts.

Women and the Environment

Women have an essential role to play in the development of sustainable and ecologically sound consumption and production patterns and approaches to natural resource management, as was recognized at the United Nations Conference on Environment and Development and the International Conference on Population and Development and reflected throughout Agenda 21.

Awareness of resource depletion, the degradation of natural systems and the dangers of polluting substances has increased markedly in the past decade. These worsening conditions are destroying fragile ecosystems and displacing communities, especially women, from productive activities and are an increasing threat to a safe and healthy environment.

Poverty and environmental degradation are closely interrelated. While poverty results in certain kinds of environmental stress, the major cause of the continued deterioration of the global environment is the unsustainable pattern of consumption and production, particularly in industrialized countries, which is a matter of grave concern, aggravating poverty and imbalances. Rising sealevels as a result of global warming cause a grave and immediate threat to people living in island countries and coastal areas.

All States and all people shall cooperate in the essential task of eradicating poverty as an indispensable requirement for sustainable development, in order to decrease the disparities in standards of living and better meet the needs of the majority of the people of the world. Hurricanes, typhoons and other natural disasters and, in addition, the destruction of resources, violence, displacements and other effects associated with war, armed and other conflicts, the use and testing of nuclear weaponry, and foreign occupation can also contribute to environmental degradation.

The deterioration of natural resources displaces communities, especially women, from income-generating activities while greatly adding to unremunerated work. In both urban and rural areas, environmental degradation results in negative effects on the health, well-being and quality of life of the population at large, especially girls and women of all ages. Particular attention and recognition should be given to the role and special situation of women living in rural areas and those working in the agricultural sector, where access to training, land, natural and productive resources, credit, development programmes and cooperative structures can help them increase their participation in sustainable development.

Environmental risks in the home and workplace may have a disproportionate impact on women's health because of women's different susceptibilities to the toxic effects of various chemicals. These risks to women's health are particularly high in urban areas, as well as in low-income areas where there is a high concentration of polluting industrial facilities.

Through their management and use of natural resources, women provide sustenance to their families and communities. As consumers and producers, caretakers of their families and educators, women play an important role in promoting sustainable development through their concern for the quality and sustainability of life for present and future generations. Governments have expressed their commitment to creating a new development paradigm that integrates environmental sustainability with gender equality and justice within and between generations as contained in chapter 24 of Agenda 21.

No Role in Policy Formulation

Women remain largely absent at all levels of policy formulation and decision-making in natural resource and environmental management, conservation, protection and rehabilitation, and their experience and skills in advocacy for and monitoring of proper natural resource management too often remain marginalized in policy-making and decision-making bodies, as well as in educational institutions and environment-related agencies at the managerial level. Women are rarely trained as professional natural resource managers with policy-making capacities, such as land-use planners, agriculturalists, foresters, marine scientists and environmental lawyers. Even in cases where women are trained as professional natural resource managers, they are often underrepresented in formal institutions with policy-making capacities at the national, regional and international levels.

Often women are not equal participants in the management of financial and corporate institutions whose decision-making most significantly affects environmental quality. Furthermore, there are institutional weaknesses in coordination between women's non-governmental organizations and national institutions dealing with environmental issues, despite the recent rapid growth and visibility of women's non-governmental organizations working on these issues at all levels.

Women have often played leadership roles or taken the lead in promoting an environmental ethic, reducing resource use, and reusing and recycling resources to minimize waste and excessive consumption. Women can have a particularly powerful role in influencing sustainable consumption decisions.

Women, especially indigenous women, have particular knowledge of ecological linkages and fragile ecosystem management. Women in many communities provide the main labour force for subsistence production, including production of seafood; hence, their role is crucial to the provision of food and nutrition, the enhancement of the subsistence and informal sectors and the preservation of the environment.

Stable Members

In certain regions, women are generally the most stable members of the community, as men often pursue work in distant locations, leaving women to safeguard the natural environment and ensure adequate and sustainable resource allocation within the household and the community.

The strategic actions needed for sound environmental management require a holistic, multidisciplinary and intersectoral approach. Women's participation and leadership are essential to every aspect of that approach. The recent United Nations global conferences on development, as well as regional preparatory conferences for the Fourth World Conference on Women, have all acknowledged that sustainable development policies that do not involve women and men alike will not succeed in the long run.

They have called for the effective participation of women in the generation of knowledge and environmental education in decision-making and management at all levels. Women's experiences and contributions to an ecologically sound environment must therefore be central to the agenda for the twenty-first century. Sustainable development will be an elusive goal unless women's contribution to environmental management is recognized and supported.

In addressing the lack of adequate recognition and support for women's contribution to conservation and management of natural resources and safeguarding the environment, Governments and other actors should promote an active and visible policy of mainstreaming a gender perspective in all policies and programmes, including, as appropriate, an analysis of the effects on women and men, respectively, before decisions are taken.

The Governments should take the following actions to involve women actively in environmental decision-making at all levels:

- Ensure opportunities for women, including indigenous women, to participate in environmental decision-making at all levels, including as managers, designers and planners, and as implementers and evaluators of environmental projects;
- Facilitate and increase women's access to information and education, including in the areas of science, technology and economics, thus enhancing their knowledge, skills and opportunities for participation in environmental decisions;
- Encourage, subject to national legislation and consistent with the Convention on Biological Diversity, the effective protection and use of the knowledge, innovations and practices of women of indigenous and local communities, including practices relating to traditional medicines, biodiversity and indigenous technologies, and endeavour to ensure that these are respected, maintained, promoted and preserved in an ecologically sustainable manner, and promote their wider application with the approval and involvement of the holders of such knowledge; in addition, safeguard the existing intellectual property rights of these women as protected under national and international law; work

actively, where necessary, to find additional ways and means for the effective protection and use of such knowledge, innovations and practices, subject to national legislation and consistent with the Convention on Biological Diversity and relevant international law, and encourage fair and equitable sharing of benefits arising from the utilization of such knowledge, innovation and practices;

- Take appropriate measures to reduce risks to women from identified environmental hazards at home, at work and in other environments, including appropriate application of clean technologies, taking into account the precautionary approach agreed to in the Rio Declaration on Environment and Development;
- Take measures to integrate a gender perspective in the design and implementation of, among other things, environmentally sound and sustainable resource management mechanisms, production techniques and infrastructure development in rural and urban areas;
- Take measures to empower women as producers and consumers so that they can take effective environmental actions, along with men, in their homes, communities and workplaces;
- Promote the participation of local communities, particularly women, in identification of public service needs, spatial planning and the provision and design of urban infrastructure.
- Take gender impact into consideration in the work of the Commission on Sustainable Development and other appropriate United Nations bodies and in the activities of international financial institutions;
- Promote the involvement of women and the incorporation of a gender perspective in the design, approval and execution of projects funded under the Global Environment Facility and other appropriate United Nations organizations;
- Encourage the design of projects in the areas of concern to the Global Environment Facility that would benefit women and projects managed by women;

- Establish strategies and mechanisms to increase the proportion of women, particularly at grass-roots levels, involved as decision makers, planners, managers, scientists and technical advisers and as beneficiaries in the design, development and implementation of policies and programmes for natural resource management and environmental protection and conservation;
- Encourage social, economic, political and scientific institutions to address environmental degradation and the resulting impact on women.
- Assume advocacy of environmental and natural resource management issues of concern to women and provide information to contribute to resource mobilization for environmental protection and conservation;
- Facilitate the access of women agriculturists, fishers and pastoralists to knowledge, skills, marketing services and environmentally sound technologies to support and strengthen their crucial roles and their expertise in resource management and the conservation of biological diversity.

The Governments should take the following actions integrate gender concerns and perspectives in policies and programmes for sustainable development

- Integrate women, including indigenous women, their perspectives and knowledge, on an equal basis with men, in decision-making regarding sustainable resource management and the development of policies and programmes for sustainable development, including in particular those designed to address and prevent environmental degradation of the land;
- Evaluate policies and programmes in terms of environmental impact and women's equal access to and use of natural resources;
- Ensure adequate research to assess how and to what extent women are particularly susceptible or exposed to environmental degradation and hazards, including, as necessary, research and data collection on specific groups of women, particularly women with low

income, indigenous women and women belonging to minorities;

- Integrate rural women's traditional knowledge and practices of sustainable resource use and management in the development of environmental management and extension programmes;
- Integrate the results of gender-sensitive research into mainstream policies with a view to developing sustainable human settlements;
- Promote knowledge of and sponsor research on the role of women, particularly rural and indigenous women, in food gathering and production, soil conservation, irrigation, watershed management, sanitation, coastal zone and marine resource management, integrated pest management, land-use planning, forest conservation and community forestry, fisheries, natural disaster prevention, and new and renewable sources of energy, focusing particularly on indigenous women's knowledge and experience;
- Develop a strategy for change to eliminate all obstacles to women's full and equal participation in sustainable development and equal access to and control over resources;
- Promote the education of girls and women of all ages in science, technology, economics and other disciplines relating to the natural environment so that they can make informed choices and offer informed input in determining local economic, scientific and environmental priorities for the management and appropriate use of natural and local resources and ecosystems;
- Develop programmes to involve female professionals and scientists, as well as technical, administrative and clerical workers, in environmental management, develop training programmes for girls and women in these fields, expand opportunities for the hiring and promotion of women in these fields and implement special measures to advance women's expertise and participation in these activities;
- Identify and promote environmentally sound technologies that have been designed, developed and improved in

consultation with women and that are appropriate to both women and men;

- Support the development of women's equal access to housing infrastructure, safe water, and sustainable and affordable energy technologies, such as wind, solar, biomass and other renewable sources, through participatory needs assessments, energy planning and policy formulation at the local and national levels;
- Ensure that clean water is available and accessible to all by the year 2000 and that environmental protection and conservation plans are designed and implemented to restore polluted water systems and rebuild damaged watersheds.
- Involve women in the communication industries in raising awareness regarding environmental issues, especially on the environmental and health impacts of products, technologies and industry processes;
- Encourage consumers to use their purchasing power to promote the production of environmentally safe products and encourage investment in environmentally sound and productive agricultural, fisheries, commercial and industrial activities and technologies;
- Support women's consumer initiatives by promoting the marketing of organic food and recycling facilities, product information and product labelling, including labelling of toxic chemical and pesticide containers with language and symbols that are understood by consumers, regardless of age and level of literacy.

The Governments should take the following actions to strengthen or establish mechanisms at the national, regional and international levels to assess the impact of development and environmental policies on women.

- Provide technical assistance to women, particularly in developing countries, in the sectors of agriculture, fisheries, small enterprises, trade and industry to ensure the continuing promotion of human resource development and the development of environmentally sound technologies and of women's entrepreneurship;
- Develop gender-sensitive databases, information and monitoring systems and participatory action-oriented

research, methodologies and policy analyses, with the collaboration of academic institutions and local women researchers, on the following:

— Knowledge and experience on the part of women concerning the management and conservation of natural resources for incorporation in the databases and information systems for sustainable development;
— The impact on women of environmental and natural resource degradation, deriving from, inter alia, unsustainable production and consumption patterns, drought, poor quality water, global warming, desertification, sealevel rise, hazardous waste, natural disasters, toxic chemicals and pesticide residues, radioactive waste, armed conflicts and its consequences;
— Analysis of the structural links between gender relations, environment and development, with special emphasis on particular sectors, such as agriculture, industry, fisheries, forestry, environmental health, biological diversity, climate, water resources and sanitation;
— Measures to develop and include environmental, economic, cultural, social and gender-sensitive analyses as an essential step in the development and monitoring of programmes and policies;
— Programmes to create rural and urban training, research and resource centres that will disseminate environmentally sound technologies to women;
— Ensure the full compliance with relevant international obligations, including where relevant, the Basel Convention and other conventions relating to the transboundary movements of hazardous wastes (which include toxic wastes) and the Code of Practice of the International Atomic Energy Agency relating to the movement of radioactive waste; enact and enforce regulations for environmentally sound management related to safe storage and movements; consider taking action towards the prohibition of those movements that are unsafe and insecure; ensure the strict control and management of hazardous wastes and radioactive waste, in accordance with relevant international and regional

obligations and eliminate the exportation of such wastes to countries that, individually or through international agreements, prohibit their importation;

— Promote coordination within and among institutions to implement the Platform for Action and chapter 24 of Agenda 21 by, inter alia, requesting the Commission on Sustainable Development, through the Economic and Social Council, to seek input from the Commission on the Status of Women when reviewing the implementation of Agenda 21 with regard to women and the environment.

6

National Policy

Sri Lanka is predominantly an agricultural country, 75 per cent of its population live in the traditional rural sector depending for their livelihood upon agriculture and allied pursuits. Since independence in 1948, successive governments have progressively attempted to transform the country into a social welfare state and have made considerable investment in social and human development activities. Sri Lanka has a democratic set of laws on ownership of property. Sri Lankan women have the right to own, acquire and manage land. Women's ownership of land and other properties and the registration record of these, enables them to be either eligible or not eligible for participation in the credit programmes implemented by the financial institutions and the local district administration.

In Sri Lanka there are mainly three major, programmes for women's development. They are Samurdhi, Sasana and Janasaviya/National Development Trust Fund (NDTF).

Samurdhi

Samurdhi means prosperity. It is the national savings and credit programme launched by the government of Sri Lanka, for the eradication of poverty on a sustainable basis through broadening development horizons and creating opportunities for income enhancement and employment.

Although this program is not specifically women focused, women have access to it and its implementation has contributed significantly towards better living standards for them. The main trust of the poverty reduction strategy, as embodied in the Samurdhi programme, is to ensure the participation of the poor in the production processes.

The main objectives of the Samurdhi programme are:

— Broadening opportunities for income enhancement and employment.
— Organising youth, women and other disadvantaged segments into small groups.
— Encouraging them to participate in decision-making activities and the developmental process at the grass roots level.
— Assisting individuals to develop their latent talents and strengthen their asset bases through productive employment.

All aspects of decision-making of Samurdhi are centred around the village and cluster levels where the programme is planned and implemented by the organisations set up for this purpose.

The programme aims to implement economic development projects identified on the basis of specific family needs, skills, assets and other abilities of parti-cipating families. They are encouraged to engage in develop-mental activities of their choice utilising locally available resources. It also attempts to enhance the capacity of the poor to make initiatives to improve the quality of life of the family on a sustainable basis. These initiatives will be supported by the provision of technical, managerial and financial resources to needy families.

Samurdhi envisages to coordinate all programmes implemented by various government and non-government agencies at the village level, with the dual objective of improving the service delivery of government sponsored programmes and eliminating unnecessary overlap.

At the initial stage of the programme, two animators named 'Samurdhi Niyamakas' are appointed and made responsible for the setting up of the 'Samurdhi Balakaya' (Task Force) at village level and for conducting elections to its Executive Committee. The members of the Executive Committee are youth who are permanent residents of the village.

The Samurdhi programme covers one-third of the popu-lation of the country. The poorest of the poor within this category earn on average about Rs. 500 per month, and include about 30,000 families scattered in all parts of the country. Their monthly income has be raised to about Rs. 1,500 by a direct income transfer of Rs. 1,000 per month. The remaining families who are estimated to earn an average of around Rs. 1,000 per month, are receiving an income transfer of Rs. 500 a month. Thus, the thrust of this programme is to raise the incomes of the poor to about Rs. 1,500 per month.

However, with the additional income that could accrue from the Samurdhi Programme's self-employment activities, the income will rise to Rs. 2,000 per month or more. All the beneficiaries of the Programme will exit from it when the income exceeds Rs. 2,000 per month for a continuous period of six months, or when at least one member of the family finds employment as Samurdhi beneficiaries exit from the programme, new entrants will be able to join the programme.

The identification of the beneficiaries is undertaken by the Samurdhi Niyamakas on the basis of participatory identification. The ultimate objective of Samurdhi is to promote self-reliance by encouraging saving habits and investment in income generating self-employment.

All Samurdhi beneficiaries are encouraged to save a part of the income supplement in order to develop a culture of thrift and savings. The resources accumulated through savings will be utilised to finance new income earning activities among the beneficiaries, along with supplementary finance from outside.

The poor households are expected to divide by choice into pure savers and groups of potential borrowers/entrepreneurs. For savers, the compulsory savings of Rs. 100 to Rs. 200 per month will accumulate in a group savings account at a selected State Bank branch with interest paid to the saver. The principle sum and the interest will only be available when the consumption component of Rs. 500 and 1,000 is terminated.

Sasana

Sasana is being implemented with the intention of alleviating poverty and improving living condition of those below the poverty line, by providing credit facilities and support services for self-employment through micro-enterprises.

The project activities to be financed under Sasana have been selected by the target group using their knowledge and skills, depending on the availability of raw materials and markets for their products or services.

Type of projects qualified to receive credit under this programme include small scale agricultural and industrial activities, small scale training activities and services genera-ting self employment.

The maximum loan granted under this scheme is Rs. 10,000 with a minimum of Rs. 2,500. The loan depending on its size to be repaid within 24 months with a concessional interest rate of 10 per cent per annum. A total of Rs. 500 million has been disbursed under this programme.

Two state-run commercial banks are used as conduits to disburse funds to selected beneficiaries. With a view to maintain a balance distribution of resources each of the Samurdhi Balakaya has been allocated Rs. 41,500/-. The beneficiaries to receive credit have been identified by the community through scrutiny of applications at a public meeting in the village.

Janasaviya/National Development Trust Fund (NDTF)

The Janasaviya/National Development Trust Fund (NDTF) was established in 1991 to address poverty alleviation throughout the country by supporting and financing local NGOs. About 250 partner organisations received support from NDTF and are executing poverty alleviation projects.

The Trust can be described as a non-profit quasi-governmental agency which is a mix between a government institution, with related non-alignment-style, government policy, administrative procedures and accountability require-ments, and an NGO, with a more diverse orientation, requiring a more differentiating approach and a less bureaucratic management-style.

The fund has four major components—Social Mobili-sation Fund, Community Projects Fund, Credit and Micro Enterprise Development Fund and Nutrition Fund. In addition, a gender and development programme too has been included subsequently.

The institutional positioning of NDTF within the national NGO network should be judged in two ways. In the first place, out of an estimated 400 established/registered development NGOs a good number, some 300, are supported by NDTF.

Women of Our World

The ratio of women to men in the population results from differences in women's and men's death rates and migration patterns, as well as sex ratios at birth. For biological reasons, boys slightly outnumber girls at birth but have higher mortality; as they age (and as populations grow older), women tend to equal or out-number men in the population. In a few regions, mainly in Asia, a deficit of women relative to men stems from various forms of lifelong discrimination against girls and women—particularly inferior nutrition and health care early in life and during the childbearing years.

In a few countries, the sex ratio at birth deviates markedly in favor of boys, because a strong traditional preference for sons places girls at risk of sex-selective abortions or infanticide. Infant girls survive in greater numbers than infant boys almost everywhere, but in a few countries gender discrimination and neglect outweigh girls' biological advantage.

From 2002 to 2020, the number of women of reproductive age (15-49) in less developed countries will grow by 24 percent. (Excluding China, the number will grow by 34 percent.) Though fertility rates—the number of births per woman—in these countries have fallen considerably in recent decades, the relatively high fertility of past decades has meant growing numbers of young women are now beginning their reproductive years. Even if these women have fewer children than their mothers did, the absolute number of children born will continue to rise for some years to come.

Women have higher life expectancy than men and therefore make up the majority of the elderly population in almost every country. Women spend a much larger part of their old age without partners than do men, because they tend to marry older men and live longer. Elderly women are also more likely to be living in poverty than elderly men. In many countries, elderly women are restricted in their employment opportunities, property rights, and social behavior.

Table:1
Deaths in the First Year of Life Among Girls and Boys, Selected Countries

Deaths under age 1 per 1,000 live births, 1995–2000

Country	*Girls*	*Boys*
Burkina Faso	96	102
Zimbabwe	65	73
Egypt	47	53
Brazil	36	48
United States	6	8
Nepal	84	81
Bangladesh	79	78
India	78	67
Papua New Guinea	64	59
China	48	35

Demography: World

	Total Fem. (in mill.)	Wom.per 100 Men	Ages Wom. 15–49 (in mill)		Life Expec. at Birth (yrs)		Total Fertility Rt.
	2002	2002	2002	2020	Female	Male	
WORLD	3,083	99	1,594	1,873	69	65	2.8
More Developed	614	106	298	268	79	72	1.6
Less Developed	2,469	97	1,296	1,605	66	63	3.2
Less Developed (Excl. China)	1,836	98	939	1,261	64	61	3.6

Demography: Africa

	Total Fem. (in mill.)	Wom.per 100 Men	Wom.Ages 15–49 (in mill)		Life Expec. at Birth (yrs)		Total Fertility Rt.
	2002	2002	2002	2020	Female	Male	
AFRICA	416	100	197	304	55	52	5.2
Sub-Saharan Africa	343101	158	195	52	49	5.6	

Northern Africa	89	98	47	63	67	64	3.6
Algeria	15.5	97	8.4	11.1	70	68	3.1
Egypt	34.7	98	18.2	24.3	68	65	3.5
Libya	2.7	93	1.5	2.1	77	73	3.9
Morocco	15.5	100	8.3	10.8	71	67	3.4
Sudan	16.2	99	7.9	12	57	55	4.9
Tunisia	4.8	98	2.7	3.1	74	70	2.3
Western Africa	118	99	54	90	52	50	5.8
Benin	3.4	103	1.6	2.6	51	49	6.3
Burkina Faso	6.3	106	2.7	5	47	47	6.8
Cape Verde	0.2	114	0.1	0.2	72	65	4
Côte d'Ivoire	8.1	95	3.9	6	47	45	5.2
Gambia	0.7	102	0.3	0.5	54	51	5.9
Ghana	10.1	101	5	7.6	59	56	4.3
Guinea	4.2	99	1.9	3.1	47	43	5.5
Guinea-Bissau	0.6	103	0.3	0.5	46	44	5.8
Liberia	1.6	99	0.8	1.5	52	49	6.6
Mali	6.1	102	2.6	4.6	47	45	7
Mauritania	1.4	102	0.7	1.1	52	49	4.7
Niger	5.8	98	2.5	4.8	41	41	7.5
Nigeria	59.5	98	27.2	45.2	53	52	5.8
Senegal	5	101	2.3	3.8	54	51	5.2
Sierra Leone	2.4	103	1.1	1.9	47	42	6.3
Togo	2.4	101	1.1	1.8	58	53	5.8
Eastern Africa	132	101	60	97	51	49	5.7
Burundi	3.4	105	1.5	2.6	47	46	6.5
Comoros	0.4	99	0.2	0.3	59	54	6.8
Djibouti	0.3	112	0.2	0.2	48	44	6.1
Eritrea	2	101	0.9	1.6	57	53	6
Ethiopia	33.2	101	14.9	23.6	53	51	5.9
Kenya	16	101	7.9	11.4	49	48	4.4
Madagascar	8.5	101	3.9	6.7	56	52	5.8
Malawi	5.9	101	2.6	4.1	40	39	6.3
Mauritius	0.6	101	0.3	0.3	74	67	2
Mozambique	9.6	102	4.4	6.3	76	69	5.6
Reunion	0.4	105	0.2	0.2	79	70	2.3
Rwanda	4.1	102	1.9	2.9	40	39	5.8
Somalia	4.8	101	2.1	4.1	48	45	7.3
Tanzania	18.5	101	8.7	14.1	54	52	5.6
Uganda	12.4	100	5.3	10.3	43	42	6.9
Zambia	5.4	99	2.4	4	38	37	6.1
Zimbabwe	6.5	100	3	4.6	39	41	4
Middle Africa	51	102	22	40	50	46	6.6

Angola	7	102	3	5.4	39	37	6.9
Cameroon	7.8	101	3.6	5.6	56	55	5.2
Republic	2	105	0.9	1.4	46	43	5.1
Chad	4.2	102	1.9	3.3	52	48	6.6
Congo	1.6	104	0.7	1.3	52	47	6.3
Congo,Dem. Rep.of	27.4	102	11.5	22.2	50	45	7
Equatorial Guinea	0.2	102	0.1	0.2	52	48	5.9
Gabon	0.7	102	0.3	0.5	54	51	4.3
Southern Africa	26	103	13	13	53	51	3.1
Botswana	0.8	104	0.4	0.5	42	41	3.9
Lesotho	1	101	0.5	0.5	55	52	4.3
Namibia	0.9	102	0.4	0.6	45	47	5
South Africa	22.4	103	12	11.4	54	52	2.9
Swaziland	0.5	102	0.2	0.3	41	40	5.9

Demography: North America

	Total Fem. (in mill.)	Wom.per 100 Men	Wom. Ages 15–49 (in mill)		Life Expec. at Birth (yrs)		Total Fertility Rt.
	2002	2002	2002	2020	Female	Male	
NORTH AMERICA	162	103	80	83	80	74	2
Canada	15.8	102	8	7.8	81	76	1.4
United States	146.2	103	72.2	75.2	80	74	2.1

Demography: Latin America and the Caribbean

	Total Fem. (in mill.)	Wom.per 100 Men	Wom. Ages 15–49 (in mill)		Life Expec. at Birth (yrs)		Total Fertility Rt.
	2002	2002	2002	2020	Female	Male	
LATIN AMERICA & THE CARIBBEAN	270	102	145	174	74	68	2.8
Central America	70	101	37	48	76	71	3.1
Belize	0.1	97	0.1	0.1	74	70	3.2
Costa Rica	2.1	97	1.1	1.4	79	75	2.6

El Salvador	3.3	104	1.7	2.3	73	67	3.5
Guatemala	6	98	2.8	4.7	68	63	4.8
Honduras	3.3	99	1.6	2.6	68	64	4.4
Mexico	51.5	102	27.9	33.7	78	73	2.8
Nicaragua	2.7	101	1.3	2.1	70	66	4.3
Panama	1.5	98	0.8	0.9	76	72	2.6
Caribbean	19	101	10	11	71	66	2.6
Bahamas	0.2	103	0.1	0.1	75	70	2.4
Cuba	5.6	100	3	2.6	77	73	1.6
Dominican Republic	4.3	97	2.3	2.7	71	67	3.1
Haiti	4.3	104	2.1	3	51	47	4.7
Jamaica	1.3	103	0.7	0.8	73	70	2.4
Trinidad and Tobago	0.7	101	0.4	0.4	73	68	1.7
South America	180	102	97	115	73	67	2.6
Argentina	19.3	104	9.5	11.5	77	70	2.6
Bolivia	4.4	101	2.1	3.2	64	60	4.2
Brazil	88.5	103	49.6	55.2	72	65	2.4
Chile	7.9	102	4.1	4.6	78	72	2.3
Colombia	22	103	11.9	14.5	74	68	2.6
Ecuador	6.5	99	3.5	4.5	73	68	3.3
Guyana	0.4	106	0.2	0.2	68	62	2.5
Paraguay	2.9	98	1.4	2.2	76	71	4.3
Peru	13.4	102	7.2	9.1	71	66	2.9
Suriname	0.2	102	0.1	0.1	74	68	3
Uruguay	1.7	106	0.8	0.9	78	70	2.3
Venezuela	12.5	99	6.6	8.6	76	70	2.9

Demography: Asia

	Total Fem. (in mill.)	Wom.per 100 Men	Wom. Ages 15–49 (in mill)		Life Expec. at Birth (yrs)		Total Fertility Rt.
	2002	2002	2002	2020	Female	Male	
ASIA	1,844	96	981	1,149	68	65	2.7
Asia(Excl. China)	1,21596	627	807	66	63	3.2	
Western Asia	96	96	49	70	69	66	3.9
Armenia	2	107	1.1	1	76	71	1.1
Azerbaijan	4.1	103	2.3	2.3	75	68	2
Bahrain	0.3	74	0.2	0.2	75	70	2.8
Cyprus	0.4	100	0.2	0.2	79	75	1.8

Georgia	2.7	109	1.4	1.1	77	69	1.2
Iraq	11.9	97	5.8	9.5	60	58	5.3
Israel	3.2	103	1.6	2	80	76	3
Jordan	2.5	93	1.3	2	71	69	3.6
Kuwait	0.8	72	0.5	0.7	73	72	4.2
Lebanon	1.8	104	1	1.2	73	68	2.5
Oman	1.3	89	0.6	1.1	73	69	6.1
Qatar	0.2	56	0.1	0.1	74	69	3.9
Saudi Arabia	10.1	88	4.6	8.8	69	66	5.7
Syria	8.4	97	4.3	6.8	70	70	4.1
Turkey	34	98	18.3	22	71	67	2.5
United Arab Emirates	0.9	52	0.5	0.7	76	71	3.5
Yemen	10	100	4.2	8.7	61	57	7.2
South Central Asia	745	95	381	515	62	60	3.4
Afghanistan	11.3	94	5.2	9.2	44	46	6
Bangladesh	69.5	94	35.7	52	59	59	3.3
Bhutan	1.1	98	0.5	0.9	66	66	5.6
India	504.5	94	260.2	337.3	61	60	3.2
Iran	35.4	96	18.8	25.7	71	69	2.6
Kazakhstan	8.3	106	4.5	4.2	71	60	1.8
Kyrgyzstan	2.6	104	1.4	1.7	72	65	2.4
Maldives	0.2	95	0.1	0.1	63	60	5.8
Nepal	11.8	95	5.6	8.9	57	58	4.1
Pakistan	72.4	95	34.1	56.4	61	60	5.6
Sri Lanka	9.4	95	5.3	5.5	74	70	2.1
Tajikistan	3.1	101	1.6	2.1	71	66	2.4
Brunei	0.2	90	0.1	0.1	76	71	2.7
Cambodia	7	105	3.3	5.2	58	54	4
Indonesia	108.4	99	59.3	70	70	65	2.7
Laos	2.8	100	1.3	2.1	54	51	5.4
Malaysia	11.4	98	6	7.8	75	70	3.2
Myanmar	24.6	101	13.2	16.2	57	54	3.3
Philippines	39	99	20.1	27.8	70	64	3.5
Singapore	2.1	99	1.2	1	80	76	1.6
China, Hong Kong	3.5	97	2	1.9	82	77	1
Japan	65.2	104	28.9	25	84	77	1.3
Korea, North	11.3	99	5.9	6.3	73	67	2.3
Korea, South	23.6	99	13.5	11.8	78	71	1.5
Mongolia	1.3	100	0.7	0.9	65	61	3.1

Demography: Europe

	Total Fem. (in mill.)	Wom.per 100 Men	Wom. Ages 15–49 (in mill)		Life Expec. at Birth (yrs)		Total Fertility Rt.
	2002	2002	2002	2020	Female	Male	
EUROPE	375	107	183	154	78	70	1.4
Northern Europe	49	104	23	21	80	74	1.6
Denmark	2.7	102	1.2	1.1	79	74	1.7
Estonia	0.7	115	0.4	0.3	76	65	1.3
Finland	2.7	105	1.2	1.1	81	74	1.7
Ireland	2	101	1	1.1	79	74	1.9
Latvia	1.3	117	0.6	0.5	76	65	1.2
Lithuania	1.9	112	1	0.8	77	67	1.3
Norway	2.3	102	1.1	1	81	76	1.8
Sweden	4.5	102	2	1.8	82	77	1.5
United Kingdom	30.3	103	14	12.8	80	75	1.7
Western Europe	94	104	44	38	81	75	1.6
Austria	4.1	105	2	1.6	81	75	1.3
Belgium	5.2	104	2.4	2.1	81	75	1.6
France	30.6	105	14.4	13.1	83	75	1.9
Germany	41.8	104	19.5	15.7	81	74	1.3
Luxembourg	0.2	103	0.1	0.1	81	75	1.7
Netherlands	8.1	102	3.9	3.5	81	75	1.7
Switzerland	3.6	102	1.7	1.3	83	77	1.5
Eastern Europe	159	112	80	66	74	63	1.2
Belarus	5.4	115	2.8	2.3	74	62	1.3
Bulgaria	4	106	1.9	1.5	75	68	1.2
Czech Republic	5.3	106	2.6	2.2	78	71	1.1
Hungary	5.2	110	2.5	2.1	75	66	1.3
Moldova	2.2	109	1.2	1.1	72	64	1.4
Poland	19.8	106	10.2	8.9	77	68	1.4
Romania	11.4	105	5.8	5.1	74	67	1.3
Russia	76.6	114	39.3	31.7	72	59	1.2
Slovakia	2.8	106	1.5	1.3	77	69	1.3
Ukraine	26.1	115	12.7	10	74	63	1.1
Southern Europe	74	105	36	30	80	74	1.3
Albania	1.5	96	0.8	0.9	75	69	2.8
Bosnia-Herzeg-ovina	2.1	102	1.1	0.9	72	65	1.6
Croatia	2.4	107	1.1	1	77	70	1.4
Greece	5.4	103	2.6	2.2	81	76	1.3
Italy	29.6	106	13.8	10.8	82	76	1.3
Macedonia[b]	1	100	0.5	0.5	75	70	1.9

Malta	0.2	102	0.1	0.1	80	74	1.7
Portugal	5.2	108	2.5	2.2	79	72	1.5
Slovenia	1	106	0.5	0.4	79	72	1.2
Spain	20.4	105	10.2	8.2	82	74	1.2
Yugoslavia	5.3	101	2.6	2.4	75	70	1.6

Demography: Oceania

	Total Fem. (in mill.)	Wom.per 100 Men	Wom. Ages 15–49 (in mill)		Life Expec. at Birth (yrs)		Total Fertility Rt.
	2002	2002	2002	2020	Female	Male	
OCEANIA	16	99	8	9	76	72	2.5
Australia	9.8	101	5	5.2	82	76	1.7
Fiji	0.4	97	0.2	0.2	69	65	3.3
New Zealand	1.9	103	1	0.9	80	74	2
Papua-New Guinea	2.4	92	1.2	1.8	55	56	4.8

Economic Status

Women's employment can raise their status by allowing them to earn income and have more control over resources. Women's participation in the labor force has increased in almost all regions of the world. Several factors explain this:

Women's use of family planning has enabled them to spend less time on child care and more on work outside the home; attitudes toward the employment of women have become more accepting; and new policies in some countries on family and child care favor working women.

In addition, economic growth and the expansion of service industries (like finance, communications, and tourism) that tend to employ large numbers of women have increased women's labor force participation.

These trends are positive, but equality in the workforce is still a long way from reality. Women typically occupy lower-paid, lower-status jobs than men and have higher unemployment rates than men. Far more women than men work in "the informal sector," occupations like street vending and market work, where wages are very low and no other benefits are afforded, such as safety standards, social security, or health insurance.

Even when women work in the same sector as men, wages are typically lower. For many women, working outside the home may not be viewed as a gain in status but as an unwelcome economic necessity.

Women are participation in the labor force in greater numbers, but they typically receive lower pay than men, even when they work in the same sector.

In addition, more women are remaining in the workforce during their reproductive years, leading to a "dual burden": working outside the home while at the same time doing a larger share of work in the home than men—such as childrearing, cooking, and cleaning. Recent UN conferences have called on governments to reduce disparities between men and women in the workforce and provide additional support to working women, such as maternity leave, child care assistance, and other flexible arrangements.

The proportion of female-headed households is on the rise globally; for a variety of reasons, these households are typically poorer than those headed by men. Female-headed households account for one-quarter or more of households in eastern and southern Africa, the Caribbean, North America, and parts of Europe and Central Asia. Women-headed households result from divorce, widowhood, men's migration for work, war and other armed conflicts, and unmarried women who begin childbearing. Elderly women living alone account for a growing proportion of female-headed households.

The connections between gender and poverty have attracked more attention recently, because women's lack of social power and lack of resources can be mutually reinforcing. Unfortunately, most income and poverty data do not reveal how many of those living in poverty are men and how many are women. Nevertheless, a growing body of evidence shows that gender disparities are greatest in the poorest countries and regions, and that promoting gender equality can contribute to greater prosperity.

Economic Status: World

	Percent of Female Headed Households	Percent in Labor Force (ages 15-64) 1980	Percent in Labor Force (ages 15-64) 2000		Gross National income per Capta PPP $US
		Female	Female	Male	
WORLD	—	57	61	86	6,650
More Developed	—	59	65	81	20,520
Less Developed	—	57	60	87	3,300
Less Developed (Excl.China)	—	51	49	86	3,210

Economic Status: Africa

	Percent of Female Headed Households	Percent in Labor Force (ages 15-64) 1980	Percent in Labor Force (ages 15-64) 2000		Gross National income per Capta PPP $US
		Female	Female	Male	
AFRICA	—	56	57	86	1,790
Sub-Saharan Africa	—	63	63	87	1,370
Northern Africa	—	30	37	82	3,070
Algeria	11	19	31	80	4,840
Egypt	13	29	37	82	3,460
Libya	—	23	26	78	–
Morocco	15	38	44	83	3,320
Sudan	13	31	35	86	–
Tunisia	11	35	40	83	5,700
Western Africa	—	59	58	87	1,000
Benin	18	78	76	83	920
Burkina Faso	7	83	78	90	960
Cape Verde	38	39	50	90	4,450
Côte d'Ivoire	15	46	45	87	1,540
Gambia	—	71	71	90	1,550
Ghana	37	83	81	82	1,850
Guinea	7	83	80	87	1,870
Guinea-Bissau	—	60	60	91	630
Liberia	19	56	56	83	
Mali	8	76	74	90	740
Mauritania	—	72	65	88	1,550
Niger	10	74	71	93	740

Nigeria	14	50	50	87	770
Senegal	18	63	63	87	1,400
Sierra Leone	11	45	46	85	440
Togo	26	55	55	87	1,380
Eastern Africa	—	74	73	88	850
Burundi	25	87	86	94	570
Comoros	25	68	64	86	1,430
Djibouti	18	—	–	–	–
Eritrea	31	78	77	87	1,040
Ethiopia	—	60	59	86	620
Kenya	33	78	77	89	1,010
Madagascar	22	73	71	89	790
Malawi	26	81	79	87	570
Mauritius	18	29	42	84	8,950
Mozambique	27	87	84	91	810
Reunion	—	37	54	72	–
Angola	—	78	75	90	1,100
Cameroon	18	50	51	86	1,490
Central African Republic	21	77	68	87	1,150
Chad	22	68	70	89	840
Congo	—	57	59	84	540
Congo,Dem.Rep.of	—	66	63	85	–
Equatorial Guinea	—	48	48	91	3,910
Gabon	—	68	66	86	5,280
Southern Africa	—	48	51	82	8,160
Botswana	47	72	67	84	6,540
Lesotho	—	50	50	85	2,350
Namibia	39	55	57	83	5,580
South Africa	—	47	50	82	8,710
Swaziland	40	42	44	83	4,380

Economic Status: North America

	Percent of Female Headed Households	Percent in Labor Force (ages 15-64) 1980	Percent in Labor Force (ages 15-64) 2000		Gross National income per Capta PPP $US
		Female	Female	Male	
NORTH AMERICA	—	58	70	82	31,260
Canada	30	57	72	84	25,440
United States	36	58	70	82	31,910

Economic Status: Latin America and the Caribbean

	Percent of Female Headed Households	Percent in Labor Force (ages 15-64) 1980	Percent in Labor Force (ages 15-64) 2000		Gross National income per Capta PPP $US
		Female	Female	Male	
LATIN AMERICA & THE CARIBBEAN	—	33	45	86	6,460
Central America	—	31	42	86	6,900
Belize	22	23	30	88	4,750
Costa Rica	20	24	40	85	7,880
El Salvador	27	32	49	87	4,260
Guatemala	20	28	38	89	3,630
Honduras	20	32	42	87	2,270
Mexico	17	31	42	86	8,070
Nicaragua	28	35	50	86	2,060
Panama	22	37	47	83	5,450
Caribbean	—	45	54	84	—
Bahamas	36	58	74	84	15,500
Cuba	—	40	57	85	—
Dominican	25	31	43	87	5,210
Haiti	39	64	58	83	1,470
Jamaica	38	73	75	84	3,390
Trinidad and Tobago	—	40	49	81	7,690
South America	—	33	46	86	6,730
Argentina	22	33	42	84	11,940
Bolivia	24	40	49	84	2,300
Brazil	18	36	47	87	6,840
Chile	25	29	42	82	8,410
Colombia	24	27	51	84	5,580
Ecuador	—	22	34	86	2,820
Guyana	—	30	44	88	3,330
Paraguay	21	34	39	88	4,380
Peru	23	26	36	81	4,480
Suriname	—	27	39	79	3,780
Uruguay	23	37	59	83	8,750
Venezuela	21	32	46	83	5,420

Economic Status: Asia

	Percent of Female Headed Households	Percent in Labor Force (ages 15-64) 1980	Percent in Labor Force (ages 15-64) 2000		Gross National income per Capta PPP $US
		Female	Female	Male	
ASIA	—	60	62	87	3,930
Asia (Excl. China)	—	50	52	85	4,130
Western Asia	—	39	42	82	4,810
Armenia	—	68	71	78	2,360
Azerbaijan	—	67	61	78	2,450
Bahrain	—	17	34	88	—
Cyprus	14	47	57	88	19,080
Georgia	—	71	66	79	2,540
Iraq	—	16	19	76	—
Israel	—	42	56	79	18,070
Jordan	—	15	28	80	3,880
Kuwait	5	21	42	80	—
Lebanon	—	21	32	81	—
Oman	—	8	20	79	—
Qatar	—	13	38	91	—
Saudi Arabia	—	10	23	82	11,050
Syria	—	24	30	80	3,450
Turkey	10	48	53	85	6,440
United Arab— Emirates	16	33	89	—	
Yemen	12	29	32	84	730
South Central Asia	—	48	47	86	2,250
Afghanistan	—	50	50	88	—
Bangladesh	9	70	68	87	1,530
Bhutan	—	60	60	91	1,260
India	9	48	45	87	2,230
Iran	6	21	30	80	5,520
Kazakhstan	—	71	69	80	4,790
Kyrgyzstan	26	69	68	78	2,420
Maldives	—	63	68	86	—
Nepal	13	59	58	86	1,280
Pakistan	7	28	37	87	1,860
Sri Lanka	—	32	46	82	3,230
Tajikistan	—	68	63	77	—
Turkmenistan	—	70	67	80	3,340
Uzbekistan	22	70	68	78	2,230

Southeast Asia	—	58	64	85	3,210
Brunei	—	31	52	81	—
Cambodia	—	85	85	86	1,350
Indonesia	13	46	58	85	2,660
Laos	—	77	78	90	1,430
Malaysia	18	43	50	81	7,640
Myanmar	—	70	68	90	—
Philippines	11	46	51	83	3,990
Singapore	—	47	55	84	22,640
Thailand	—	80	78	90	5,950
Vietnam	32	75	78	84	1,860
East Asia	—	72	77	89	5,750
China	—	76	80	90	3,550
China, Hong Kong SAR	27	51	57	85	22,570
Japan	17	52	62	85	25,170
Korea, North	—	66	67	85	—
Korea, South	17	50	58	80	15,530
Mongolia	—	76	77	86	1,610

Education

Recent UN conferences have called for universal access to and completion of primary education, and for reducing the "gender gap"—differences in boys' and girls' enrollment—in secondary education. Many governments now recognize that female education can foster economic growth and improve the health of women and children.

Women with more education have smaller, healthier families because they usually make a later transition into adulthood: They have their first sexual experience later, marry later, want smaller families, and are more likely to use contraception and other health care than their less educated peers.

Primary and secondary school enrollments for both girls and boys increased during the 1990s in almost all regions of the world. The gender gap has closed somewhat in recent years but remains pronounced at the secondary school level.

Girls are more likely than boys to discontinue their schooling because of household duties, early marriage and/or childbearing, parents' perceptions that education is more beneficial for sons, and worries about girls' safety at school.

During the 1990s, the gender gap in education closed somewhat in countries where girls have historically lagged behind boys—in northern Africa, sub-Saharan Africa, western Asia, and southern Asia.

Nevertheless, in regions where almost one-third of the world's women live (in southern Asia and sub-Saharan Africa), the gender gap in education continues to be wide. The populations of these two regions are among the world's fastest growing, suggesting that the absolute number of illiterate and poorly educated women in these regions will continue to grow.

Political Leadership

Around the world, women's lack of representation in government, especially high-level ministerial (executive) and legislative bodies, limits their influence over governance and public policies. Worldwide, women held only 14 percent of seats in parliaments in 2001, a slight increase from a decade earlier. In many countries in northern Africa and southern and western Asia, women hold fewer than 10 percent of seats in legislative bodies. There are a small number of exceptions: In Rwanda, Mozambique, Vietnam, and Cuba, women hold more than 25 percent of seats; and in Sweden, women hold 43 percent of parliamentary seats.

Viewed over the long term, women have made some political progress: Over the last century, voting rights have been extended to women in all but a few countries. Women's right to equal participation in political life is guaranteed by a number of international conventions, notably the Convention on the Elimination of All Forms of Discrimination Against Women (CEDAW), which was adopted in 1979 but not ratified by all governments. Women have also become a growing part of the international political landscape, helped in part by the growing influence of women's groups in UN conferences such as the 1994 International Conference on Population and Development and the 1995 Fourth World Conference on Women. These conferences concluded that more action was needed to increase women's participation in decisionmaking and entry into politics. Many of the political inroads women have made are due to gender quotas designed to seat more women in legislative bodies, from national parliaments to local village councils.

A number of countries, including Brazil, France, India, the Philippines, and Uganda have established such quotas in the last decade. In South Africa, the proportion of women in Parliament rose from 1 percent to 30 percent following the establishment of a new constitution that promoted women's rights.

Reproductive Health Challenges

Family Planning. The ability to space and limit childbearing can increase women's autonomy and allow women and men greater control over their lives. Use of family planning also improves health by enabling women to bear children during the healthiest times for themselves and their children. About 57 percent of couples in the less developed world use family planning today, a dramatic increase from earlier decades. This increase in family planning use has brought about a marked and widespread decline in fertility.

Still, more than 100 million women in less developed countries would prefer to prevent a future pregnancy but are not using contraception. The reasons may vary. Many women and their husbands fear the side effects of contraceptive methods. Other women are dissuaded by their husbands' disapproval or by family pressure to have more children.

Some couples oppose contraception for religious reasons. Difficulties in obtaining contraceptives and a shortage of trained health personnel can restrict access to modern family planning methods.

Studies have shown that providing a range of contraceptive methods, improving interactions between providers and clients, and informing family planning clients about the risks and benefits of contraceptive use can help couples achieve their reproductive goals.

Safe Motherhood. More than 500,000 women die every year from causes related to pregnancy, childbirth, and abortion. Ninety-nine percent of these deaths occur in less developed regions, particularly in Africa and Asia. The ratio of maternal deaths to live births varies greatly throughout the world—from fewer than 10 maternal deaths per 100,000 live births in many European countries to more than 1,400 deaths per 100,000 live births in some countries in sub-Saharan Africa.

In addition, for every woman who dies, the World Health Organization (WHO) estimates that bout 30 suffer from long-term health problems such as infertility and damage to the reproductive organs.

Though policymakers and health professionals are more aware of the problem and possible solutions than a decade ago, there is no evidence that maternal death rates have declined significantly.

Maternal deaths are strongly associated with substandard health services and a lack of medical care during and immediately after childbirth. All pregnant women, even healthy women, face some risk of complications that cannot be predicted in advance but require skilled medical care when they arise.

Yet only about half of deliveries in less developed countries take place in the presence of a skilled attendant—a health professional such as a doctor, nurse, or midwife.

Women often lack access to well-functioning transportation and health systems that would enable them to reach and obtain appropriate care in the event of life-threatening complications. The WHO estimates that 13 percent of maternal deaths result from complications of abortion. These complications arise from unsafe procedures, which usually occur where abortions are illegal or inaccessible. In countries where abortion is illegal or where safe abortion services are not available, women with unwanted pregnancies may seek clandestine abortion services or abortion drugs and other means of self-induced abortion.

Many of these cases lead to injuries that require emergency care. Women's deaths due to complications of pregnancy and childbirth are strongly associated with inadequate medical care at the time of delivery. The HIV/AIDS epidemic has had a profound impact on the lives of women, especially those whose economic dependence on men and low social status render them powerless to reject risky behaviors or negotiate preventive actions. Women and girls also provide the main sources of support for those suffering from the disease. Globally, women account for 48 percent of adults who are infected with HIV/AIDS. In sub-Saharan Africa, however, where HIV is spread mainly through heterosexual activity, women account for 55 percent of adults infected with HIV.

The situation is most severe for young women, who are becoming infected in far greater numbers than their male peers. In regions where HIV/AIDS is spread mainly through heterosexual activity, young women are becoming infected in far greater numbers than young men. Adolescent girls are vulnerable for both biological and social reasons. Young women are especially vulnerable to HIV infection for both biological and social reasons. Physiological differences make transmission of the virus through sexual contact more efficient from men to women than vice versa. Adolescent girls have an immature reproductive tract that makes them even more susceptible to infection.

Girls and young women often have sex with older partners who have already been exposed to HIV, and they may lack the knowledge or self-confidence to resist sexual advances or persuade older men to use a condom. Poverty is also a factor, as girls and women may exchange sex for money or gifts. Studies in sub-Saharan Africa have shown that young women are two to six times more likely than young men to contract HIV. Health experts are advocating ways to combat HIV that take into account the distinct social roles and circumstances of men and women—for example, by giving information and counseling to women to help them gain negotiating skills.

International Legal Framework

International law provides a framework of protection for individuals affected by armed conflict. International humanitarian law, the body of law which comes into operation at the outbreak of international or non-international armed conflict, regulates the conduct of hostilities and protects those who are not taking part in hostilities or are no longer doing so. It is the area of law that is of primary relevance to the protection of women and girls during armed conflict. International human rights law is also applicable in times of armed conflict, and is of particular importance in the context of internal armed conflict, where international humanitarian law may not apply.

International criminal law has also come to assume increasing significance in relation to crimes against women and girls during armed conflict, in particular crimes of sexual violence. The protections offered by the provisions of international refugee law are also of relevance to women and girls prior to, during and in the aftermath, of armed conflict.

An overview of the application of these complementary strands of international law. It also considers procedural innovations that address the particular needs of women and girl victims of international crimes in armed conflict. Avenues for compensation for war-related injuries, which is of particular relevance for women and girls as they seek to reconstruct their lives, are also described.

International Humanitarian Law and Human Rights Law

International humanitarian law consists of both conventional and customary rules, the principal conventional instruments of relevance to the protection of victims of armed conflict being the four Geneva Conventions of 1949 and their two Additional Protocols of 1977, which deal with international armed conflicts and non-international armed conflicts respectively. International humanitarian law is binding on both States and organized groups. Many of the rules provided by these treaties form part of customary international law, and are thus binding on all States.

The protections and guarantees laid down by the Geneva Conventions and their Additional Protocols are granted to all without discrimination. Accordingly, women combatants and civilians enjoy the protection of the general rules of international humanitarian law on a basis of equality with men. Some of the provisions of international humanitarian law are of particular importance to women, including those relating to the maintenance and restoration of family ties. The Conventions and their Additional Protocols also include special provisions that offer additional protection to women. These require women to be treated with all consideration due to their sex, and seek to reduce their vulnerability to sexual violence, or provide protections for pregnant women and mothers of young children. There are no special provisions in relation to women in the rules determining the legitimate conduct of hostilities.

The conventional rules proscribe any attacks on the 'honour' of civilian women, with Article 27 of the Fourth

Geneva Convention providing that such women are to be "especially protected ... in particular against rape, enforced prostitution or any form of indecent assault". Article 27 does not protect women from the activities of the State of which they are a national, but Protocol I extends protection to all who are in the territory of a party to a conflict. Article 75.2 of that Protocol prohibits, in relation to both women and men "outrages upon personal dignity, in particular humiliating and degrading treatment, enforced prostitution and any form of indecent assault", whether committed by military or civilian personnel. Article 76 of the Protocol applies specifically to women, and provides that women "shall be the object of special respect and shall be protected in particular against rape, forced prostitution and any other forms of indecent assault".

Female prisoners-of-war, internees and detainees are to be treated with all the regard due to their sex, and are to be provided with female supervision and accommodation and sanitary conveniences separate from those provided to men. Punishments in excess of those applicable to male prisoners -of-war may not be imposed on women prisoners.

Additional protection is provided to pregnant women and mothers of young children. They are accorded special treatment in relation to medical care; food; physical safety; release, repatriation and accommodation in neutral countries and criminal sanctions.

Girls also fall under the protection of the special provisions of international humanitarian law dealing with the protection of children. For example, Protocol I Additional to the Geneva Conventions provides that all children shall be the object of special respect and are to be protected against sexual assault.

The protection afforded by international humanitarian law is applicable in situations amounting to an "armed conflict". In general terms, an armed conflict exists when there is a resort to the use of force between two or more States, or protracted armed violence between governmental authorities and organized armed groups, or between such groups within a State. The determination of whether a violent confrontation within a State goes beyond the realms of domestic criminal law and can be categorized as armed conflict to which international humanitarian law applies can be difficult, especially when the State concerned indicates that it has the situation under control.

The legal consequences of characterizing a conflict as solely internal are significant, as Protocol II, which applies to internal conflicts provides fewer protections than the Geneva Conventions provide to those affected by inter-State armed conflict. Moreover, those protections do not apply in "situations of internal disturbances and tensions, such as riots, isolated and sporadic acts of violence and other acts of a similar nature". Basic protections are also provided to civilians affected by non-international armed conflict through Article 3, common to the four Geneva Conventions of 1949.

That Article prohibits violence to life and person, in particular murder of all kinds, mutilation, torture, cruel treatment and the taking of hostages, outrages upon personal dignity, in particular humiliating and degrading treatment and the passing of sentences and the carrying out of executions without previous judgement carried out by a regularly constituted court, affording judicial guarantees. In addition, where war crimes are concerned, although there have been important recent developments in this area. The Geneva Conventions create criminal liability only for those violations committed in international armed conflict.

Most conflicts which occur in the world today are non-international in nature. Although some reach the threshold of violence and organization required for the application of Protocol II, common Article 3 is perhaps the area of international humanitarian law most applicable to contemporary conflict. International humanitarian law generally ceases to apply on the general close of military operations or on the final repatriation of protected persons. In the case of an occupied territory, the Fourth Convention generally ceases to apply one year after the general close of military operations, but an occupying power which exercises effective control over a territory, continues to be bound by a significant part of the Convention for the duration of that occupation. A significant part of the conventional rules of international humanitarian law relating to conflict and occupation apply to protected persons only, that is, to persons who find themselves in the hands of a Party to the conflict or Occupying Power of which they are not nationals.

The Fourth Geneva Convention, which deals with the protection of the civilian population, provides protection for the whole of the population of the countries in conflict. The protection provided by international humanitarian law to women and girls in times of armed conflict are complemented by those provided by international human rights law, with the Preamble to Protocol II to the Geneva Conventions recalling that international instruments relating to human rights offer a basic protection to the person. Human rights norms are particularly significant in the context of non-international armed conflicts where the protection provided by conventional international humanitarian law is more limited. Human rights obligations relating to the rights to life, to freedom from torture and other inhuman or degrading treatment, and to freedom from slavery provide legal protection against the majority of the worst abuses suffered by women and girls during armed conflicts. The International Covenant on Civil and Political Rights defines these rights as non-derogable, including in times of public emergency that threatens the life of a nation. International human rights law is fully applicable in the pre-conflict and post-conflict stages, where international humanitarian law does not apply.

The legal protection available under international human rights law, including those provided by the International Convention on the Elimination of All Forms of Racial Discrimination, the International Covenants on Civil and Political Rights and Economic, Social and Cultural Rights, the Convention against Torture and Other Cruel, Inhuman and Degrading Treatment and Punishment and the Convention on the Rights of the Child, apply to women and girls on the basis of non-discrimination.

The 1979 Convention on the Elimination of All Forms of Discrimination against Women is the most comprehensive treaty on women's human rights, imposing legally binding obligations on States parties to end discrimination against women in the enjoyment of the full range of civil, political, economic, social and cultural rights. This Convention also expressly addresses issues, such as traffic in, and the exploitation of prostitution of women, which may occur in times of conflict or its aftermath. An Optional Protocol to the Convention, which entered into force in December 2000, enables individuals and groups of individuals who have fulfilled certain admissibility criteria, including exhausting domestic remedies, to submit petitions on violations of the rights in the Convention to the Committee on the Elimination of Discrimination against Women, the monitoring body established by the Convention.

The Protocol also enables the Committee to initiate inquiries into situations of grave or systematic violations of the Convention in those States which have accepted this procedure.

Girls benefit from the specific protections for children set out in the almost universally accepted 1989 Convention on the Rights of the Child which are to be respected and ensured by States parties without discrimination of any kind, including on the basis of sex. By virtue of Article 38 of this Convention, States parties undertake to respect and ensure respect for rules of international humanitarian law applicable to them in armed conflicts which are relevant to the child, and to take all feasible measures to ensure protection and care of children who are affected by armed conflict.

Further protections are provided by the Optional Protocol to the Convention on the Rights of the Child on the sale of children, child prostitution and child pornography, which provides detailed requirements for criminalization of these activities, and the Optional Protocol to the Convention on the Rights of the Child on the involvement of children in armed conflict, which seeks to limit the use of children in armed conflict, including through raising the minimum age of recruitment to 18 years. Both these treaties were adopted in 2000, and entered into force on 18 January and 12 February 2002, respectively.

A number of abuses associated with armed conflict or its aftermath, such as trafficking in women and girls, which have emerged as a particular concern in these contexts, are specifically addressed by international law. The first consolidated instrument on trafficking, the Convention for the Suppression of the Traffic in Persons and of the Exploitation of the Prostitution of Others was adopted by the General Assembly in 1950. Article 6 of the Convention on the Elimination of All Forms of Discrimination against.

Women, and Articles 34 and 35 of the Convention on the Rights of the Child are also directed at the elimination of this abuse, while the International Labour Organization's 1999 Convention 182 on the Worst Forms of Child Labour requires each State party to take immediate and effective measures to prohibit and eliminate the worst forms of child labour, which include slavery, or practices similar to slavery, such as the sale and trafficking in children.

In 2000, the General Assembly adopted the United Nations Convention against Transnational Organized Crime, and its supplementary Protocols: the Protocol to Prevent, Suppress and Punish Trafficking in Persons, Especially Women and Children, and the Protocol against the Smuggling of Migrants by Land, Sea and Air.

The Convention provides, among other things, for cooperation in investigation, mutual legal assistance, extradition where trafficking is concerned, while the Trafficking Protocol provides the first international definition of trafficking, and requires States parties to criminalize such activity and makes provision for assistance to and protection of victims of trafficking, and elaborates preventive measures and preserves existing rights, obligations and responsibilities with respect to refugees.

Responses by United Nations system organizations to address trafficking have included principles developed by OHCHR to ensure the integration of a human rights perspective into national, regional and international anti-trafficking laws, policies and interventions, which require the human rights of trafficked persons to be at the centre of all efforts to prevent and combat trafficking and to protect, assist and provide redress to victims. The principles indicate that States have a responsibility under international law to act with due diligence to prevent trafficking, to investigate and prosecute traffickers and to assist and protect trafficked persons. They also make clear that anti-trafficking measures should not adversely affect the human rights and dignity of persons, in particular the rights of those who have been trafficked, of migrants, internally displaced persons, refugees and asylum-seekers.

Redress for Women and Girls for Conflict-related Abuses

At the international level, the main avenues of redress for women and girls who have experienced conflict-related abuses are through claims of war crimes, crimes against humanity and genocide. In some situations, such women and girls may also be able to claim financial compensation for their war-related injuries. Legal developments during the last decade have focused on individual responsibility for abuses committed during armed conflict, with the Statutes of the two ad hoc Tribunals created by the Security Council to address crimes committed in the former Yugoslavia and Rwanda providing redress for victims through the international criminal law process. The Statute of the Special Court for Sierra Leone provides similar relief.

The Rome Statute of the ICC, which recognizes that Court's competence with regard to war crimes committed in both international and non-international armed conflict provides worldwide jurisdiction to try individuals charged with the most serious crimes. Other extra legal mechanisms have also been introduced to provide alternative, and in some cases, complementary avenues for redress. These include truth and reconciliation processes designed to address the violations of international humanitarian law and human rights law, which are intended to supplement traditional judicial proceedings.

It is through these developments that the international community has sought to address the culture of impunity for violations in armed conflict, including gender-based violence, such as rape, enforced prostitution, and trafficking in armed conflict, with such violence being included within definitions of war crimes, crimes against humanity, and forming components of the crime of genocide, as well as torture or other cruel, inhuman and degrading treatment, and enslavement. Their goals are not only to deal with past atrocities, but also to form part of peace and reconciliation which is fundamental to nation-building or rebuilding.

Those who commit war crimes incur individual criminal responsibility for their actions. The four Geneva Conventions of

1949 codify war crimes in provisions which identify 'grave breaches', with each of the Conventions containing its own list of grave breaches, which are expanded by Additional Protocol I. Under the Conventions and the Protocols, States are obliged to look for those who commit grave breaches and prosecute them, or hand them over to a State willing to do so. States also undertake to enact the necessary legislation to provide effective penal sanctions for those who commit or order grave breaches. Many of the abuses women and girls experience during armed conflict, such as wilful killing, torture or inhuman treatment, are classified as grave breaches of the Geneva Conventions and Additional Protocol I, but gender-specific abuses, such as sexual violence, are not expressly classified as grave breaches. Article 2 of the Statute of the International Criminal Tribunal to address crimes committed in the former Yugoslavia (ICTY) States that Tribunal jurisdiction with respect to grave breaches of the four 1949 Geneva Conventions and Protocol I, including torture and inhuman treatment and wilfully causing great suffering or serious injury to body and health. Article 3 of the Statute also criminalizes violations of the laws and customs of war.

As a result of gender-sensitive prosecutorial policies, sexual violence has been charged under the Statute of the ICTY as a grave breach of the Fourth Geneva Convention relative to the Protection of Persons in Time of War in several cases. For example, in its 1998 Celebici decision, the Trial Chamber of the ICTY considered whether rape constituted torture within the definition of a grave breach for the purposes of Article 2 of the Statute. In concluding that rape at the instigation of a public official or with such an official's acquiescence in situations of armed conflict was torture within the Statute, the Trial Chamber emphasized that gender discrimination was a prohibited purpose for the offence of torture.

Other decisions of the ICTY have also determined that rape constitutes torture within Articles 2 and 3 of its Statute. Similar decisions have been reached by the ICTR, as well as the Inter-American Court on Human Rights and the European Court of Human Rights. In addition, the ICTY has determined sexual violence consisting of outrages on personal dignity, including rape, to constitute a violation of the laws and customs of war.

Article 8 of the Rome Statute of the ICC defines war crimes as grave breaches of the 1949 Geneva Conventions. It also defines 'other serious violations of the laws and customs applicable in international armed conflict...as war crimes. Included within this list of crimes are gender-specific offences, namely: rape, sexual slavery, enforced prostitution, forced pregnancy, ... enforced sterilisation, or any other form of sexual violence also constituting a grave breach of the Geneva Conventions. The crime of committing outrages upon personal dignity, in particular humiliating and degrading treatment is also included as a war crime.

Traditionally, war crimes were considered to arise from breaches of the law committed during international armed conflict only. Article 3 common to the 1949 Geneva Conventions, relating to non-international armed conflicts, is not included in the grave breach provisions of the Conventions, while Additional Protocol II Relating to the Protection of Victims of Non-International Armed Conflicts contains no provisions on grave breaches. However, recent State practice has established that certain breaches of the laws regulating non-international armed conflicts constitute war crimes, and they therefore attract individual criminal responsibility. Article 4 of the Statute of the ICTR criminalizes serious violations of Article 3 common to the Geneva Conventions and of Additional Protocol II, including outrages upon personal dignity, in particular humiliating and degrading treatment, rape, enforced prostitution and any form of indecent assault.

The ICTR has concluded that sexual violence constitutes a violation of the laws and customs of war and has articulated the elements required to establish the crimes of humiliating and degrading treatment, rape, and indecent assault. Notably, in the absence of a commonly accepted definition of rape in international law, in its judgement in Akayesu in 1998, the ICTY defined rape as a physical invasion of a sexual nature, committed on a person under circumstances that are coercive.

It has also described sexual violence, which includes rape, as any act of a sexual nature that is committed on a person under circumstances that are coercive and continued that sexual violence is not limited to physical invasion of a human body and may include acts that do not involve penetration or physical contact. In Akayesu itself, where evidence existed that girls were forced to perform gymnastics naked for the entertainment of soldiers, the Trial Chamber cited forced nudity as falling within the definition of sexual violence.

In the case of a non-international armed conflict the Rome Statute defines war crimes to include serious violations of Article 3 common to the Geneva Conventions. These include, committing outrages upon personal dignity, including humiliating and degrading treatment. In non-international armed conflicts that take place in the territory of a State when there is protracted armed conflict between governmental authorities and organized armed groups or between such groups, the following acts are within the jurisdiction of the ICC: committing rape, sexual slavery, enforced prostitution, forced pregnancy ... enforced sterilization, and any other form of sexual violence also constituting a serious violation of Article 3 common to the four Geneva Conventions.

Article 3 of the Statute of the Special Court for Sierra Leone establishes jurisdiction over serious violations of Article 3 common to the Geneva Conventions. These are defined to and include outrages upon personal dignity, in particular humiliating and degrading treatment, rape, enforced prostitution and any form of indecent assault. The Statute also empowers the Court to prosecute those who have committed certain crimes under Sierra Leonean law, which include offences relating to the abuse of girls.

Crimes Against Humanity. Like war crimes, crimes against humanity are also subject to universal jurisdiction and may therefore be tried by any State. Although long part of internationally customary law, Article 6 of the Charter of the International Military Tribunal (Nuremberg Tribunal) provided the first definition of crimes against humanity in positive international law. Several indictments of the International Military Tribunal for the Far East included charges of sexual violence as crimes against humanity, but the Nuremberg Charter did not include gender-based crimes.

The Statute of the ICTY includes gender-based and sexual violence expressly in its definition of crimes against humanity, with Article 5 of the Statute of the ICTY conferring power on the Prosecutor to prosecute persons responsible for, inter alia, rape when committed in armed conflict, whether international or internal in character, and directed against any civilian population. Article 3 of the Statute of the ICTR, which deals with crimes against humanity, also expressly includes rape.

The Prosecutor has issued indictments in relation to both conflicts charging rape as a crime against humanity and the Tribunals have found individuals guilty of crimes against humanity for, inter alia, rape. Acts of sexual violence other than rape have also been charged as crimes against humanity, being categorized as inhumane acts, before both the ICTY and the ICTR. The classification of serious sexual assault as a crime against humanity via the categorization of inhumane acts has also been confirmed by the ICTY.

Similarly enslavement, another of the acts defined as a crime against humanity, has also been interpreted to reflect the perspective of women. The Trial Chamber of the ICTY in its Foca decision convicted defendants who had held women captive for sex and domestic service of crimes against humanity by way of sexual enslavement, thereby indicating that existing crimes are, increasingly, being interpreted to reflect the perspective of women.

The Statutes of both Tribunals and the Rome Statute provide that torture may constitute a crime against humanity if it is directed against any civilian population. The Prosecutor has issued indictments against defendants before the ICTY for crimes against humanity on the basis of sexual violence as torture and has successfully prosecuted sexual violence on political, racial and/or religious grounds as persecution constituting a crime against humanity.

The Rome Statute extends the range of gender-related crimes within the definition of crimes against humanity to include rape, sexual slavery, enforced prostitution, forced pregnancy, enforced sterilization, or any other form of sexual violence of comparable gravity", provided these crimes are committed as part of a widespread or systematic attack directed against any civilian population, with knowledge of the attack. The Rome Statute further provides that the term enslavement means the exercise of any or all of the powers attaching to the right of ownership over a person, including the exercise of such power in the course of trafficking in persons, in particular women and children, thereby taking into account particular experiences of women.

Accordingly, trafficking in women and children committed as part of a widespread or systematic attack directed against any civilian population meets the definition of a crime against humanity. The Rome Statute also includes gender as one of the impermissible discriminatory grounds in the definition of the crime of persecution. The Statute for the Special Court for Sierra Leone is similar to that of the Rome Statute and includes within its definition of crimes against humanity in Article 2 "[r]ape, sexual slavery, enforced prostitution, forced pregnancy and any other form of sexual violence".

The 1948 Convention on the Prevention and Punishment of the Crime of Genocide defines genocide, a term used in indictments of major war criminals at Nuremberg, as a specific example of the broader category of crimes against humanity. Genocide requires a physical act, such as killing, causing serious bodily or mental harm, deliberately inflicting conditions, calculated to bring about physical destruction, imposing measures intended to prevent births and forcibly transferring children. It is distinguished from other crimes against humanity, however, because a specific mental element is required: a specific intent to destroy a "national, ethnical, racial or religious group in whole or in part.

Although referring to the imposition of measures intended to prevent births within the group in Article II (d), the distinctive ways in which women and girls experience genocide are not expressly reflected in the Genocide Convention. Both the Statutes of the ICTY and the ICTR include genocide within the jurisdiction of the Tribunals. In its Akayesu decision, the Trial Chamber of the ICTR found the defendant guilty of genocide in that he abetted the infliction of serious bodily and mental harm on members of the Tutsi group, through acts of sexual violence, mutilations and rape, with the necessary intent to destroy the group in whole or in part.

The classification of sexual violence as genocide has been subsequently confirmed by the ICTR. It is to be noted that the definition of genocide in the Genocide Convention requires attacks on a national, ethnical, racial or religious group, and does not expressly cover the targeting of women solely on the basis of their sex. When women are specifically targeted, it is usually because they are within one of the specified groups and they are covered as constituting part of a group, within the meaning of Article II of the Genocide Convention. However, in cases where women are targeted for destruction solely on the basis of their sex, judgements of the ICTR provide support for the proposition that a flexible interpretation of genocide should be adopted. For example, in the Akayesu decision, the Trial Chamber noted that the drafters of the Genocide Convention intended to include only 'stable' groups, constituted in a permanent fashion and membership of which is determined by birth, with the exclusion of more 'mobile' groups which one joins through individual voluntary commitment, such as political and economic groups.

In considering whether additional groups meeting this criterion might also be covered, the Chamber stated that "the intention of ... the Genocide Convention, ...was patently to ensure the protection of any stable and permanent group", thereby providing support for the proposition that targeting women, exclusively on the basis of their sex, may fall within the existing definition of genocide. Article 6 of the Rome Statute includes the crime of genocide within the jurisdiction of the Court, but does not make any specific reference to rape or sexual violence, adopting verbatim the definition of the crime contained in the Genocide Convention. However, the work of the Preparatory Commission of the ICC specifically acknowledges that, in certain circumstances, sexual violence may fall within the definition of genocide, thereby confirming the approach of the ICTR in such cases as Akayesu.

In addition to explicitly recognizing gender-based crimes, the constituent documents of the ICTY, the ICTR, the ICC and the Special Court for Sierra Leone include provisions to ensure the delivery of gender-sensitive justice. For example, the Statutes of both the ICTY and the ICTR provide for measures to protect the victim's identity and the Rules of Procedure and Evidence of both Tribunals contain specific rules relating to evidentiary matters in cases of sexual assault. A Victims and

Witnesses Unit is also a feature of the Registry of both Tribunals. The aim of the Unit is to "recommend protective measures for victims and witnesses, and to provide counselling and support for them, in particular in cases of rape and sexual assault.

There is no requirement in the Statute of either Tribunal for gender balance in the composition of the Tribunals themselves, in the staff of the Registry or in the Office of the Prosecutor. The only exception is in the context of the Victims and Witnesses Unit of the Registry, where consideration must be given to the employment of qualified women. The Rome Statute requires that in its "application and interpretation of law", the International Criminal Court "must be consistent with internationally recognized human rights, and be without any adverse distinction founded on grounds, such as [inter alia] gender, as defined in Article 7, paragraph 3 [of the Statute] ...". Provisions also seek to ensure that the Court has a balanced sex composition and gender expertise in all three organs of the Court namely, the Office of the Prosecutor, the Registry and the members of the Court. To provide protection for victims and witnesses, the Registrar is required to set up a Victims and Witnesses Unit. Trials before the Court must be conducted with full respect for the rights of the accused, and with "due regard for the protection of victims and witnesses".

With that balance in mind, the Court is required to "take appropriate measures to protect the safety, physical and psychological well-being, dignity and privacy of victims and witnesses, and must have regard to, among other things, gender considerations, and the nature of the crime, in particular, but not limited to, where the crime involves sexual or gender violence or violence against children. Victims and witnesses also have the right to participate in the process at the ICC, a development intended to give victims a more empowered role in the process.

Reparations for Victims of Conflict

There are several legal avenues for victims of armed conflict to pursue claims for compensation. First, compensation may be payable by a State that is in breach of its obligations under international law. It is a well-established principle of international law that a State must make reparation (which can include the payment of compensation) for its internationally wrongful acts. The United Nations Compensation Commission, specifically recognized and compensated gender-based harms, such as sexual violence to women and girl children, injury to pregnant women, as well as other harms experienced by women, (albeit not exclusively), such as health effects of conflicts and certain types of economic loss. Notably, the Commission acknowledged the difficulties associated with reporting sexual violence, particularly during times of armed conflict, and regarded all forms of sexual assault to be compensable, regardless of whether these acts were part of a widespread campaign of sexual violence.

Another possible source of compensation for victims of criminal acts during armed conflict are the perpetrators of the offence themselves. As the international community has assumed greater responsibility for prosecuting international crimes committed during armed conflict, this issue has received some attention. Neither the Statute of the ICTY nor of the ICTR expressly includes the power to order compensation as part of the penalties imposed on convicted persons, although both confer the power on the relevant Tribunal to order the return of property and proceeds acquired by criminal conduct.

The Rome Statute includes a provision on reparation for victims, which can include restitution, compensation and rehabilitation which entitles the Court, either on request or its own motion to determine the scope and extent of any damage, loss and injury to, or in respect of victims. The provision does not explicitly refer to gender issues, although these might be taken into account by the Court when it establishes principles relating to reparations. Reparations can be ordered directly against a person convicted by the Court, and in appropriate circumstances, may be paid through the Trust Fund established for the benefit of victims of crimes within the jurisdiction of the Court, and their families.

Protecting Refugee and Internally Displaced Women and Girls

International legal protection for refugees, IDPs and returnees, is provided by international human rights law, humanitarian law, and, increasingly, criminal law. Provisions within refugee law further strengthen the international legal regime protecting women and girls during times of armed conflict which are of particular significance in the aftermath of conflict. Policy directives and guidelines on the protection of refugee women, children and reproductive health, and against sexual violence, predominantly formulated by UNHCR over the past 15 years have led to the de facto expansion of protection for women and girls in this context. Under international law, the fundamental rights of refugees, returnees and internally displaced persons are essentially the same.

Moreover, everyone within the territory or under the jurisdiction of a State has a right to the protection of, and is subject to, the laws of that country, regardless of migratory status, or sex. Under the 1951 United Nations Convention relating to the Status of Refugees, those who meet the definition of a refugee in Article 1 (2) of that Convention, have access to a wide array of rights and protections, including legal aid and material protection, as well as the right not to be returned to the place where they face persecution.

Successive conclusions of UNHCR's Executive Committee have emphasized the importance of gender-sensitive interpretation of the Convention definition, and women and girls have been classified as refugees on the basis of gender-based persecution, including through sexual violence, and because they are at risk of severe discrimination as a result of transgressing social mores.

Persons who are internally displaced fall outside the framework of the Refugee Convention, but are protected by the international human rights framework, and, in many cases, international humanitarian law. While there is no international organization with the global mandate to protect or assist internally displaced people, a number of steps have been taken to address their needs. ICRC provides protection to civilians, including IDPs, in the context of armed conflict. Although UNHCR's governing Statute makes no reference to internally displaced persons, UNHCR increasingly provides assistance and protection to internally displaced persons on the basis of General Assembly resolutions and Article 9 of its Statute when called upon to do so by the United Nations General Assembly,

Security Council or Secretary-General. Nonetheless, the absence of internally displaced persons from its mandate prevents UNHCR from taking the initiative and planning long-term for the protection that this group of forced migrants requires.

The 1998 Guiding Principles on Internal Displacement, which are not legally binding, consist of 30 principles to provide protection and assistance throughout displacement and against arbitrary future displacement, and establish guidelines for safe return, resettlement and reintegration. These principles, which are based on the binding rules for the protection of IDPs found in international humanitarian law and human rights, seek to provide guidance to United Nations and international and national actors in working with internally displaced persons. They pay particular attention to the rights and needs of children, including prohibitions on the sale of children into marriage, sexual exploitation, forced labour and recruitment or use of children during hostilities. The principles also stress equal educational opportunities for girls.

Challenges

A comprehensive legal framework exists at the international level to provide protection to women and girls during armed conflict and its aftermath, and this legal framework has been increasingly responsive to the experiences of women and girls in this context, in particular where sexual violence is concerned. The international criminalization of activities in non-international armed conflicts has been of great significance, as have gender-sensitive prosecutorial policies and procedural innovations that address the singular experiences of women and adolescent girls in the enforcement process. Another major advance has been the determination of command responsibility for many of the offences involving sexual violence against women and girls in armed conflict, which has undermined the culture of impunity that previously pervaded in this context.

It is essential that these positive developments are maintained and further advanced. Although there is now a greater understanding of the use of sexual violence against women and girls in armed conflict, other important aspects of women's experience in this context must also be recognized and acknowledged adequately in the legal regime. Significant attention must also be paid to improving compliance with existing international norms. Steps must be taken to ensure that the requirements of international humanitarian and human rights law are widely known and applied, particularly at the national level. Here measures are required at international, regional and national levels to ensure that perpetrators are punished for violations of international standards in this area. Measures are also required to ensure that violations are prevented. This latter objective is affected significantly by the changed nature of armed conflict, with a large number of actors, including non-State actors, private militias and children taking part as combatants.

Many of these actors are unaware of the rules of international human rights, international humanitarian and international refugee law which provide minimum protection for women and girls in conflict, or if they are aware of these rules they disregard or openly flout them. In particular, many of these actors target civilians, including women and girls, often in gender-specific ways.

Issues and trends in multifaceted human and national development in Sri Lanka are currently being examined by researchers from the vantage point of fifty years since political independence was regained in 1948. Yet gender issues continue to be missing in several of these reviews, despite being pushed into public consciousness by the momentum generated in the international environment after the United Nations International Women's Year in 1975.

The need to examine developmental trends and issues from a gender perspective is supported by two conclusions that have surfaced in gender studies. With the exception of leaders, women tend to be 'lost' in history which, it has been claimed, is presented largely as 'his-story'. The fifty years since independence have also seen the emergence of development paradigms and debates flowing from the polarisation of countries into developed and developing nations since the 1950s, and increasing international interdependence and globalisation. Boserup's (1970) contention that development trends and programmes have had a differential impact on men and women has been echoed in subsequent gender-related literature and has spawned 'women in development' (WID) and 'gender and development' (GAD) programmes. Women's rights as human rights have been underscored, particularly in the 1990s.

This introduction contextualises the gendered nuances and issues that have been part of the historical process and that are reflected in the contemporary scene, as a preface to six chapters on special themes and the sixteen interviews of women in diverse circumstances. It presupposes the need for a holistic framework to situate the political, social, economic and intrafamilial changes that have taken place over five decades.

Sri Lanka's recorded history is over 2,500 years old. For most of this period the country was a monarchy with a semi-feudal agrarian society. The religio-cultural orientations of its majority Sinhalese and Buddhist population intermingled over the years with those of a Hindu Tamil minority, and subsequently a Muslim minority of chiefly Arab descent. Western imperial powers in turn established colonial rule from the sixteenth century till the mid-twentieth century. While the Portuguese and the Dutch could control only the coastal areas, the British penetration into the whole island in 1815 introduced to its traditional society the political and social institutions of a modern state and a commercially oriented economy.

Sri Lanka emerged as an independent state in 1948. However, the country had the useful experience of a transitional period of semi-representative government from 1931 to 1947. While the colonial economy continued unchanged, the political developments and social policies initiated during these years blurred the dividing line between the period before and after independence, and shaped some of the contours of post-independence development. In this context, there was greater continuity before and after 1948 than before the end of direct colonial rule and the late 1930s and 1940s.

Political and Legal Framework

Sri Lanka has been largely a functioning democracy over the five decades since 1948, with regular elections and changes of government, and policy stances determined by the ideologies of the two major parties and their alliances. The most significant development took place before political independence when universal franchise was introduced in 1931, and both men and women over 21 years of age were given the right to vote, in contrast to the earlier system of limited male franchise.

Sri Lanka has had three constitutions since 1948 (R.K.W. Goonesekere, 1998). The independence constitution (1948-72) provided for a parliament comprising a house of representatives and senate, a prime minister and cabinet, a governor-general appointed by the prime minister and an independent judiciary and public service. The autochthonous 1972 constitution established a republic, replacing the Queen of England with a president appointed by the prime minister, giving sovereignty to the people through the national state assembly, the prime minister and the cabinet, and eroding the independence of the judiciary. The politicisation of the bureaucracy began with the appointment of senior officials by the prime minister and cabinet ministers rather than by the Public Service Commission.

The 1978 constitution transformed the political power structure by providing for an executive president elected by the people, with the prime minister and cabinet ministers appointed by the executive president responsible to a parliament elected on the basis of the system of proportional representation. The judiciary and public service continued to be vulnerable to political control, but the function of judicial review given in the constitution contributed to empowering the judiciary. The 13th Amendment to this constitution in 1987 abruptly devolved power to eight elected provincial councils in a process of sharing power to satisfy the aspirations of the Tamil population particularly in the north. Below these provincial councils are the pre-independence urban local government institutions and the new divisional councils—the smallest local units. A new draft constitution (1997) attempts to grapple with the problems of devolution.

From a 'rights perspective', the fundamental rights of all citizens have become progressively enshrined in constitutional provisions. From a situation of no safeguards for rights and concern only for minorities in 1948, the 1972 constitution incorporated the general concept of equality before law, but the 1978 constitution included gender equality as a fundamental right and made such rights justiciable. The space provided for the Supreme Court to review new legislation for violation of rights and for individuals to challenge executive and administrative discriminatory action has strengthened human rights, but gender discrimination has yet to be challenged even after two decades (R.K.W. Goonesekere, 1998).

The momentum in safeguarding women's rights has come chiefly from international pressures—the ratification of the United Nations (UN) Convention on the Elimination of All Forms of Discrimination against Women (CEDAW) in 1981 and the UN Convention on the Rights of the Child in 1990, and the endorsement of the UN Declaration on Elimination of Violence against Women in 1993. This momentum has led to the formulation and acceptance at the national level of the Children's Charter (1992) and the Women's Charter (1993). The establishment of a Human Rights Commission in 1996 and the move to strengthen fundamental rights in the new draft constitution are further steps in the direction of equality.

The legal system in Sri Lanka—the general law based on Roman-Dutch and English law, the personal laws of the three ethnic communities, and the developments since 1948—has both egalitarian and discriminatory provisions. The provisions of the Citizenship Act (1948) that discriminated against women marrying foreign spouses continue to devolve the rights of women. The inheritance rights in the Land Development Ordinance (1934) favour male succession in settlement areas. The penal code was not revised for around a hundred years, and violence against women did not become an overt issue till international pressure and local agitations mounted in the 1990s and led to the revision of the code in 1995, with higher sentences for rape in contrast to its trivialisation in courts earlier, and the criminalisation of incest, grave sexual abuse and sexual harassment. It is apparent that these changes have been the outcomes also of heightening awareness of violation of human rights in conflict situations in recent decades. Procedural delays in obtaining legal redress have continued to bedevil the dispensation of justice to all citizens.

The personal laws of the Kandyan Sinhalese, the northern Tamils (Thesavalamai) and the Muslims (Islamic laws) embody varying degrees of gender discrimination with regard to aspects such as inheritance, marriage and divorce; discrimination that is in violation of the constitution. Sporadic efforts to enforce a non-discriminatory common personal law have failed in the context of an increasing sense of ethnic identity and consequent resistance from some ethnic communities (S. Goonesekere, 1995).

On the other hand, an area in which much progress was made even before independence is labour legislation. Labour laws were introduced in Sri Lanka in the plantation sector in the early decades of the twentieth century, and were extended to the rest of the formal sector. They have increasingly conformed to international norms through ratification of several International Labour Organisation (ILO) conventions. In particular, equal minimum wages have been enforced in the formal sector and maternity leave was introduced in 1985. But weak enforcement of legislation and the exclusion of the large, amorphous informal sector from the ambit of legislation have exposed a high proportion of women and men workers, and even children, to economic exploitation. The protracted delays in finalising the Workers' Charter are symptomatic of the conflict between he concern for workers' rights and the increasing pressure to deregulate in an 'open' market economy.

In Sri Lanka's democracy, political consciousness has been very high among women and men, with a high turnout of voters and volatile elections. Sri Lanka has the disinction of having had the first woman prime minister in the world in 1960. A woman was elected as executive president and another woman became prime minister in 1994. Nevertheless, all national and local assemblies have been consistently male-dominated. The proportion of women members in parliament or the national state assembly has never exceeded 5 per cent since 1931, and the proportion has been around 2 per cent in provincial, municipal and divisional councils (de Silva, 1995). The fact that very few women have held the posts of cabinet minister, chairperson of a provincial council or mayor reflects the low level of their participation in decision making.

The public service has expanded over the years. Women were admitted to the foreign service in 1958 and to the prestigious administrative service in 1963. In terms of participation, however, the 'glass ceiling' appears to have prevailed since independence in the public and private sectors and in trade unions, with change occurring chiefly at the heights of political power. In the administrative structure, the national machinery for women's affairs—the Women's Bureau established in 1978 and the Ministry of Women's Affairs set up in 1983 during the UN Decade for Women, as well as the National Committee on Women appointed in 1993 to oversee the implementation of the Women's Charter and its interests—had tended to be marginalised in the national policy making, implementation and monitoring structures. The fact that 'women's affairs' is not a devolved subject under the 13th Amendment to the constitution has created confusion at local levels in administration.

A strong rights orientation is juxtaposed with weak participation and implementation in meeting needs that have surfaced over the years in the politico-legal framework. However, the rights issues have also been obscured, challenged and even jettisoned in the ethnic and social conflicts that have ravaged the country at different times since the mid-1950s. The political instability and violence arising from these conflicts are other facets of political change that have impinged on the lives of thousands of men and women. Two sources of political conflict emerged in the years after independence, both stemming largely from inequalities created by the policies of the colonial administration.

The rise of communal conflict in Sri Lanka's multi-ethnic society may be traced to the Sinhala majority community's perception of disadvantage under the colonial administration, the unequal distribution of social and economic opportunities, and the resentment of perceived ethnic discrimination by Tamil youth as a consequence of the policies of 'Sinhala only' as the official language introduced in 1956 and of university admissions on the basis of district quotas from the 1970s. What had been sporadic riots since 1958 escalated in 1983 into a civil war with the demand for a separate Tamil state in the north and east of the country, and with Indian intervention in the late 1980s.

While the medium of instruction in educational institutions had been the 'mother tongue' of students since the 1940s and 1950s, as an outcome of the ethnic war the 13th Amendment to the constitution (1987) made Sinhalese and Tamil the official languages with English as the link language. Provincial councils were created to devolve power, and a power sharing political package is now being discussed. The war, however, continues in the north and east, with loss of life incurred by both sides—army and rebels—as well as by civilians, the exodus of Tamil refugee families to India, to the West and Australia, internal displacement of thousands of Tamil, Muslim and Sinhalese families, and loss of livelihood and economic deprivation.

Another strand of violence surfaced at the end of the 1960s as slow economic growth and consequent unemployment frustrated the aspirations of a generation of educated Sinhala youth emerging from universities and secondary schools. The first Janatha Vimukthi Peramuna (JVP) insurgency in 1971 was an effort to take power from the state, and was suppressed in a less than a year. A large number of youth, chiefly young men, died during the insurgency, while several others were imprisoned and/or rehabilitated. Indian intervention and the India-Sri Lanka Accord in 1987 triggered an open confrontation between the JVP and the state which lasted until the capture and death of the leader in 1989. The violence unleashed by the JVP and counter-violence by the state resulted in loss of life, temporary displacement and loss of assets and livelihood. In the 1990s the JVP entered mainstream policies and the parliament.

In both conflicts, men have been the main victims of war. But women too have lost their lives, as civilians caught in the crossfire, as LTTE combatants and as personnel in the state army. They have been victims of rape and other forms of sexual abuse, and have borne a large share of the burden of displacement. They have lost spouses and livelihoods, and the number of female heads of households has increased steadily. The psychological trauma they and their children have undergone has long-term consequences (Perera, 1998).

In restrospect, despite some constitutional and legal advances, Sri Lanka has endured a violence that has brutalised its society for several decades. Persistence of poverty, uneven socio-economic development, Tamil perceptions of injustice, the resentment of Sinhalese youth towards elite domination of the economy and society, and politicisation of employment have torn the social fabric and continue to threaten political stability and social integration.

The Social Sector

Social policies and their impact on the quality of life of the population have been perceived as Sri Lanka's 'success story' in the post-colonial years. The commitment to improving living standards through education and health policies sufaced in the transition years as a concomitant of universal franchise. The welfare package introduced chiefly in the early 1940s included free education and health services and a subsidised food scheme, creating a momentum in social development that continued till at least the mid-1960s. Policy directions, therefore, had already been determined before 1948.

Education: Policies and Consequences

Education policies formulated in the 1930s and 1940s had the expressly stated objective of reducing the socio-economic inequalities created by British colonial educational policies. The latter had privileged a minority by setting up a dual-language structure consisting of free-levying, urban, English schools and under-resourced, free, mass, 'vernacular' schools in the two local languages. The entrenched power of the Christian minority had contributed to greater disparities in the dual system of state and denomination schools. The right to education in a democracy, and to equal educational opportunity for upward socio-economic mobility, were recognised and articulated in official statements (*Report of the Special Committee on Education*, 1943). Fifty-four central schools were set up between 1940 and 1947 to extend secondary and university education to the rural sector. Free primary, secondary and university education were introduced in 1945, and the mother tongue became the medium of instruction in primary schools as an initial step towards dethroning English as the language of education. At the same time, public school examinations were delinked from British universities and the first local university was established in 1942.

The two decades after independence till the mid-1960s saw continuity in the implementation of policies to extend educational opportunity, despite the opposition of vested interests and efforts to introduce selection processes that would result in the social exclusion of the poor. The number of schools nearly doubled from 5,726 in 1945 to 9,550 in 1965, remaining at around 10,000 from the late 1970s onwards. The majority of denominational schools were absorbed into the state system in 1961, so that around 97 per cent of all school are now within the free state education system. The number of co-educational schools increased from 77.6 per cent of all schools in 1945 to 89.2 per cent in 1963, and subsequently to around 96 per cent since 1982. The number of teachers also doubled over this period. Most importantly, enrolment in secondary education increased sharply between 1952 and 1965, with local languages being progressively introduced as the medium of instruction from 1953 to 1959. Enrolment increased fourfold in Grades 9 and 10 and sixfold in Grades 11 and 12. Consequently, education participation rates in the 5-14 age group rose from 57.6 per cent in 1946 to 71.7 per cent in 1953 and 74.4 per cent in 1963

(*Census of Sri Lanka*, 1946, 1953, 1963). Enrolment rates increased faster than the relatively high population growth rates during this period. The University of Ceylon saw an explosion in enrolment in the early 1960s as the cumulative result of free education and the change in the medium of instruction. The number of universities was increased from one to four. What is significant is the rapid increase in educational participation within a short period of time in a low-income country such as Sri Lanka.

Educational opportunity was thrown open to hitherto disadvantaged socio-economic groups (Alailima, 1997). Women were major beneficiaries of policies that were implemented without gender differentiation, and parents were not compelled now to invest their scarce resources only in the education of sons. Gender disparities in educational participation in the 5-14 age group were almost eliminated by 1963 and, from the mid-1960s onwards, more girls than boys were enrolled in secondary grades. The social composition of a university students had been transformed by the mid-1960s into a rural and non-affluent majority (Jayaweera, 1984; Strauss, 1951; Uswatte-Arachchi, 1974), and the proportion of women students rose from 10.2 per cent in 1942 to a peak of 44.5 per cent in 1970. Literacy levels rose from 76.5 per cent male and 46.2 per cent female literacy in 1946, to 85.6 per cent male and 67.1 per cent female literacy in 1963, to 90.5 per cent and 82.8 per cent respectively in 1981.

The high incidence of unemployment from the late 1960s, and the influence of human capital theories and attendant 'manpower' projections from the West, resulted in a shift in priorities with reduced concern for extending educational opportunity. Efforts are focused, with little success, on meeting employment needs at a time when slow economic growth limited the absorptive capacity of the labour market. From 1972 to 1978 pre-vocational subjects were made compulsory in secondary schools, and job-oriented courses were introduced in arts faculties to increase the employability of the products of the education system. But neither these reforms nor the efforts to open junior university colleges in the late 1960s and affiliated university colleges in the early 1990s reduced the gap between supply of and demand for labour in the context of a sluggish economy. University admissions were frozen from 1967 to 1976 to restrict the output of graduates, and the universities progressively lost their autonomy through legislations enacted in 1966, 1972 and 1978.

Regional imbalances persisted, and the solution adopted was not the extension of educational opportunity by replicating the model of the 'central schools' in districts, but the adoption since the 1970s of a scheme of district-based quotas for university admissions with special quotas for disadvantaged districts. These quotas have prevailed for nearly three decades without concomitant expansion in senior secondary science facilities. Consequently, although some students from disadvantaged districts have entered universities, inter-district and intra-district disparities continue to exist. This policy has also had an adverse impact on educationally developed districts such as Colombo and Jaffna, manifested in the growing resentment among Tamil youth towards the perceived discrimination against them, leading them in the 1980s to take up arms against the state. It is also manifested in the flight of professionals all communities overseas to ensure access to higher education for their sons and daughters.

In the 1980s, International Monetary Fund/World Bank (IMF/WB) structural adjustment programmes reduced social sector expenditure and increased income disparities. Expenditure on education, that had increased from 2.7 per cent of GDP in 1945 to nearly 5 per cent of GDP in 1970, declined to 2.3 per cent in the mid-1980s, resulting in deterioration in the quality of educational inputs and in the levels of student achievement (Alailima, 1995). The network of educational institutions survived, but disparities persisted in provision and partitcipation and there was stagnation in enrolment and literacy rates in the 1980s. The only significant expansion took place in university education, with the number of universities increasing from four in 1970 to twelve in 1997. Nevertheless, universities accommodate less than 3 per cent of the relevant age group, and the absence of adequate alternative opportunities at the tertiary education level has created intense competition and frustration at the point of entry to higher education.

In the 1990s, educational opportunity and the quality of education resurfaced as issue in response to the norms set by the UN Convention on the Rights of the Child (1990), the Jomtien UN Declaration on Education for All (1990), and by the SAARC summits. In a context of increasing poverty and hardship in the

1980s, free midday meals and free uniforms were provided to reduce non-schooling. Compulsory education regulations for the 5-14 age group were enforced from January 1998.

Universal primary education, however, has yet to be achieved. Male and female participation rates in the 5-14 age group increased slowly from 83.7 per cent and 83.6 per cent respectively in 1981 to 89.4 per cent and 89.5 per cent in 1994, and in the 15-19 age group from 41.2 per cent and 42.7 per cent in 1981 to 53.4 per cent and 55.3 per cent in 1994 (*Census of Sri Lanka*, 1981; *Demographic and Health Survey*, 1994). The number of girls in total enrolment has been 51 per cent in Grades 9-11 and 56 per cent in Grades 12-13, and has fluctuated from 40 to 45 per cent in universities since 1970. Achievement levels of all students in basic competencies have been relatively low, particularly in disadvantaged districts (Wijesuriya, 1994).

The weakest sector in the education system has been technical and vocational education. Further educational opportunities at the tertiary level tend to be concentrated largely in the service sector—in teaching, health-related programmes, accountancy, and secretarial and word processing skills. Several islandwide networks in technical and vocational education at the secondary level have developed in ad hoc fashion since the 1950s, but are hardly adequate to meet the needs of even 50 per cent of school-leavers from different exit points. With the exception of the National Apprenticeship and Industrial Training Authority established in 1972, all other institutions or centres—technical colleges, non-formal technical units and vocational centres of the Departments of Labour and Agriculture and the National Youth Services Council—have had no linkages with the labour market and have therefore have little success as intermediate agencies between schools and employment (Kelly and Culler, 1990). Women have been further disadvantaged by wide gender imbalances in enrolment and under-representation in technical courses (Jayaweera, 1991, 1998).

In reviewing educational development over the last fifty years, several trends can be identified. Education has reduced socio-economic inequalities, although the poorest have yet to be brought within the ambit of the education system. Gender differences hardly exist in access to general education or in performance. Horizons have widened, and the quality of life has improved significantly, particularly as education and literacy have promoted better utilisation of health services. The education of women and their subsequent employment have delayed marriage and thereby reduced family size and population growth.

In the early decades after independence, the expansion of secondary and higher education contributed to increased female labour force participation and to upward occupational mobility. This trend was nearly reversed with the high incidence of unemployment particularly among secondary-educated youth and university graduates, with globalisation and the demand created by the international division of labour for low-cost female workers for semi-skilled labour-intensive employment, and with the expansion of the private sector, with its requirement of proficiency in English, at the expense of the public sector under the structural adjustment programmes. Consequently, there has been in recent years an adverse trend in socio-economic mobility, particularly for educated women: vertical mobility for the affluent, and horizontal mobility in low-skilled jobs for those without family resources.

After independence, the emergence on the political scene of those who perceived themselves to have been a disadvantaged majority under colonial rule resulted in emotive intra-nationalism and divisive language and education policies and structures. Sinhalese was adopted as the official language in 1956, and efforts were made to redress ethnic imbalances through artificial mechanisms. Education policies and programmes made no effort to counter ethnic tension, to build 'bridges' and promote mutual understanding, respect for diversity and national harmony in a multi-ethnic society.

The examination-dominated curriculum, with centralised, uniform courses and state monopoly of textbooks, left little space for the encouragement of initiative, creativity, personality attributes and life-skills, or for the promotion of human values and human rights perspectives. While women have had equal access to general education, there has been little awareness of the need to counter gender role stereotypes and gendered behavioural norms reflected in the school and in the 'hidden' curriculum that has bedvilled their social and economic empowerment (Jayaweera, 1993).

The progress made in education over fifty years may be assessed accurately from the fact that the National Education

Commission appointed in 1991 proposed virtually the same goals and policies—those of extending educational opportunity, improving the quality of education, promoting national harmony and establishing links with the world of work—as were recommended fifty years earlier (*Report of the Special Committee on Education*, 1943; *First Report of the National Education Commission*, 1992).

Health Policies and Programmes

The provision of health services followed the same trend as education—limited reach under colonial rule; expansion initiated in the transition years as an outcome of the social policy orientation of those years; and continuity in progress after independence until financial constraints were imposed in the 1980s. In 1950, free health services were recognised as a state policy and a network of health units focusing specially on maternal and child care services was developed throughout the country. These increased in number from 8 in 1945 to 91 in 1950 and 929 in 1997. The number of doctors per 100,000 population was 9 in 1950 and 25 in 1995, and the number of nurses 18 and 74 respectively. Institutional births increased from less than half in 1945 to 86.3 per cent in 1996 (Samarasinghe, 1998).

The 'basic needs' approach prioritised by international agencies for economically developing countries in the 1970s popularised the concept of primary health care and the provision of integrated facilities at the local level. These are currently provided at primary health care complexes in every administrative division. With support from the United Nations Children's Fund (UNICEF), a Child Survival and Development initiative in the 1970s extended immunisation programmes to around 90 per cent of the child population. Through an Act of Parliament in 1961, state support was made available to indigenous schools of medicine, from research institutes and universities to the local level.

In the 1980s, the IMF/WB structural adjustment package reduced state expenditure and partially introduced the concept of 'user fees'. State health facilities survived, but there was visible deterioration in the quality of services, and the poor were compelled increasingly to seek treatment in the expanding private health sector and to cope with rising costs of drugs (Alailima, 1997). In recent decades, too, curative services have expanded at the expense of preventive services, as the demand for sophisticated services grows with the increase of diseases that are symptomatic of the changing pace of development.

The provision of extensive services over several decades has resulted in sharp improvement in demographic and health indicators that have reached levels atypical in a low-income country. In this process, women have been major beneficiaries of maternal and child care services and primary health care facilities.

Mortality rates declined sharply from 19.9 per 1,000 in 1945 to 14.3 per 1,000 in 1950, partly as a result of the campaign to eradicate malaria, and then steadily to 8.5 per 1,000 in 1965 and 5.5 per 1,000 in 1995. Infant mortality rates declined from 131 per 1,000 in 1945 to 100.5 per 1,000 in 1950 and further to 15 per 1,000 in 1995, and maternal mortality rates fell from 16.5 per 1,000 in 1945 to 5.6 per 1,000 in 1950, 2.4 per 1,000 in 1963 and 0.4 per 1,000 in the 1990s. Life expectancy rose from 43 years in 1946 to 52 years in 1952 and 72 years in 1994. What is significant is that female mortality rates, which were higher than male mortality rates in 1946, declined faster and were lower than male rates from the mid-1960s. Male and female life expectancy were 43.8 and 41.5 years respectively in 1946, 63.6 and 65 years respectively in 1965, and 70 and 74 years respectively in 1994. These overall indicators, however, conceal disparities consonant with socio-economic differences, reflected particularly in unacceptably high maternal and infant mortality rates in urban low-income neighbourhoods, plantations and pockets in the eastern province.

It is an index of the whole development process in Sri Lanka, however, that despite the decline in mortality rates, the incidence of morbidity has remained relatively high. Communicable diseases were controlled by immunisation programmes, but environmental diseases such as diarrhoea and dysentery persisted largely because of environmental factors and access to water, sanitation and housing became issues of concern only in the 1980s and 1990s. Even in 1994, only 53.7 per cent of the total population, 87 per cent of the urban population and 49 per cent of the rural population had access to safe drinking water, and 61 per cent, 67 per cent and 60 per cent respectively had sanitation facilities. Sri Lanka also had to cope with the 'double burden' of environmental, infectious and parasitic diseases seen in economically less developed countries as well as the common diseases of adults in industrialised countries, such as hypertension, heart diseases, diabetes and cancers and the degenerative disease of an ageing population (Samarasinghe, 1998). Currently, therefore, healthy growth and reduction in morbidity have emerged as a critical need in the health sector.

This situation has been exacerbated by the persistence of undernutrition as debilitating factors. The food subsidy or food ration scheme introduced during the Second World War in the early 1940s continued after independence to safeguard minimum nutritional levels among the poor. In 1979, as a part of the structural adjustment programme, the food ration was converted into food stamps that were not indexed to the cost of living. The erosion in the value of the stamps with spiralling costs of living in the 1980s reduced the calorie intake of the poor and increased undernutrition. Evidence from national studies indicates that undernutrition—stunting, wasting and underweight—increased among the under-5 population in the 1980s and declined slightly in the 1990s. The relatively high incidence of low birth weight–around 20 per cent—is said to be a result of maternal undernutrition and, of course, of poverty. Women, especially pregnant women, appear to be more vulnerable to anaemia, iodine deficiency and protein energy malnutrition, which are relatively widespread in Sri Lanka (UNICEF, 1997).

Overall, the population of Sri Lanka increased from 6.6 million in 1946 to over 18 million in 1994. A significant achievement over the years, however, has been a decline in fertility and reduction in family size contributing to a considerable fall in population growth rates from 2.8 per cent in the 1950s to 1.2 per cent in the 1990s. The crude birth rate remained high, between 35 per 1,000 and 40 per 1,000, till 1960 and then declined to 28.2 per 1,000 in 1981 and 19.9 per 1,000 in 1993. The total fertility rate was 5.3 in 1953, 4.2 in 1971, 3.8 in 1981 and 2.3 in 1993. The rising educational levels and labour force partipation rates of women and the consequent increase in their age of marriage to 25 years, alongwith the extension of family planning services since the 1960s resulting in a contraceptive prevalence rate of 72 per cent in 1993, have contributed to this trend.

Other manifestations of health problems that are life-threatening or adversely affect the quality of life of families have surfaced in recent years—sexually transmitted diseases and HIV/AIDS, alcohol and drug dependence, mental illness and suicide, and unsafe abortions. The paradigm shift to a life-cycle approach in health has generated needs that were peripheral in the past, such as the health needs of adolescents, occupational health hazards of workers, especially women workers, domestic violence, and geriatric care for a rapidly ageing population.

Economic Development

Sri Lanka's economic development over fifty years has lagged behind progress in the social sector, creating dissonances and tensions that have negated some social gains and have resulted in political instability and violence.

The colonial economy—with its dependence on exports of three primary commodities, tea, rubber and coconut, a plantation sector juxtaposed with peasant agriculture and chiefly cottage industries, and an expanding public service—continued to dominate the economy in the early years after independence. Women had been economic producers in the traditional economy for centuries, and also acted as wage earners on plantations. A booming export market and financial assets generated during the World War created a facade of prosperity until a negative external environment in the late 1950s exposed its vulnerability.

Falling commodity prices from the late 1950s resulted in deterioration in terms of trade, depletion of assets, and decline in average economic growth rates from 4.6 per cent in 1950-60 to 3.9 per cent in 1960-77. The state responded by promoting import substitution in agriculture and industry and protecting domestic industries. Import quotas and controls, and foreign exchange restrictions, were introduced progressively till a closed economy came into operation in the 1970s. The socialist stance of the government that was in power for much of the period from 1956 to 1977 meant that central planning, nationalisation, and state intervention and monopolies in all sectors of the economy, were key policies. The State Industrial Corporation Act of 1957, the Government Business Acquisition Act of 1971 and the nationalisation of plantations in 1974 are illustrative of this trend. At the same time, the land reforms of 1972 and the ceiling on housing imposed in 1973 were strategies to distribute assets more equitably (Indraratne, 1998).

In agriculture, large scale alienation of state lands—through land settlement schemes in the dry zone and village expansion schemes in the wet zone—increased the resources of some of the large landless population. In the 1960s, Green Revolution technologies and inputs were promoted through state subsidies to promote self-sufficiency. Land reform in 1972, however, brought little significant improvement in productivity in plantations and in domestic agriculture, or in the working and living conditions of women and men in the agriculture sector.

The low priority given to industrialisation in the early years gave way from the late 1950s to active promotion of import substitution industries. Large-scale, state-owned, capital-intensive industries were established for the manufacture of products such as plywood, paper, ceramics, tiles and steel, and small-scale private enterprises sprang up to meet the demand for consumer goods such as food, textiles, garments, footwear, and rubber and plastic products. Foreign exchange and import restrictions stifled export industries. They also limited drastically the availability of capital and intermediate inputs, and consequently limited the import substitution industries to low levels of capacity utilisation and poor-quality products (Abeyratne, 1997). These industries, however, gave a fillip to male and female employment in existing and new industries in both the traditional and modern small sectors within a protected domestic market. The services sector expanded as state institutions proliferated.

Nevertheless, slow economic growth in the closed economy limited the capacity of the labour market to absorb a labour force that had expanded with high population growth rates in the 1950s and 1960s and with the output of increasing numbers of women from educational institutions. Consequently, male and female unemployment rates, which had been 8.9 per cent and 7.6 per cent respectively in 1963 (*Census of Sri Lanka*, 1963; *Socio-Economic Survey*, 1969-70) increased to 11.4 per cent and 21.2 per cent respectively in 1969-70 and 18.9 per cent and 36.3 per cent respectively in 1973, with female unemployment rates at double the male unemployment rates. This high incidence of unemployment and the frustration of expectations among the youth contributed to the insurgency of 1971.

Stagnation in economic growth led the new government in 1977 to initiate a radical shift in economic policy accompanied by the introduction of an IMF/WB-sponsored structural adjustment programme. This shift to market liberalisation and an open economy survived the change of government in 1994. Tariffs were reduced and import controls virtually removed, facilitating trade and the movement of capital and labour. The currency was devalued. Incentives were offered for foreign and local investment, and infrastructural support provided through institutions such as the Export Development Board and the establishment of three export processing zones in 1978, 1985 and 1990, to promote export-oriented production, particularly in light manufacturing industries.

The economic growth rate increased to an average of 6 per cent in 1978-83, but declined to 4.9 per cent in 1983-86 and 3.1 per cent in 1987-90. It later rose again in the 1990s to around 5 per cent. As a consequence of the increase of both imports and exports, terms of trade continued to deteriorate, and budget deficits and external debt increased. Decontrol of prices and removal of consumer subsidies such as those for food led to rising costs of living. The removal of producer subsidies increased costs of production to levels unaffordable for small producers. The reduction of social sector expenditure resulted in deterioration in the quality of services.

Not only was private enterprise promoted, but the public sector was reduced in size and in employment potential through 'voluntary retirement' packages, the privatisation of state enterprises, and privatisation of the management of plantations during the second phase of structural adjustment in the 1990s. Private enterprise and private financial institutions flourished, but inflation, high costs of living and the exclusion of small producers from the benefits of market-led growth caused hardship to the poor, widened income disparities and increased poverty. Women in low-income families appear to have borne a disproportionate share of the burden of poverty and of adjustment to the structural adjustment programme.

In the agriculture sector, the Accelerated Mahaweli Development Scheme translocated around 100,000 families from overcrowded locations to newly opened and irrigated lands in the dry zone. But the withdrawal of the fertiliser subsidy in 1989, and the privatisation of input supplies and consequent rise in costs of production, depressed the fortunes of small farmers who comprise two-thirds of all cultivators.

With the removal of protection and control, local industries failed to compete with imports, and those that depended on imported inputs, such as the handloom industry, the forte of women, collapsed. With no support to cope with market forces, thousands lost their livelihood (Atukorale, 1986). Export-oriented industrialisation expanded rapidly, the percentage of manufacturing in total exports increasing from 5.7 in 1970 to 34 in 1983, 60 in 1993 and 75 in 1995. These export-oriented industries were largely labour-intensive and low-technology. Garment manufacture, which had a high import content and low value addition, dominated the industry sector and there was little diversification. The relocation of these industries to countires such as Sri Lanka by multinational corporations was motivated by the need to reduce production costs by recruiting low-cost female labour perceived as a trainable, docile and dispensable workforce. Consequently, 80 per cent of the labour force in the three export processing zones, 60 per cent in factories outside the zones, and 90 per cent in the rural garment factories established in the 1990s, were women. The demand was chiefly for young women aged between 18 and 30 for semi-skilled, low-technology and relatively low-wage jobs.

Employment opportunities in the public services, which had been a niche for women, declined. On the other hand, the phenomenon of labour migration for employment abroad became widespread during the mid-1970s. While there was a demand for skilled male workers and construction workers in the oil-rich Middle East and West Asian countries, the strongest demand has been for female domestic labour in the Middle East, in Southeast Asia and elsewhere. Women in the low-income informal sector and in other poverty groups responded to this demand for reasons of family survival, and their proportion among overseas workers increased to 80 per cent in the 1990s. They were left largely at the mercy of market forces and subjected to economic exploitation, sexual abuse and family dislocation, while their remittances made a crucial contribution to solving the country's balances of payments problems. It was only in the mid-1990s that the Foreign Employment Bureau instituted measures to protect them from exploitation and to provide them support.

In retrospect, therefore, the structure of the economy has changed since the 1980s, with the share of agriculture in GDP declining from 49.8 per cent in 1950 to 24.6 per cent in 1982 and 20.8 per cent in 1994; the share of manufacturing increasing from 3.9 per cent in 1950 to 14 per cent in 1982 and 20 per cent in 1994;

and the share of trade rising from 8.2 per cent to 20.1 per cent and 22 per cent over the same period. There has been a shift in employment from agriculture to jobs in industry or in the services sector. Globalisation has resulted in the incorporation of the labour force into the international labour market. Economic development had depended increasingly over the years on female labour chiefly in jobs of poor quality and prospects.

Income disparities declined to some degree till the 1970s as a consequence of positive social policies in education and health and the provision of food subsidies. The implementation of the economic reforms initiated in 1977 widened disparities, but there appears to have been a slight improvement in the 1990s. The highest decile had 42.5 per cent of total income in 1946, 30.5 per cent in 1973, 43 per cent in 1981-82, and 40 per cent in 1996-97. The bottom 40 per cent had 12 per cent, 15.8 per cent, 11.6 per cent and 12.4 per cent of total income in these years. It appears, too, that there has been no sustained shift to a more equitable distribution from 1946 to 1996 (Colombage, 1998). Poverty is said to have increased from 18 per cent in 1978 to 27 per cent in 1986, and to have then declined to 22 per cent in 1991. Estimates differ, however, and are higher when a different poverty line is used for computation.

The urban population is said to be most affluent on an average, as macro-economic policies have had an urban bias and the rural hinterland and remote villages have been excluded from the benefits of economic growth (Lakshman, 1997a and b). The percentage of women income receivers rose from 25 in 1963 to 31 in 1986-87. Women earned half the income of men in the 1960s and 1970s, and two-thirds in 1985-86. Though education has contributed to reducing income inequalities among the population, employment appears to have widened differences as the business community, concentrated in a small number of firms, has prospered with the economic reforms of 1977 while the majority of men and women workers are still employed in casual, marginal, low-skill, low-income employment or are self-employed. Violence culminating in armed conflict has exacerbated the constraints to economic development and increased income inequalities.

It has been suggested that Sri Lanka was late in adopting economic development strategies such as market liberalisation and export orientation in comparison with other countries in the region (Lakshman, 1997a and b). Overall, the absence of evidence of sustained economic growth has made it difficult to reduce unemployment or poverty in the country. Priorities shifted in a dichotomous manner from social policies to economic policies, so that the emergence of social unrest and political conflict necessitated special poverty alleviation programmes—or income transfer programmes such as the Janasaviya Programme in 1989 and the Samurdhi Programme in 1995. Another recent dichotomy, between macro-economic policies that result in increasing poverty and peripheral 'safety net' programmes that are merely appendages to these policies, bedevils the current economic development scene, while the victims of armed conflict and the victims of social exclusion continue to be vulnerable groups within the political economy.

Changing Social Structures and Relations

Inevitably, social structures including the family have not remained static over a period of fifty years in the context of a changing environment. The constitutional and legal changes and social and economic policies outlined earlier contributed to changes in or the reinforcement of existing structures. International pressures through the process of globalisation and particularly through new and rapidly expanding information channels have engendered both positive and negative trends.

Sri Lanka's plural and multi-ethnic society has seen some changes in social composition. The western-oriented Burgher population, which contributed greatly to professional and civic life at the time of independence, has diminished drastically in numbers as a consequence of migration to Australia and to the West following changes in language policies. The plantation community of recent Indian origin brought to the country by the colonial administration, though still resident in enclaves, has moved from immigrant to citizenship status. Language rather than religion became a divisive issue between the Sinhala majority and the chief minority, the Tamil population, in the mid-1950s as intranationalism replaced anti-colonialism as an emotive issue. Regrettably, the failure to resolve contentious issues early has resulted in open confrontation escalating into ethnic war since the mid-1980s in a seeming political impasse, and continuing violence in the north and east of the island.

Caste as a traditional basis of social organisation has weakened in force in the Sinhala community except in the institution of marriage. It is likely that the upheaval in the north has had some impact on the more rigid caste-based hierarchy in this region. Social class is a more visible manifestation of structural impediments to social integration. The extension of educational opportunities may have promoted socio-economic mobility, but poverty groups continue to be the victims of social exclusion. Democratic political structures and universal franchise have reduced the salience of social hierarchies, but politicisation of the administrative processes, corruption and abuse of power have compounded social exclusion. The frustration of educational and employment expectations in this context led to the alienation of educated youth, to social unrest and to conflict with the state, resulting in violence and counter-violence by the state in 1971 and in the late 1980s.

The family as the primary social unit has been buffeted by these pressures. The traditional nuclear-cum-extended family has not been transplanted wholesale into the urban environment in view of spatial separation from natal families. While land allocations and the provision of rural services have limited the magnitude of rural-urban migration in Sri Lanka, urban families, particularly middle-class professional families, have tended to be deprived of direct support from the extended family. The emergence of increasing numbers of female heads of household, relationships outside the formal institution of marriage and diminishing parental authority are other indicators of change. Social norms and values are being continually assailed by the consumerism and value orientation purveyed in the mass media and on the Internet.

Concomitantly, gender roles and relations in the economy, in society and within the family have been influenced by social changes and economic policies. Gender equality in access to education has fuelled the highest aspirations, reduced the preference for sons and promoted a more equitable allocation of resources within and outside the family. Access to health and family planning facilities has reduced family size and given women greater control over reproduction. Their expanding economic roles, reflected in their increasing participation over the years in the professions, in agriculture, in industry and particularly in export processing zones and overseas employment away from family control, accompanied by economic independence and control over the resources they generate, have entailed greater equality in gender relations, a more equitable division of labour and sometimes even role reversals in the family. Less overt male dominance and more joint decision making are manifestations of emerging patterns of relationships, except in resistant cultures such as the plantation resident community.

The legal system has yet to be fully supportive of women's rights as human rights. Fundamental rights in the constitution, international conventions that have been ratified, such as CEDAW, and amendments to the penal code to eliminate gender-based violence, have introduced a positive framework since the 1980s. But anachronistic family laws, land succession regulations in settlements, and citizenship regulations regarding marriage to foreigners continue to entrench inequality. It is doubtful whether any policy over the years has been purposefully directed at countering the social construction of gender. Consequently, gender role stereotypes, misperceptions of 'masculinity' and 'femininity' and ideologies of women's domestic role have been perpetuated. Social control over female behaviour through puberty rituals, restrictions on mobility and on female autonomy in choice of spouse, dowry bargaining and virginity tests, and male control of female sexuality as illustrated in sexual harassment, incest, domestic violence and rape, continue to vitiate gender relations.

'Civil Society' Organisations

Finally, parallel to the development of state institutions, policies and trends, and partly as a response to them, there emerged over the period of a century non-state, voluntary organisations as autonomous institutions/agencies to meet the specific needs of interest groups.

In pre-independence decades, these voluntary organisations had been virtually transplanted from metropolitan society, sometimes as purveyors of colonial norms and practices. Whether of religious, social or welfare orientation, they were usually differentiated on the basis of gender, and had at this time a relative elitist ethos, e.g., the YMCA and YWCA, and the Boy Scouts and Girl Guides Associations. In addition to the local anti-colonial men's organisations formed around 1930 at the end of direct rule, the short-lived Women's Franchise Union and Women's Political Union were formed by a small number of women from affluent families to support the demand for political rights for women. In a different environment, the Lanka Mahila Samithi (established in 1930) worked for 'the upliftment' of rural women and continues to do so.

In the early years after independence, international organisations continued to be the model for local voluntary organisations. Both welfare-oriented elitist organisations and organisations of professional women were affiliated to international women's organisations. An endogenous conceptualisation of development needs inevitably surfaced with political changes in the mid-1950s, beginning with the Sarvodaya Movement and its community orientation. The state enlisted the cooperation of these non-governmental organisations (NGOs) for the delivery of services under its 'basic needs' approach and for organising 'women in development' programmes during the UN Decade for Women. While this expanded the quantum and scope of activities of these voluntary organisations, it increased their dependence on donor funds.

In the 1980s and 1990s, the human rights lobby was active in the context of political violence, and multifarious organisations emerged to promote the rights of citizens including the victims of such violence. The conflict situation also engendered temporary 'Mothers' Fronts' in the north, east and south, but many women's organisations concerned themselves increasingly with the promotion of women's rights as human rights and with advocacy to eliminate gender-based violence.

A 'women's movement' as popularly conceptualised has not emerged in Sri Lanka. What is interesting is the rich diversity of activities of women's organisations, moving from an earlier era of welfare orientation to multi-faceted activists encompassing, research, economic empowerment through entrepreneurship, propagating women's issues through the media, fighting domestic violence, promoting political awareness and participation, advocacy and lobbying on gender issues, and 'social mobilisation' and activism, at both the national and community levels. Voluntary organisations, including women's organisations, are moving towards coordinating structures to increase solidarity, however retaining their distinctive orientations. The state and non-governmental organisations have had relatively harmonious relations, albeit with intermittent bouts of mistrust in recent years.

References

Abeyrante, Sirimal (1997). Trade Strategy and Industrialisation, in W.D. Lakshman (ed.) *Dilemmas of Development*, pp. 341-85. Sri Lanka Association of Economists, Colombo.

Alailima, Patricia (1995). Post Independence Evolution of Social Policy and Expenditure in Sri Lanka. Working Paper No. 9, CENWOR, Colombo.

— (1997). Social Policy in Sri Lanka, in W.D. Lakshman (ed.) *Dilemmas of Development*, pp. 127-70. Sri Lanka Association of Economists, Colombo.

Atukorale, P. (1986). The Impact of 1977 Policy Reforms on Domestic Industry. *Upanathu*, Vol. 1, No. 1, pp. 69-105.

Boserup, Ester (1970). *Women's Role in Economic Development*. George Allen and Unwin, London.

Census of Sri Lanka (various years). Department of Census and Statistics, Government of Sri Lanka, Colombo.

Colombage, S.S. (1998). Trends in Income Distribution, in A.D.V. de S. Indraratne (ed.) *Fifty Years of Sri Lanka's Independence*, pp. 557-74. Sri Lanka institute of Social and Economic Studies, Colombo.

Demographic and Health Survey (1994). Department of Census and Statistics, Government of Sri Lanka, Colombo.

De Silwa, Wimala (1995). Political Participation of Women in Sri Lanka, 1985-1995, In *Facets of Change*, pp. 229-63. CENWOR, Colombo.

First Report of the National Education Commission (1992). Sessional Paper V of 1992, Government Publication Bureau, Colombo.

Goonesekere, R.K.W. (1998). Changes in Constitutional Government, in A.D.V. de S. Indraratne (ed.) *Fifty Years of Sri Lanka's Independence*, pp. 35-36. Sri Lanka Institute of Social and Economic Studies, Colombo.

Goonesekere, Savitri (1995). Realising Gender Equity through Law, in *Facets of Change*, pp. 6-57. CENWOR, Colombo.

Indraratne, A.D.V. de S. (1998). Economic Development and Policy: An Overview, in A.D.V. de S. Indraratne (ed.) *Fifty Years of Sri Lanka's Independence*, pp. 1-34. Sri Lanka Institute of Social and Economic Studies, Colombo.

Jayaweera, Swarna (1984). Access to University Education—The Social Composition of University Entrants. *University of Colombo Review*, Vol. 1, No. 4, pp. 6-40.

— (1991). *Women, Skills Development and Employment*. Institute of Policy Studies, Colombo.

— (1993). Education and Socialisation, in *Shadows and Vistas*, pp. 148-82. CENWOR, Colombo.

Velmurugu v. Attorney-General (1981). 1 Sri LR 406.

Warnapala, Wiswa (1974). *Civil Service Administration in Ceylon.* Department of Cultural Affairs, Government of Sri Lanka, Colombo.

Wijesekera, Chitra (1995). *Women in Our Legislature: A Sri Lankan Study from 1921 to 1947.* Sarvodaya Visva Lekha, Ratmalana.

Wijesuriya v. State (1973). 77 NLR 25.

William Silva v. Shirani Bandaranayaka (1997). 1 Sri LR 92.

Wilson, A.J. (1973). The Development of the Constitution, in K.M. de Silva (ed.) *History of Ceylon*, pp. 359-71. University of Ceylon, Peradeniya.

Workshop for Provincial Council Officials (1998). Organised by the National Committee for Women, Colombo.

7

Women in Politics Sri Lanka: Prime Minister Srimavo Bandarnaike and Prime Minister Chandrika B. Kumartunga

I. The Setting

Party System. It was a consequence of the British departure from India that Sri Lanka then known as Ceylon, secured its independence in 1948. Ceylon became a Republic and changed its name to Sri Lanka. Sri Lanka came to be governed alternatively by two main parties. These were the United National Party (UNP) and Sri Lanka Freedom Party (SLFP). The United National Party was led in turn by D.S. Senanayake, his son Dudley Senanayake and his nephew Sir John Kotelawala. The Sri Lankan Freedom Party was founded and led by Solomon Bandarnaike and after his murder led by his widow Srimavo Bandarnaike. Solomon. W.R.D. Bandarnaike had defected from the United National Party before forming SLFP. The People's Alliance also formed the government later with Bandarnaike's party as one of its constituents. One of the important leader of Peoples Alliance was Chandrika B. Kumartunga.

India and Sri Lanka were liberal democracies with well established parties. Till 1977 there was one great difference between the two. Where as one of the special feature of the Indian Political System was one dominant party alongwith several other with little chances for forming governments, in Sri Lanka UNPSLFP and the People's Alliance formed government alternately.

This made a great difference between the two countries, in the role and status of opposition. The UNP in Sri Lanka governed from 1948 to 1956 and from 1865 to 1970, the SLFP and the People's Alliance (PA) the rest of the time. The 1956 election campaign was one of the most important campaigns. In that Bandarnaike defeated the UNP by running on a combined racial and religious ticket. The combination was pro-Sinhala and Pro-Buddhist. The Tamil Minority who formed 25 per cent of the Sri Lankan population, were discriminated against and persecuted. The Buddhist establishment enjoyed a permanent increase in its political influence. Both the UNP and the SLFP began wooing and Buddhists. These two were the ruling parties for most of the time. Besides, these there were several left wing parties. The most important among these was the Lanka Sama Samaj Party. It was born in 1935 as a reaction against colonialism. It had a membership in the Trotskyist International. After the year 1963, this party joined Mrs. Srimavo Bandarnaike's government, but had to leave in 1975. Srimavo's government was joined by the pro-Russian communist Party also in 1965. Srimavo's co-alition had fair chance of winning elections of that year. But it could not be successful because of dismal economic situation, which deteriorated alarmingly during the sixties when the SLFP was in the governmental saddle. The population was rising very, fast and doubled in 1975. The external debt jumped four times. Unemployment rose.

Srimavo and her allies won the election of 1970. But in 1971 they received severe jolt because of an well organised armed peasant rising. It was carefully planned and directed by Janatha Vimukthti Peramuna (JVP) or Popular Liberation Front. It was a break away group of Maoist communist party. It regarded both SLFP and UNP as a post imperialist and neo-colonialist bourgeoisie. In 1977 the UNP returned to power under J.R. Jaywardene. Srimavo reverted to the opposition as its leader.

Family Syndrome

In Sri Lanka, there are smaller circles within the narrow confines of the political classes. These circles based on the network of relationships were created by the caste-system and the custom of cross cousin marriage Mr. and Mrs. Bandarnaike and Mrs. Kumartunga belonged to one family and S.D.S. Senanayake, Dudle Senanayake and Sir John Kotelawala belonged to another.

Bandarnaike's father was Maha Mudaliyar—an high official. Due to this marriage into the high caste (Radala) Ratwattes in 1940, the Low country and Kandyan aristocracy were brought together. Srimavo was the wife of Bandarnaike. She was the daughter of a Dissawe, the highest royal title. (L.C. Weeramantry, 1969, and D.B. Dhanapalu, 1960). Chandrika Bandarnaike Kumartunga was the daughter of above two Prime Ministers—Solomon and Srimavo Bandarnaike.

The Bandarnaike family tree was said to be complicated especially with regard to Kandyaan reaches. Solomon Bandarnaike and Sam D Bandarnaike were the founder of the SLFP. J.P. Obeyesekers another kinsman, took over the 'family seat' of Attangalla after Bandarnaike's assassination in 1959. He duly handed over the seat to Mrs. Bandarnaike in 1965. Felix Dias Bandarnaike-nephew of Bandarnaike took over the other half of the seat. Dompe, served in Srimavo's cabinets of 1960 and 1970. In 1970 about eight relations of Srimavo were elected to the Parliament on the SLFP tickets. Many relations of Srimavo reached high political positions between 1962 and 1966. Srimavo appointed her daughter Sunetra as her political secretary. Her son Anura became the leader of the SLFP Youth League, just as Indira Gandhi's son Sanjay had become the leader of the Youth Congress. After Chandrika B. Kumartunga assumed Presidentship of Sri Lanka, she administered oath of Prime Minister's office to her mother Srimavo Bandarnaike even though she had attained the age of 78. (Hindustan Times, Patna November 15, 1994).

Srimavo Bandarnaike was not keeping good health at the age of 78 in the year 1994. Yet the ruling People's Alliance needed her at that juncture to occupy an essentially ceremonial office. This underlined the "family syndrome" afflicting the Sri Lankan polity. Apart from Chandrika, the widows of other slain leaders like Lalith Atthulamudali, Gamini Dissanaike and Rana Singh Premdasa were catapulated to the centre stage of Sri Lankan Politics. Srimavo herself had come to power in the wake of her husband's assassination. Except one or two estrangements, as was the case, when Mrs. Bandarnaike's son Anura, broke away from her, the filial bonds served well to keep the heirs of politicians in importance.

Political Assassinations Violence

Assassinations had been a part of Sri Lankan politics, since Chandrika's father former Prime Minister Solomon Dias Bandarnaike was shot by a Buddhist mark in 1958. President Rana

Singhe Premdasa was blown up at the Armor street junction, a naval chief was killed on Galle Road, a defence Minister died in a carbomb explosion on Havelock Road, a Presidential candidate (Gamini Dissanayake) was killed like Premdasa by a suicide bomber at Thotalanger on 24th October 1994. (Hindustan Times, Patna, 12 November, 1994, p. 8).

Sri Lanka became a melancholy nation since 1990 because of the assassinations of the leaders, front rank politicians and military officers. Hundreds of bystanders died alongwith them. These political murders put the country's capital on the same map as Beirut and Belfast. At Chandrika's victory speech meeting, special Task Force officers had to open reporters pens and flipp through their note pads as security measures. Alterwards she was whisked away, while a dummy convoy diverted attention (Hindustan Times, Patna, November 11, 1994).

The politics of assassination had catapulated contended wives to the hottest chair in the politics of Sri Lanka. The magazine week (Vol. 12, No. 46, November 1994) called Sri Lanka as "Island of Widows". The Sri Lanka Freedom Party fell back for leadership on the widow of Solomon Bandarnaike after he was murdered, When Late President Premdasa was killed, his widow Hema Premdasa stepped into politics. The Assassination of Lalit Athulathmudali threw his wife Srimani Athulathmudali into political role. She became a Minister in Chandrika's cabinet. The boiling ethnic strife in 1983 led to the murder of Vijay Kumartunge by V.P. rebels. He was a Sinhalli Superstar and was the husband of Chandrika B. Kumartunga. Chandrika left for London after the death of her husband, when she returned she rejoined the Sri Lankan Freedom Party and took up the command of her party. Then in the list of widowed politicians came Srima Dissanaike—the wife of late Gamini Dissanaike killed by a human bomb in November 1994 while he was convassing as a candidate for Presidential Election.

II. Leader and the Style

The British Press extended a hearty welcome to Srimavo, when she came to the position of the Prime Minister of Ceylon. The British press was fascinated because a woman had assumed the powers of a Prime Minister in Ceylon. According to them, it was for the first time in the history of any country, that people make a choice for a woman Prime Minister. The Sri Lankan Freedom Party (SLFP) found it safe for its popularity to fall back upon Srimavo after Solomon Bandarnaike was killed. She was a mother of three children. The men in SLFP thought they could control her. But they were shocked when she began edging out some of them form their entrenched positions.

The British press was anxious about Srimavo's probable attitude towards British interests. She seemed to led her party with left leanings. They were worried about British bases in Ceylon, the establishment of a Republican form of government, nationalisation of essential industries consisting foreign owned plantations, transports, banking and insurance. The balance had actually titled against the West, especially against U.K. the Nationalisation of Life Insurance and establishment of a state Petroleum Corporation made the position of foreign companies untenable.

During Srimavo's regime, Ceylon made friendship with Communist China and the Soviet Union. She stood for the entry of People's China into the U.N. She considered it unrealistic to keep out communist China from the World body.

The left orientation of Srimavo was perceptible in her stand taken on British arm sale to South Africa, as it was taken in defiance of the U.N. Sri Lanka under her, was opposed to the establishment of Diego Garcia military base in Indian Ocean. Srimavo reiterated Sri Lanka's earlier proposal for turning Indian ocean into a neutral Nuclear Free-Zone. The Afro-Asian, countries supported Srimavo when addressing the U.N. She advocated for an "Indian Ocean Zone of Peace".

Srimavo encouraged cultural ties with several countries, specially with USSR, Poland and Czechoslovakia. She sent about twelve delegations to USSR to participate in Moscow World Youth Festival. Srimavo herself visited Czechoslovakia, Poland and Soviet Union. Treaties for setting up a State Tyre and Tube Factory in Ceylon with Soviet assistance was signed. In May 1970, Srimavo had returned to power. She headed at that time the left oriented coalition. Her government announced radical economic programmes like nationalisation of banking system and import trade in essential goods. Her government also proclaimed its intention to take over the control of the agency houses because according to her they were "major vehicles" through which imperialism dominated the plantation economy.

Under her nationalisation programmes Srimavo brought in the subsidiary companies of Shell, Caltex and Esso. On 1st January 1971, her government took over marine banking services, and the manufacturing chemicals and pesticide industries. In order to regulate internal and external trade, the State Trading Corporation Bill was passed in December 1970. Its aim was to party nationalise and partly Ceylonize the different economic sectors. This was made necessary in view of the fact that the import export and the wholesale were largely in foreign hands.

Srimavo vehemently criticized the attitude of the West which was "a very real threat to the possibility of peaceful co-existence between nations." (Ceylon Daily News, 10 March, 1961), Srimavo placed emphasis upon cooperation between Asian countries. "We in Asia must turn to Asia again and re-establish the close contacts with our neighbours which were denied to us when we were colonies of foreign powers." (Ceylon Daily News, 3 January, 1963).

S.W.R.D. Bandarnaike had established a Ministry of Cultural Affairs in 1957. Srimavo Bandarnaike encouraged the use of the symbols of Sinhalese Buddhist culture at state functions. Her husband had established two Buddhist universities. Vidyalaya and Vidyalankara. Religious discrimination came to be practised against the Christian and Hindu minorities. Srimavo got enacted a law, according to which she took over the Christian Schools. The Buddhist state-aided educational institutions were left out of the purview of this law. When the new constitution of the Republic of Sri Lanka was declared as duly passed, its emblem carried "Buddhist chakra and the Pot of prosperity". Before the declaration of the constitution a Buddhist ceremony took place at Navarangahala.

The Mahajana Eksath Peramuna (M.E.P.) or the People's United Front was led by S.W.R.D. Bandarnaike in the general elections of 1956 in Sri Lanka. He was the former leader of the opposition. The various political parties and groups supported his SLFP were the Viplavakari Lanka Sama Samaj Party (VLSSP—a left wing group led by Philip Gurawardene) and the Bhasa Permuna, (a Sinhalese communal organisation associated with W. Dalanayake) and some independent members (Jacob M. Lucy, 1973, 64).

Buddhist Revivalism, linguistic nationalism and resurgence of traditional culture influenced the rural middle class and swayed them in favour of MEP and identified the UNP with western values. Though MEP won, it lacked a common programme as it heterogeneous. S.W.R.D. having won the election in 1956 had to remain on his toes in order to maintain a balance in his government. He was assassinated in 1959. Srimavo stepped into the shoes of her husband and became the Prime Minister after the election of 1960. Hardly and she continued for about four years that in 1964 she had to face defeat. The Parliament had to be dissolved. Her defeat was caused by the defection of C.P. de Silva. The Bandarnaike had helped Ceylon emerge with a changed perception in external affairs. They declared Ceylon's non-alignment stand on 12th Arpil, 1956.

S.W.R.D. Bandarnaike had said that he "was in general agreement with the policy pursued by Mr. Nehru". (Times of Ceylon (Colombo), 13th April 1956). As a leader of the opposition he showed his preference not for Nehru's non-alignment but for a neutralist policy like that of Switzerland. He had observed that Ceylon should retain friends but remain aloof and follow a neutralist policy. (Ceylon Daily News, (Colombo) 25 May, 1956). For him co-existence and Neutralism were essential for Ceylon's external affairs, and western idea of democracy alongwith Soviet Union Socialism was proper in the domestic field.

In 1960 Srimavo Bandarnaike continued the policies of her husband. On 21st July, she observed before the Press that "her party would follow the neutralist policy pursuaded by her late husband". (Time of Ceylon, 22 July, 1960). This was supported by the Governor General in his speech from the throne at the opening of the Parliament (Ceylon H.R. Debate, Vol. 39, 1960, Col. 51).

Srimavo intended to follow the "Definite Centre Party Policies" of her late husband because those policies represented the interest of the rural people. "No government" she observed "serving the interests which we do can be extreme left or Marxist. Nor are we a left wing government serving vested interests. It would be correct to describe as a Central Party Government". (The Hindu, Madras, 30 July 1960) Many like C.P. de Silva did not accept her stand. He alleged that she was aligning with the left. It was on this ground that he had walked out of Srimavo's government in December 1964, resulting into her defeat.

In 1970 the UF government initiated a resolution with regard to constituent Assembly. The resolution was considered to be a mandate of the representatives of the people to form a constituent Assembly. Srimavo as Prime Minister convented the constituent Assembly on July 1970. (Lucy M. Jacob, 1973, 174-175).

Since the Governor General was the representative of the crown, it was Srimavo—the elected head as the Prime Minister, who convened the meeting of the Constituent Assembly. It met at Navarangahala—the autitorium of the Royal Preparatory School and not in the Parliament Hall. According to Srimavo, the aims and objectives of the constitution were "unity". She explained—"the new constitution will help strengthen the oneness of the Ceylonese nation and overcome the stress caused by various racial, linguistic and religious differences". (Lucy M. Jacob, 1973, 175). Srimavo's stand was supported by the leader of the opposition J.R. Jaywardene "we are partners in a common material enterprise and the purpose of which is not to secure an advantage for a political party, but to benefit the people of our country of all races and religion". (Lucy M. Jacob, 1973, 175).

On May 22, 1972, the Constitution was duly passed and the President of the Constituent Assembly Stanleg Tillekaratne declared its acceptance. A Republic was born. The new emblem was Buddha's Chakra and the Pot of Prosperity. The main entrance to the Hall of the Parliament was decorated with it.

Srimavo was a supporter of parliamentary system and showed active interest in politics as an opposition leader. In an interview with Srimavo Bandarnaike, published in the Frontline, October 12-25, 1991, 124-125) by (N. Ram and Thomas Abraham) she was described as a formidable opposition leader. "A manipulator"and "Schemer". Srimavo who was seventy five years old in 1991, was a SLFP leader of the opposition. She had been the Prime Minister of Sri Lanka between the years 1960-77. She supported the UNP rebellions leaders—Lalit Athulamuddali and Gamini Dissanaike, in opposing President Premdasa. The interviewers described her as tough, uncompromising in her determination to end the system of Executive Presidency which according to her was disastrous. She called for survival of democracy. She had been characterised as outspoken in her assessment of politics, issues and personalities. At the time of the senior active politician in the world.

The interviewers asked Srimavo about the no confidence motion which was on the anvil against the government. What should have been the alternative? Srimavo was bitterly opposed to the Presidential system" My one objective was to see that this (Presidential) system should be done away with. In fact in 1972, when we were bringing in our constitution we turned Parliament into a constituent Assembly. J.R. Jaywardene's party was also there. He told me "why don't you have the presidential system." I said "No. That's a dangerous thing. In a country like ours, we do not need a system like that". I said "listen, suppose Rohana Vijeweera becomes President of Sri Lanka. What happens then? I said I did not want this, I was going to see to the old (Parliamentary) system with a few more seats in Parliament. As soon as Jayawardene came he amended one clause in that and he became President automatically without an election. He came in as Prime Minister and he became President by changing the Constitution". "Of course", she alleged, "latter on he had an election two years later and prevented her from contesting by taking away her civic right. "...we are only thinking of what happened in other countries... Now it has happened in here. You see from the experience we had from other countries, like the Idi Amins and soon, it is virtually a dictatorship".

To a question whether Srimavo had the same authority which Premdasa had as President, she said "We did not have this kind of power. I had a Parliament and a cabinet, didn't I? I did certain things but with cabinet's approval. They say that I kept the Emergency too long. My civil rights were taken away for that "Abuse of Power". There is no such thing as Abuse of Power in any law book today. But they took away my civil rights for that I kept the Emergency too long. Why did I do it, for the same reason they are keeping it today. Because we had thousands in camps (after the 1971 JVP insurrection)... If we removed Emergency all these persons were going to be released. We rehabilitated them. "Some were hard core. Some were in custody to be tried". (Interview, 127).

Srimavo Bandarnaike observed that she could not accept Prime Ministership under Presidential system even if there was an opportunity for that. The method for changing the political system she thought referendum would be the best.

Srimavo alleged that Premdasa was anti-Sri Lanka. She collected information about Lorry-loads of weapons being sent to the LTTE so that the TNA is destroyed. "Boys of 15 or 16 were just massacred. They are also our brethren Sri Lankan... And also to fight the IPKF not only to destroy the TNA but to fight the IPKF." She also alleged that air-conditioners which were supplied to Sri Lankan Army in bunkers, passed on to the LTTE. Srimavo suspected that the LTTE were even entering the Sri Lankan Parliament.

Srimavo had arrogance in her personality. She accused Premdasa of doing any thing just to get the votes to the LTTE, who were entering the Parliament. She remarked that Premdasa was badly shaken on the day impeachment motion was to be introduced. She did not like to show any respect to him.

"On Parliament day, we said we wouldn't go in before he came in because we would have to stand up and we did not want to stand. But we have to stand for the Speaker and the Mace. So we thought we would stay out. We stayed outside the door... after as went in, we went in. The signal was there and we went in on the other side and sat down." (In the Interview, 126).

It was interesting to note how politicians indulge in all sorts of magic and witchcraft for achieving success. Srimavo Bandarnaike displayed superstition and seemed to believe in witchcraft. She said "And there is another interesting thing. He is supposed to have bought two Malyalis and done some witchcraft". "He is supposed to have applied oil on our chairs and sprinkled dust al over the place... He (Premdasa) is supposed to have sat on his chair. I do not know quite what they did... drew something round his feet, various thing... He had gone in around 6.30 p.m. On the previous day with his secretary and two others... He went in because he believes in (Black magic) (In the Interview, 127).

Srimavo's anti-Indian feeling made her suspect the two "others" as Malayalees coming from India. Srimavo went in the Parliament hall where Premdasa had supposedly practiced black magic she said "But we all went in and wiped our chairs. And with holy water, we rubbed our chairs."

Srimavo was not only a formidable leader in the Opposition but also ambitious. Her ego was wounded by President J.R. Wardene following his victory in the 1977 elections. He ushered in a new constitution and assumed charge as the Executive President. He got a parliamentary enactment passed under which Srimavo Bandarnaike was deprived of her civil right to vote, for a full six year term. Srimavo could not forget this humiliation. She entered the contest for Presidential chair in 1988 but lost o Mr. Rana Singhe Premdasa by less than one per cent vote. She was revengeful. In a press interview she said that she had been defeated in elections several times which she took in sportsman spirit. But his was one time when she had been deprived of her due by electoral rigging and other malpractices. "I have been cheated of my victory". This was the reason why Srimavo considered it necessary for the vindication of her personal honour to rise to be the country's President. She would not mind even if the post became merely titular.

A great deal of pursuasion was needed to get Srimavo to step aside and let her daughter stand for the Presidency. She had resisted even the advice of the doctors, not to take the strain of election as she had undergone an operation and had attained the age of '78. President D.B. Wijetunga decided to change his earlier scheme for elections. He ordered for Parliamentary elections before the Presidential elections. Srimavo was insistent that she was unfairly deprived of her right to vote and kept out of the topmost post by two successive Presidents.

The second period of Srimavo's Prime Ministership started in November 1994. The Sri Lankan cabinet nominated the Septuagenarian leader as Prime Minister of Sri Lanka, after her daughter Chandrika B. Kumartunga took over as the new Executive President in the same month. A daughter-mother team formally took charge of the Sri Lankan government on the 14th November 1994. (Hindustan Times, Patna, November 15, 1994, 12).

Srimavo Bandarnaike, had the privilege of being the first woman Prime Minister as early as in 1959. But she entered into her second Prime Ministership, seemingly for keeping the chair warm for her daughter Chandrika B. Kumartunga, after the Executive Presidentship was abolished by July 15, 1995. This was the deadline before which Constitution had to be amended and the Parliamentary system restored.

In Sri Lanka the Second Woman Prime Minister Mrs. Chandrika B. Kumartunga

Mrs. Chandrika Bandarnaike Kumartunga was the second woman Prime Minister of Sri Lanka within a period of about forty years. As mentioned earlier she came from a family of politicians. Both her parents had been Prime Ministers of Sri Lanka. Her husband and actor—turned politician was killed by a Sinhala radical during a rebellion against the government. In August 1994, she led her Leftist People's Alliance to victory in parliamentary elections after remaining out of power for seventeen years. Her victory in August election was by a thin majority. She remained Prime Minister of Sri Lanka for three months only, after which she led her ruling People's Alliance (PA) to a victory in Presidential election. The magnitude of Chandrika's electoral victory in Presidential election was beyond the expectation of even the best optimist in her ruling party. She won by a margin of two million votes over her nearest rival Srima Dissanaike of the United National Party (UNP), in the biggest victory in any elections in this island. It must be mentioned here that before contesting the post of Prime Ministership, Chandrika became the Chief Minister of Western Province after fighting her first election in May 1993. She was the first woman Chief Minister in Sri Lanka.

Along with Parliamentary elections Mrs. Chandrika B. Kumartunga's popularity was demonstrated also in Presidential elections. She won with heavy support from the war weary eastern Sri Lankan Zone. It consisted of Tamil and Muslim majority. She brought a rich "political heritage, a history of tragedy and a headstrong manner to Sri Lanka's most powerful post" (The Hindustan Times, 12 November, 1994).

The Sri Lankan Muslims Congress (SLMC) said, "This victory is an endorsement of Chandrika's stewardship, the PA's performance within a short span a governance" (*Ibid.*, 11 November, 1994, 14).

Chandrika's overtures to the Tamil's earned her accolades from the TULF leaders. One of them remarked "The government is certainly moving in the right directions". Sticking to the election manifesto by a new administration was a rare thing.

The groups/organisations who were in support of Chandrika represented a wide spectrum. Her support came from Sri Lanka Progressive Front, Ceylon Workers Congress, Nav Sama Samaj Party, Sri Lanka Muslim Conference (SLMC). The SLMC leaders felt that Chandrika was the "best bet to resolve the ethnic problem" "We don't want that opportunity to slip by". (Chakravarti Sudeep with Jayakar, 165).

As Prime Minister Chandrika had pledged to the Sri Lankan people that she would abolish Executive presidency within eight months and transfer more powers to the Parliament and the

Cabinet. Like her mother Srimavo, Chandrika also believed that powers of the Executive President could be too easily abused. Hence the constitution should be amended in order to bring a change into this system.

Interestingly, the November 9 election (1994) for the Executive Presidentship was over an office which both the Peoples Alliance (PA) of Chandrika and the United National Party of Gamini Dissanaike wanted to abolish. Peoples Alliane, vowed to the people that once it came to power it would abolish Executive President's office.

Chandrika's stand on the abolition of Executive Presidentship depended upon reasons different from her mother Srimavo. Many youths belonging to JVP had supported the former in both the national elections because they were committed to a radical change in the constitution, especially on the issue of Presidential powers. Sri Lanka Progressive Front, which was a constituent of Chandrika's Peoples Alliance was also committed to abolition of Executive Presidency. They had even threatened to set up their own candidate, if she failed to uphold her pledge.

During three months of her Prime Ministership, Chandrika had begun dialogue with the Tamil Tiger rebels. It was the first peace talk in four years. She reduced the prices of some food stuffs.

Prime Minister Chandrika B. Kumartunga differed a bit from Prime Minister Srimavo Bandarnaike, in her ideological approach. Chandrika said her party was not overtly socialist. There were no plans for the nationalisation of expropriation of private property domestic or foreign. Other issues covered in her policy statements were that all bilateral agreements were to be honoured without any investment protection. A National Council was to be constituted with state sector, Private Sector and labour representatives. Public intervention was to be limited to the areas where market failed to function effectively. These were to be principally in the areas of human development, health, creating of employment opportunities. There were other issues like rationalisation of indirect taxation etc.

Chandrika created record like her mother Srimavo in South Asian region. Chandrika became the first woman Executive President while her mother had became the first women Prime Minister. Chandrika had created another record in 1993, by becoming the first Woman Chief Minister in any province of Sri Lanka.

Chandrika was criticised by her cabinet and members of the Legislature for being autocrat. She had not informed her cabinet or the legislature regarding her trip to Singapore. The House had to be adjourned because of that.

III. Political Impact

Srimavo Bandarnaike encouraged the symbols of Sinhalese Buddhist Culture in her country. That led to discriminatory practices against the Christian and Hindu minorities. All this encouraged sessionism among the Tamils. Terrorism started raising its ugly head not only among the Hindu Tamilians but as a reaction among the Buddhist Sinhalese also. The JVP created great difficulties for the stability of Sri Lanka. Extremist in the island led to LTTE, violence even outside Sri Lanka. The Indian Prime Minister Rajiv Gandhi was alleged to have been killed by them in 1991 on May 21st. Srimavo gave a socialist bent to her foreign politics as well as to her domestic decisions and actions. She took steps to establish Sri Lanka as a neutral Nation, following the policy of co-existence with the socialist countries and the Third world. Her importance in U.N. was accepted by the Afro-Asian countries. She advocated the "Indian Ocean Zone of Peace."

Srimavo stressed Sri Lankan values in politics and rejected UNP's seemingly Western values. The Republic of Sri Lanka was born May 22, 1972 during her premiership.

Chandrika in her short span of Prime Ministership, seemed to have restored confidence among the war-weary of eastern Sri Lanka. The LTTE may appreciate her gesture. She also took same pupulist measures in reducing the prices of food stuffs which was not easy within a period of three months when she was the Prime Minister.

But now as the Executive President of Sri Lanka, she will have to be walking on tight rope. Abolition of the post in which she has come and entrenched herself will not be easy. The procedure for constitutional reform would be difficult and yet she could not forget that she won this chair on the pledge that she would abolish it.

In pre-independence Ceylon, the situation of women varied according to class and ethnicity. Capitalism under colonial conditions was both good and bad news for women, bringing economic exploitation for some, and educational and employment opportunities as well as franchise and democratic rights for others. The post-colonial experience was also a mixed bag, resulting in new forms of exploitation of female labour in export processing zones and domestic work abroad, along with a growth of women's organisations and an increased feminist consciousness on issues ranging from equal pay to the ethnic conflict.

In fact, the progress of the women's movement in Sri Lanka since independence over fifty eyars ago cannot be discussed without taking into account such a movement's antecedents in women's collective activism under British colonialism. Be it in the sphere of religious, social, economic or political reform, Ceylonese women have been at the forefront during the nineteenth and early twentieth centuries. They were not only dynamic and valued members of reformist and/or anti-colonial organisations such as the Social Reform Society (founded in 1906), the Social Service League (1914), the Young Lanka League (1915) and the Ceylon Labour Party (1928), but also formed autonomous groups and movements such as the Women's Education Society (Nari Shiksha Dana Sangamaya) founded as early as 1889, the Ceylon Women's Union (1904), Tamil Women's Union (1909), Women Franchise Union (1927), Lanka Mahila Samiti (1930), Women's Political Union (1930), the All Ceylon Women's Conference (1944) and the Eksath Kantha Peramuna (1947).[2]

Even such a cursory listing must surely illuminate the varied nature and formulation of women's activism prior to independence. However, given the circumstances of colonial rule and the emergence and proliferation of nationalist movements during this period, it is clear that such public and collective participation—however varied they may have been—predominantly reflected nationalist and/or anti-colonial sentiments and aspirations. For example, even the performance of social service (which was the chief avenue for women's participation in the public sphere) was pried out of the stranglehold of religious philanthropy and conversion and produced as one of the chief duties of a patriot. In fact, in 1918, the *National Monthly of Ceylon* reported with satisfaction that one of the 'most hopeful features of national awakening of the people of Ceylon' was their 'growing desire to engage in efforts for the social, moral as well as the political uplift of their countrymen's (quoted in Jayawardena, 1972). One could thus argue the social service was a politically contingent form of activism for women during colonial rule since it highlighted the conditions of the poor, the unemployed, the working class, etc., under colonialism. That is to say, social service played a particular political role at a specific historical moment; it enabled a critique of the colonial government for its inability to provide the basic necessities of life, while also providing an opportunity for the Ceylonese to work for the upliftment and self-sufficiency of their own people.

In this chapter, we shall think about the women's movement in Sri Lanka from a similar perspective. We suggest that it is a broad-based movement that encompasses a variety of organisations and groups that have arisen out of different struggles and conflicts, at different historical moments. While some organisations have been short-lived, others have continued for several decades; while some have formed alliances, others have worked alone. As a matter of fact, the complexity and even contradictions encompassed within the rubric of a 'women's movement' have frequently led us to assert that there are several women's movements in Sri Lanka. Thus, our central concern here will be to highlight different kinds of political struggles in which Sri Lankan women have participated both collectively and publicly. It is the specificity of the struggle, we wish to argue, which informs activism and thus, rather than reading a particular response as either reactionary or progressive, essentialising or empowering, we wish to focus on its political efficacy and contingency. In this chapter, then, we will concentrate on exploring three different articulations of the 'political' through a selective discussion of specific women's organisations in Sri Lanka.

The Battle for Political Rights and Representation

Sri Lankan feminists have always been proud of the fact that Ceylon was one of the first colonies to achieve women's suffrage in 1931. What is unfortunate, however, is that the role of the Women's Franchise Union (WFU) in this campaign has been frequently minimised and misrepresented. While there is no doubt that the WFU was made up of bourgeois women who were nowhere as bold or as militant as their British or Indian counterparts, and who presented relatively conservative proposals to the Donoughmore Commission in 1927, the fact that it was the first autonomous, multi-ethnic women's organisation in Sri Lanka that was founded with the sole purpose of claiming their political rights, is in itself noteworthy (see De Alwis and Jayawardena, 2001).

Though the WFU was frequently criticised by many of its male peers as well as the press, the organisation perserved for several years and, along with its breakaway group, the Women's Political Union (WPU) founded in 1930, provided invaluable support to the women candidates (though few and far between) who chose to contest the general elections under the Donoughmore Constitution of 1931 (Wijesekera, 1995). In fact, Adeline Molamure, a member of the WPU, was the first woman to be elected to the newly constituted state council in 1931. She was soon followed in 1932 by Neysum Saravanamuttu, who also received the support of the Ceylon Tamil Women's Union. In 1936, the Colombo Municipal Council amended its laws to enable women to sit on the council, which resulted in yet another member of the WPU—Dr Mary Rutnam—becoming the first woman councillor in 1937 (Jayawardena, 1993; Wijesekere, 1995). In 1960, Ceylon led the world in electing the first woman prime minister—Sirimavo Bandaranaike.

Despite the fact that every woman elected to national office in Ceylon/Sri Lanka has been enabled by her male kin (i.e., due to the demise or defeat of a father or husband), there is no doubt that they have been pathbreakers in their own right and have proved to be important role models for other women. This was especially well illustrated when Mrs Bandarnaike was first elected prime minister in 1960; the enthusiasm of her women supporters, noted the *Ceylon Daily News* (22 July 1960), 'was particularly noticeable' during her inauguration, and she was mobbed by 'a crowd consisting mainly of women' when she visited Horagolla (*Observer*, 24 July 1960).

Political Participation Today

However, while women have turned out in great numbers to exercise their vote in all elections, to date, they continue to be grossly under-represented in legislative assemblies—both at the local and the national level—as well as in administrative and decision making positions. Several decades later we are beginning to see a committed and concerned effort being made to rectify this imbalance, albeit in a small way. For the first time in the history of Sri Lanka, an independent women's political group came forward to contest the 1998 provincial council elections in the district of

Nuwara Eliya. This group, led by Vimali Karunaratna, comprises a multi-ethnic conglomeration of eighteen women and four men, the majority of whom belong to the Sinhala-Tamil Rural Women's Network in Nuwara Eliya. The main objective of this group, as stated in their manifesto, is to 'enhance women's contribution to governance and the creation of a peaceful and prosperous society.'

What was particularly heartening about this new development was that this group received unprecedented support and encouragement from an umbrella feminist organisation, the Sri Lanka Women's NGO Forum, which is a broad network of autonomous women's groups based all over the island representing community-based development workers and activists as well as scholars and researchers who are committed to women's advancement. One of their main areas of focus is monitoring the implementation of the Platform of Action agreed upon by the Sri Lankan government at the Fourth World Conference on Women held in Beijing in 1995. The promotion of women's active participation in political and decision making processes has also been a central part of the NGO Forum's mandate, and it has recently begun a campaign to appeal to all Sri Lankan political parties to include more women candidates in their nomination lists, and to address women's concerns in their election campaigns and manifestos. It is also working with various grassroots organisations across the country to disseminate in the political and public spheres, both at the local as well as the national level. Two other organisations currently engaged in promoting women's political participation at the community level are Kantha Shakthi and Agromart.

This renewed concern regarding women's political participation is also reflected in the research being conducted by many women scholars at universities as well as research institutes, including the Social Scientists' Association and the International Centre for Ethnic Studies, who are working on projects entitled 'Rural Women in Political Participation' and 'Women and Governance' respectively. One of the earliest studies that initiated such research was conducted by the Centre for Women's Research (CENWOR, 1994) under the theme "Women, Political Empowerment and Decision-Making'. The present government's commitment to assigning a quota of 25 per cent for women in local government elections, as announced in its proposals for constitutional reform, is also indicative of the extensive impact of such feminist lobbying over the years.

The Battle against Cultural and Economic Exploitation

We have discussed so far the development of a particular public discourse that has sought to debate and transform women's participation in what is most narrowly, and most commonly, called the political sphere—the world of governance. In this section, we explore another formulation of the 'political' which was greatly influenced by feminist struggles in Euro-America in the 1960s and 1970s, and led to the production of a discourse that was encapsulated by a popular slogan of the time—'the personal is political'. While this slogan is now frequently reduced to a mere catch phrase, the paradigmatic shift it signals cannot be underestimated. It sought to problematise the hitherto rigid separation between the 'private' and the 'public' and insisted instead that everyday activities within the private sphere—which was also primarily defined as the woman's sphere—had political relevance; women's domestic roles were as significant as their public roles, and what went on in one sphere informed and changed what went on in the other sphere. Issues concerning women's reproductive choices, their sexuality, and the domestic burden they shouldered thus became as important as issues concerning women's rights to vote and equal employment.

In Sri Lanka, this move towards the extension of the 'political' was particularly well illustrated in the increasing frequency of consciousness raising rallies and discussions and assertiveness training workshops that feminists began to organise across the country—from Jaffna to Hambantota—from the mid-1970s onwards (Jayawardena, 1985a). One of the central foci of these meetings and workshops was the identification and critique of patriarchal norms which, manifesting under the sign of cultural traditions, sought to discipline, oppress, and exploit women. To aid their activist work, feminists also began to systematically study and analyse women's status and position within Sri Lankan society. This involved a feminist re-evaluation of cultural and religious texts and practices, historical myths and legends, school textbooks, media representations and advertisements.

Paralleling this strand of cultural critique was also one that was concerned with understanding and protesting against the economic exploitation of women. The latter project in fact was an extension of the first, as it was the argument of many Sri Lankan feminists of this period that the patriarchal cultural norms of society helped sustain the exploitation, oppression and discrimination of women, be it in the economic, political or cultural spheres. The espousal of such an ideology was also what distinguished socialist feminists from their male colleagues in the left; the latter were willing to protest against the economic exploitation of women but not their cultural oppression. The 1970s and 1980s thus witnessed a concerted effort by middle-class feminists to form alliances with their working-class counterparts. While their primary foci of protest were the exploitation of (predominantly Tamil) women in the tea plantations, and those in the newly set up free trade zones (FTZs) who were barred from forming trade unions, the most significant moment of cross-class solidarity among feminists occurred during the series of strikes that were held outside the FTZs, between 1980 and 1984, by over 1,000 women workers at the Polytex Garment Factory. The conscientisation of some of these workers led them to join other feminists in founding the Women's Liberation Movement in August 1982 (which set up the Ja Ela women's Centre as a refuge for the now out-of-work and wage-less strikers). The strikers were also supported by a network of other small feminist organisations who participated in their pickets, distributed handbills, printed posters, collected funds and canvassed international feminist groups on their behalf.

Voice of Women and the EKP

The intertwining of these cultural and economic critiques is best captured in the first feminist magazine that was published in Sri Lanka, *Voice of Women.* The first issue, published in 1980 in English, Sinhala and Tamil, provides an excellent example of the varied issues that were taken up by its founders during this period. The English issue, for instance, contained several articles with a cultural focus, such as the analysis of a newspaper advertisements including an account of a protest campaign that was launched against a particularly offensive one; studies of women's representations in local films, radio, comic strips, literary texts and school textbooks; discussions on the persistance of traditional concepts of femininity in contemporary society; and domestic violence. Articles with an economic focus included those on sexual discrimination in the workplace, unequal pay, the exploitation of women in the plantation sector, hazardous working conditions in the free trade zones, a day in the life of a rural activist, and the biography of a woman leader of the working class. Subtitled 'A Sri Lanka Journal for Women's Emancipation', its logo was (and still is) fashioned from a photograph of protesting women workers at the Wellawatte Spinning and Weaving Mills.

The Voice of Women Collective founded in 1978 comprised a group of socialist and other feminists—both academics and activists—who belonged to several different organisations and ethnic groups. These women were adamant about the fact that while they were committed to breaking down the 'oppressive structures that keep women in a subordinate position', they did not perceive this as a conflict between men and women; the emancipation of women was part of the general struggle for emancipation, 'for if the women of a country are slaves, the men can never be free' (Editorial, *Voice of Women*, January 1980). The objectives of the Voice of Women Collective are reminiscent of those espoused by a previous group of socialist women, the Eksath Kantha Peramuna (EKP) or United Women's Front. The EKP, which was formed in 1947, united women who belonged to the two main left parties at that time, the Lanka Sama Samaja Party (LSSP) and the Communist Party (CP), as well as those without party affiliations who were left-wing sympathisers (de Mel and Muttetuwegama, 1997). The members of the EKP not only represented different ethnic groups—including some foreigners, foremost among them being Doreen (Young) Wickremasinghe and Edith (Gymroi) Ludowyck—but also different classes; though the leadership was almost exclusively middle-class, several of the live wires in the organisation were also rural and urban working-class women, such as the CP trade union leader Pansinahamy. Since the WFU's meetings were conducted in all three languages, these women received many opportunities to speak at its sessions. (ibid.).

The EKP, which was dedicated to the achievement of socialism and the removal of all discrimination against women, agitated for the inclusion of women in the public services, campaigned for the improvement of living conditions in the slums, and persistently protested against the rising cost of living (Jayawardena, 1986). Its work and ideas received much publicity in the press due to its allies in the press corps, such as the editor of the *Times of Ceylon*, D.B. Dhanapala, who was a personal friend of some of the members, as well as through the many articles that the women themselves contributed to the newspapers (de Mel and Muttetuwegama, 1997). Indeed, it is especially apposite here to recall one article in particular by Doreen Wickremasinghe, written soon after Ceylon achieved independence on 4 February 1948. She castigates Prime Minister D.s. Senanayake for winning and dining, at public expense, over a hundred guests at the Independence Day celebrations, and for then having the audacity to request the masses to practise austerity and make sacrifices for the common good of the new nation. The people of Ceylon, she warns, 'despite the praise of their "dignity" and "parience" showered upon them by monocled lords, will neither forgive nor forget the circumstances in which, on their money, their so-called freedom was ushered in (*Times of Ceylon*, 6 March 1948).

Particularly interesting also was the EKP's public criticism of the Lanka Mahila Samiti (LMS) founded in 1930 by Dr Mary Rutnam, especially since one of the EKP's secretaries and indefatigable organisers was Dr Rutnam's daughter, Helen Gunasekera (Jayawardena, 1993). Not surprisingly, the EKP's ideas on social reform differed drastically from those of the LMS, which had become the largest autonomous women's organisation by this time. While the EKP was careful not to openly denounce the LMS, noting, in fact, that they recognised 'the merits' oif the LMS's work and that they honoured 'the women whose toil and sweat' had gone into this organisation, they made no bones about the fact that they disagreed with the LMS's ideology as well as practices. The members of the EKP asserted that though they, like the LMS, deplored 'the poverty and degradation of village life', they were not content to merely work within 'a village economy of a slave colony' like the LMS; 'we see our duty not merely to help people to make the best of a bad world, but to understand why it is bad and to help them realize, through experience in fighting for their rights, that they can change it' (quoted in de Mel and Muttetuwegama, 1997).

The EKP also warned the LMS about the possible ramifications of receiving financial aid from a colonial government, and was quite scathing about the patronising attitude of its middle-class members. The consequence of such a double standard, the EKP warned, was 'a tendency for the village woman to conclude that middle-class benevolence is all she should expect or hope for', to accept that the general framework of society was unalterable and the only way to progress was through patronage (quoted in de Mel and Muttetuwegama, 1997). The EKP's radical critique of social service thus sought to shift significantly the focus of philanthropy as a moral and patriotic project to one that also sought to transform oppressive colonial as well as class structures.

Unfortunately, the EKP did not last more than a year. Its existence had been largely dependent on the active support of the two left parties, and when the CP decided that it could no longer co-operate with the LSSP, the CP members in the group had to withdraw from the EKP leading to its dissolution. The attempt of some members to form an independent women's organisation, was also unsuccessful (Jayawardena, 1986). It is heartening to note, however, that by the late 1970s, the feminists in Sri Lanka had made sufficient inroads into the public sphere to sustain themselves within independent socialist women's organisation, such as the Voice of Women Collective, as well as others that were formed in subsequent years, such as the Women's Liberation Movement in Ja-Ela (which ran the Women's Centre and published the Sinhala magazine *Da Bindu*), the Progressive Women's Front in Ibbagamuwa (an offshort of the All Lanka Peasants' Congress which focused on the problems of peasant women as well as the broader issues of women's oppression and subordination within Sinhala society) and several other smaller socialist feminist organisations which belonged, along with many other groups, to the women's coalition founded in 1982–the Women's Action Committee.

Roping in the State and the Shift to Research

It is now an acknowledged fact that the increased presence and visibility of autonomous women's organisations in Sri Lanka primarily resulted from the significant attention paid to women and women's issues with the UN declaration of the 'Year of the Woman' in 1975 and the Decade for Women from 1976 to 1985. Foreign funders, also pressurised by feminist movements in their own countries, began to support local women's groups and projects focused on women at both governmental and non-governmental levels. Thus, with the formation of autonomous feminist groups (representing various shades of feminism), the state also founded the Women's Bureau in 1978 to promote women's issues and programmes. A similar national institution for the promotion of women's interests had been unsuccessfully mooted in the 1960s by the All Ceylon Conference (founded in 1944), but now a combination of factors enabled the creation of such an institution. Among these were international interest in the establishment of national machineries, the lobbying of women's NGOs—initiated by the Sri Lanka Federation of University Women and spearheaded by the Sri Lanka Women's Conference—and the co-operation of Norwegian women's NGOs who facilitated funding through NORAD—the Norwegian Agency for Development (Jayaweera, 1989). In 1983, a Women's Affairs Ministry was established and soon became the token cabinet position that was assigned to a woman.

Due to further pressures exerted by feminist groups, the Sri Lankan government also signed the Covenant for the Elimination of Discrimination against women (CEDAW) in 1981. In 1992, a Women's Charter was drafted by several academics, members of women's associations, and women's ministry officials as a statement of intent on economic, social and political rights for women. Another innovation was the setting up of the National Committee of Women (which was also stipulated in the Women's Charter) to advise policy makers on women's issues. With the change of government in 1994, the new minister of justice, acting under pressure from feminist groups, framed new laws on rape, the age of consent, and marriage, to replace the obsolete, colonial laws still in the statute book (Jayawardena, 1995).

In the north of Sri Lanka, the Jaffna University, founded in 1974, provided an important site for consciousness raising during this period. With the encouragement of many members of the faculty, the Women's Progressive Association (which initially included several male students as well) was formed by women students in 1980 to develop awareness among their peers. In 1981, several members of this association, alongwith others not affiliated to the university, founded the Women's Study Circle in order to extend their influence outside the university. These women held weekly discussions on current feminist literature, including Engels's writings on women's liberation (Maunaguru, n.d.). They also identified Tamil cutural values as one of the main mediums through which women's oppression was legitimised, and particularly concentrated on providing a critique of religion by organising several seminars on this topic. Nevertheless, they did not shy away from harnessing the drawing power of religion to their own end; their first publication, a Tamil translation of *Feminism is Relevant* which had been published by the Feminist Study Circle, Colombo, was launched at a temple festival where it sold like hot cakes *(ibid.)*.

This move towards forming reading groups and holding seminars, as well as producing translations and disseminating publications, was accompanied by a concerted effort to do original research on women's 'lost histories', to expose male biases and lacunae in the research that had been produced to date, and to promote women's studies as an academic discipline. In the 1980s, many Sri Lankan women went abroad to follow courses in women's studies, especially at the Institute of Social Studies at the Hague and the Institute for Development Studies in Sussex (Jayawardena, 1995). Those studying at other foreign universities were also influenced by the women's studies courses they followed as well as by the activities of the feminist movements in those countries. Many returned home to start their own research organisations. The Women's Education Centre (WEC) was formed in 1982 [the precursor of the Women's Education and Research Centre(WERC)], the Centre for Women's Research (CENWOR) was set up in 1984, and the Muslim Women's Research and Action Forum (MWRAF) was revived in 1986. Other non-governmental research organistions, such as the Social Scientists' Association, the International Centre for Ethnic Studies and the Centre for Society and Religion, also began to fund feminist research, as a result of which there exists today a substantial body of literature on a variety of feminist as well as women's issues (*ibid.*).

Many of these research organisations have been assiduous in organising seminars and workshops to disseminate the results of these new studies as well as to encourage debate and discussion. In this regard, the National Conventions on Women's Studies that have been organised annually by CENWOR have been particularly productive and stimulating. The launching of a master's programme in women's studies in 1991 (and recently a diploma in this field as well) at the University of Colombo, followed by establishment of women's courses in the Department of Sociology at the University of Peradeniya, have also enabled the formalisation of a course of study previously conducted at a more ad hoc level by various women's groups and non-governmental organisations.

Academic feminist research in Sri Lanka has always been an extension of feminist activism, and much of the research undertaken clearly reflects the trajectory of economic and socio-political events in the country. It has also exerted a crucial influence on Sri Lankan scholarship in general. The absence of gender awareness in the work of Sri Lankan and Sri Lankanist male scholars both at home and abroad as well as the continuing chauvinism and sexism among sections of the local academic community are now being seriously challenged. At another level, the launching of 'gender sensitising' programmes by women's groups such as CENWOR and WERC which target organisations of both women and men in both the private and the public sectors (including the police) are making participants aware of women's subordination in society and the need for change no matter how small the scale (Jayawardena, 1995).

Anti-feminist Backlash and State Hypocrisy

Unfortunately, the increasing visibility of feminist organisations has also produced consistent and concerted efforts to undermine the legitimacy of feminists within Sri Lankan society. The accusations most frequently levelled against them are that they are westernised, belong to bourgeois families, and are against local traditions and cultures. For example, an editorial on International Women's Day published in a mainstream English newspaper in 1984 predictably perpetuated a common myth about Sri Lankan society being matriarchal in order to sustain the argument that 'traditional' women are always already liberated. It is only elite women, estranged from their culture and their traditional roots, who do not realise this (*The Island,* 8 March 1984). Ironically, an editorial in a left-wing Sinhala newspaper which appeared the same day was even more virulent. It referred to feminists as 'bourgeois canaries' who believe that if men 'crept into the kitchen and helped in scraping coconut... equality would be achieved' (*Kamkaru Viththi,* 8 March 1984). Commenting on feminist protests against domestic violence, the editorial further noted: 'The relationship between a man and a woman is a complex one... To outsiders it may look as if a man is harassing and beating a woman. But if we look closer, it is merely a bit of fun and games between husband and wife' (*ibid.*).

In their discussion of the anti-feminism of the left movement in South Asia, Jayawardena and Kelkar (1989) argue that one of the reasons that all males, including those of the left, refuse to support women's liberation is that they do not want to lose the benefits of patriarchy in their homes as well as in society. They further speculate that such an attitude is the result of 'a high degree of conservatism within the Left—perhaps due to the largely petty bourgeois origin of many South Asian Left party leaders and cadres' (*ibid.:* 2125). As de Alwis (1998b) has suggested, such a backlash against feminism is also intimately tied to the articulation of nationalism in South Asia. Following Chatterjee (1989), de Alwis argues that bourgeois Ceylonese women were produced as repositories as well as reproducers and nurturers of communal identity and cultural traditions in nationalist discourses during British colonial rule in the nineteenth and early twentieth centuries. Their seclusion within the domesticated spaces of the 'inner world' and their circumscription within domesticated subject positions such as wife and mother were perceived to be crucial to the struggle for independence and the subsequent construction of a new and modern nation-state (de Alwis, 1998b).

A discourse that was constructed in opposition to colonialism, de Alwis further notes, could also easily slide into one that was anti-western and anti-modern; any critique of what have now become neutralised as age-old traditions of family and community is thus immediately attributed to western fads, ignorance, elitism and cultural intensitivity. As one Sinhala editorial noted, feminist slogans are not only borrowed from the West, but feminists are also paid by foreign funders to promote sexual licentiousness and thus bring about the cultural decline of the Sinhala nation (quoted in the de Alwis, 1998b). This equation of feminists with tarts and traitors is a new addition to the already existing list of invectives which includes canaries, elitists, home-wreckers, male-bashers, alcoholics, smokers and lesbians (*ibid.*).

What is particularly interesting, de Alwis also points out, is that through similar accusations could be levelled at the leftists—after all, Marx and Engels were westerners and the left in Sri Lanka has also received funding from foreign sources—they are not vouched in the idiom of corruption and moral decay. This takes us back to de Alwis's point above that women are placed within 'culture' in a way that men are not. Thus, while a classed critique may be viewed with trepidation as it lays bare economic and political privilege, a gendered one is simply not tolerated as it is perceived as attacking the cultural core of society—the family—and the protectors and maintainers of that core—the men (de Alwis, 1998b).

In light of such a perspective, it is not surprising that the Sri Lankan state could pursue the harassment and intimidation of feminists without undue censure. After the change to an executive presidency in 1978, the state became obsessed with political stability, and any demonstrations or protests by women's groups as well as by trade unions or student organisations were brutally dealt with. International Women's Day celebrations in the 1980s thus became occasions not only for the demonstration of feminism in the media but also for state violence against women. In 1982, women demonstrating on 8 March in Colombo were teargassed and 8 March 1983 became a *cause célèbre;* women of the SLFP, CP and LSSP had organised a picket outside the US Embassy against US army bases in the Indian Ocean. On their return home, they also protested outside Temple Trees against the rise in the cost of milk foods. The Kollupitiya police removed their banners and arrested a photographer, and when the women went to the police station to inquire after him, they were attacked (de Rosairo, 1992). Former LSSP Member of Parliament Vivienne Goonewardena recalled: 'A policeman threw me like a sack of potatoes across the room and kicked me twice… and stood with one foot on top of my stomach' (quoted in de Rosairo, *ibid.*). Violence continued in subsequent years; on 8 March 1984, 1985 and 1986, women were teargassed, baton-charged and arrested.

After the presidential elections of 1989 in which R. Premadasa took over the presidency from his party boss, J.R. Jayewardene, there occurred a further centralisation of state power, now also undergirded by populist ideology; rather than attacking feminists, the state sought to appropriate International Women's Day along with feminist discourses and symbols. Such a project was especially facilitated through the leadership of Hema Premadasa, the President's wife, who also happened to inherit the mantle of the largest women's organisation in the country, the Seva Vanitha Movement (SVM). Inspired by the Dharma Vanitha Movement, a brainchild of the military dictatorship in Indonesia, the SVM was founded in June 1983 under the auspices of Elena Jayewardene, the wife of President J.R. Jayewardene. In its heyday in 1993, it was estimated to have over 250,000 registered members. Though the SVM called itself a non-political national movement, it was funded by the President's Fund, and its members were the wives of all government officials from the grassroots level to the ministries. The president's wife was automatic head of the SVM, while the wife of each cabinet minister was the head of that ministry's SVM, and so on.

With its main objective being 'to harness the support of Sri Lankan women in National Development projects through service', the SVM was mainly involved, during its early years under the stewardship of Elena Jayewardene, in promoting charitable projects such as opening day care centres, training centres and welfare shops, maintaining hospital wards, distributing goods to displaced persons and the armed forces, etc. (de Alwis, 1995). However, the SVM went through a rapid transformation with Hema Premadasa's assumption of its presidency. She recognised the spectacular and populist potential of her husband's pet schemes, such as Gam Udawa (village upliftment), Janasaviya (poverty alleviation) and Independence Day celebrations, and sought to organise her own versions which paralleled these; the celebration of International Women's Day was one among many other celebrations of womanhood that she made her own (*ibid.*). The 8 March celebrations were held every year under the auspices of the SVM in different parts of the country. They drew mammoth crowds mainly due to their inclusion of performances by stunt riders and acrobats from the armed forces (who usually performed at Independence Day celebrations), the donation of various goods ranging from umbrellas to sewing machines, and Hema Premadasa's own innovations such as the air drop of cash vouchers to the tune of Rs. 100,000 over the stadium in which the celebrations were taking place *(ibid.)*.

With the change of government in 1994, the state began to focus on issues that it had hitherto ignored. For example, the theme for the 1995 International Women's Day celebrations organised by the state was 'Violence Against Women', and the messages issued on that day by President Chandrika Kumaratunga, Prime Minister Sirimavo Bandaranaike, and Minister of Transport, Environment and Women's Affairs Srimani Athulathmudali focused on women workers, violence against women and issues of women's rights, rather than the usual platitudes about motherhood trotted out by their predecessors (de Alwis, 1998a).

The Politicisation of Violence

Sri Lanka's history in the latter half of the twentieth century was dominated by much violence—the Sinhala (Janatha Vimukthi Peramuna [JVP]) uprising in the south in 1971 and a more extended one in 1987-89, several anti-Tamil riots in the 1950s and 1970s, the worst occurring in 1983, and a protracted civil war in the north and east fought between the Sri Lankan state and Tamil separatists, spanning over fifteen years. Women's lives continue today to be framed by the contours of war while they also bear the scars—both physical and psychological—from previous events and processes of violence. While it is beyond the scope of this chapter to adequately document the events of violence or their repercussions, we will briefly explore several responses by women's groups to different contexts of violence. We argue that no matter how different these responses may be, they nevertheless illuminate how violence has become politicised and thus requires, in turn, politicised responses.

Women for Peace

One of the most significant and unfortunate splits that occurred within the feminist movement in Sri Lanka had to do with the 'Tamil question'. After the anti-Tamil riots of 1983, feminists who sought to question the pervasiveness of Sinhala hegemony within Sri Lankan society and began to critique Sinhala nationalism and militarism, diverged drastically from those who refused to perceive these issues as being central to the conflict between Sinhalese and Tamils. In addition, feminists were suddenly confronted with a refugee crisis due to the thousands of Tamils who were displaced and traumatised as a result of the riots. Over the 1980s this crisis situation expanded in dimension and intensity due to the acceleration of the war in the north and east which resulted in the increased displacement of Tamils, Sinhalese and Muslims from the conflict regions and border zones, and in human rights violations by both the Sri Lankan state and Tamil militants.

An excellent example of the new direction taken by feminist activism in response to these transformations in Sri Lankan society is the multi-ethnic group Women For Peace (WFP), formed in

October 1984 to agitate for a peaceful and politically negotiated settlement of the ethnic conflict. This group was initially begun as a signature campaign which called for the cessation of hostilities in the north and east of the island. The original petition was signed by 100 women among whom were many feminist activists as well as leading professionals in the fields of education, law, medicine, the arts, etc. By 8 March 1985, the signatories had increased to 10,000 women from all walks of life, religions and ethnicities.

Through the organisation of marches, vigils and pickets and the distribution of newsletters, pamphlets, posters and postcards, Women For Peace consistently spoke out against the increased militarisation of Sri Lankan society. It organised peace education programmes in schools and worked along Tamil women refugees and prisoners. The WFP's committed efforts not only to call for an end to the war but also to highlight the shared suffering of both Tamil and Sinhala women as a result of this war was paralleled by the work of many other activist and research organisations which sought to stress the shared histories and cultures of the Sinhalese and Tamils through articles, songs and videos, as well as to foster greater understanding between the two groups by offering free Tamil classes and organising goodwill missions to the north.

However, Colombo-based feminist groups' increased concern with Tamil women refugees, prisoners and detainees, as well as with Tamil women civilians in the north and east who were being raped and abused by the Sri Lankan military, once again invited the censure of the Sinhala press. As de Alwis has pointed out, the extremely nationalist, mainstream Sinhala newspaper, the *Divaina*, has been at the forefront of a campaign to 'expose' Sinhala feminists—funded by foreigners and controlled by religious (meaning Christian) organisations—who are publicising the plight of the Tamil people all over the world, and are thus not only discrediting their own country, but their race and religion as well. The lead article published in the *Divaina* on 25 May 1986 even went to the extent of quoting 'unofficial reports' that accused several feminist organisations of participating in a project to procure funding for 'Tamil terrorists' (de Alwis, 1998b).

De Alwis further notes that a feature article also published in this issue of the *Divaina* sought to document, in detail, the various 'atrocities' that had been perpetrated by Sinhala feminists. The article consistently insinuated the extent of the supposed pro-

Tamil sympathies of Sinhala feminists by suggesting that they highlighted only the rapes of Tamil women by Sinhala soldiers. It further accused them of having their own Tamil representatives in Jaffna as well as links with south India, thus doubly jeopardising the Sinhala race, religion and nation-state by forming alliances with Tamils both within and across national borders (de Alwis, 1998b; 24-25). Worse still, these feminists were dishonouring their country by publicising 'private' and local problems internationally. Interestingly, only the few groups that voiced their concern for Tamil women, notes de Alwis, were singled out as feminists and tarred with the brush of treachery. Associating with the 'Other' seemed to be even more heinous than the criticism of Sinhala culture and tradition (*ibid.*).

Women in Need

The rapid militarisation of Sri Lankan society has triggered marked increase in violence against women, be it rape, sexual harassment or domestic violence. While one could argue that the increase in the number of complaints to the police and in press reportage is a result of feminist consciousness raising and reduced tolerance for such forms of violence, it is an unfortunate and irrefutable fact that many Sri Lankan and Indian soldiers raped Tamil civilian women in the territories they occupied, and that mass rapes have taken place in the context of inter-ethnic clashes in the border villages of the north and east. In addition, many feminist activists now working among Tamil, Sinhala and Muslim internally displaced populations have observed an alarming increase in domestic violence as a result of new insecurities and marginalisations faced by these groups, and by men in particular. What has not yet been adequately studied or understood is the extent of the threat posed by the thousands of military deserters who are both armed and traumatised by war, and the increase in armed violence, harassment and rape of women in areas that have now been transformed into rest and recreation (R&R) zones such as Anuradhapura.

In light of such troubled and dangerous circumstances facing a large percentage of women in Sri Lanka, be it within or without the home, it is especially disheartening to note the limited resources at their service to help them combat abusive relationships and situations. While the People's Alliance government, which came into power in 1994, has introduced several innovations such as women-only buses (to reduce the harassment of women using public transportation), special sections in police stations staffed by policewomen (to increase the comfort level of women making complaints of a sensitive nature), framing more stringent rape laws and even appointing (after much pressure from human rights and feminist groups) a commission to look into the recent rape and murder (by soldiers) of Krishanthi kumaraswamy, a Tamil schoolgirl, no effort has yet been made to help battered women. Though feminist groups, such as Suriya in Batticaloa and the Women's Development Centre in Kandy, as well as trauma counselling programmes and centres initiated by feminist groups including the Family Rehabilitation Centre, have attempted to help battered women while also providing other forms of support and services, there is only one organisation, even today, that deals exclusively with the issue of domestic violence—Women In Need (WIN).

Women In Need was formed in 1987 to deal with the increased incidence of violence against women and to advise battered women. In its first six years, WIN had 4,700 'drop-in' clients who visited its offices for advice, as well as 2,530 postal inquiries. While WIN provides free, confidential, listener-friendly service as well as legal and medical advice, the overwhelming demand for its services has especially hampered its ability to provide adequate shelter for many of its clients. The strategy adopted by WIN with regard to battered women has been urge them to think primarily in terms of rescuing their marriages rather than leaving such abusive relationships, thus drawing criticism from some feminists.

Birds of Freedom

While women have been the victims and supervisors of violence, they have also been its perpetrators. Though many women participated in the JVP youth insurrection of 1971, and to a lesser extent in the JVP insurrection of 1987-89 (see de Mel, 1998; Senanayake, 1996), the issue of women militants has really come to the force in the 1990s with the increased participation of Tamil women militants in combat. In fact, the women's wing of the Liberation Tigers of Tamil Eelam (LTTE)—Suthanthirap Paravaikal (Birds of Freedom)—has acquired almost as much notoriety as their male counterparts since a female suicide bomber killed Rajiv Gandhi, former Prime Minister of India, in 1993. The increased visibility of these women in recent LTTE campaigns against the

Sri Lankan forces has also generated much discussion among feminists in Sri Lanka on the role of female militants in anti-state movements, a familiar question to those who have studied the positioning of female fighters in guerrilla groups. Much of this feminist debate is framed in terms of whether the women in LTTE are liberated or subjugated (Coomaraswamy, 1996; M. de Silva, 1994), agents or victims (de Mel, 1998).

Sitralega Maunaguru's finely nuanced and historicised paper, on the other hand, has been able to transcend such a dichotomising debate by locating 'women warriors' within the border context of other male and female subject positions in Tamil society. Manuaguru also complicates this category of 'woman warrior' by making two distinctive phases of its mobilisation by militant groups. In the first phase, spearheaded by the LTTE, which 'owed more to its militarism than to an ideological allegiance with feminism' (Maunaguru, 1995), the ideal Tamil woman was expected to be a mother as well as a fighter, thus integrating the subject position of 'brave mother' with that of 'woman warrior', i.e., a 'warrior mother'. The second phase, facilitated by the women's wings of the more progressive Tamil militant groups (which have since disbanded or been decimated by the LTTE) such as the Eelam People's Revolutionary Liberation Front (EPRLF), enabled a formulation of the 'new woman' who contested 'patriarchal aspects of Tamil cultural ideology' and insisted on linking national liberation with women's liberation (*ibid.*).

A later phase of the 'woman warrior', which Maunaguru does not discuss but which has been addressed by de Alwis (1994, 1998a), as well as by M. de Silva (1994), Coomaraswamy (1996) and de Mel (1998), can be described as the 'masculinised virgin warrior'. In a context where the LTTE reigns supreme, having exiled, incorporated or killed all dissenters and critics (including many feminists), it is this ideal of womanhood that now seems to be foregrounded within Tamil society (through LTTE propaganda). As Radhika Coomaraswamy (1996) points out, the 'armed virgin' is a purely LTTE innovation, having no precedence in Tamil literature or culture.

While the LTTE woman's internal make-up is expected to be 'pure', 'chaste' and 'virginal', her outer body is marked as masculine; her hair is cut short and she wears a beret, combat fatigues, boots and a cyanide capsule around her neck (just like her male counterparts), but no make-up or jewellery (Coomaraswamy, 1996). The poetry of Vanati, a female 'martyr' of the LTTE, captures the 'woman warrior's' desire to transform her biologically as well as culturally marked body (as feminine) to 'heroic' masculinity while simultaneously proclaiming her virginity and chastity—she refuses the red *kumkumum* and *thali* and embraces weapons, not men (quoted in Schalk, 1992: 95). This celebration of 'martial feminism'—through extensive LTTE propaganda as well as through its ideologues such as Balasingham (1983, 1993) and Schalk (1992, 1994)—has also been critiqued by feminists, who, in turn, have been vilified by the LTTE.

Women's Action Committee

The numerous violations of human rights by both the state and militant groups in the north and east as well as the south of the island in these past two decades have led feminists to concern themselves with this issue and to be actively involved in monitoring and advocacy work. Feminists have played key roles in many human rights organisations, including the Civil Rights Movement, formed as a response to state repression during the JVP uprising of 1971, the Human Rights Organisation, the Movement for the Defence of Democratic Rigths (MDDR), the Movement for Inter-racial Justice and Equality (MIRJE), the human rights documentation centre INFORM, the Movement for Peace with Democracy, the Centre for Human Rights at the University of Colombo, and Home for Human Rights in Batticaloa.

Of the autonomous women's organisations that have been primarily concerned with human rights issues, the Women's Action Committee (WAC), a coalition of several women's organisations founded in 1982, stands at the forefront. One of the central platforms of the WAC was the establishment of a democratic culture that respected women's rights and human rights. The WAC consistently linked the ethnic conflict and the politics of violence to the deterioration of democracy and its consequences for all ethnic communities and marginalised groups (Samuel, 1998). It was one of the many coalitions that welcomed the signing of the Indo-Lanka Peace Accord in 1987 as a right step towards a political solution of the ethnic conflict. As a result of their support for the Accord, however, the WAC came under threat from the JVP which had formulated a violent campaign against the Accord and the government that signed such an Accord. The coalition had to disband, and many feminists went into hiding during the height of the JVP uprising from 1987 to 1989 (*ibid.*).

With the increase of both state and JVP violence resulting in extra-judicial killings on a mass scale and the 'disappearance' of thousands of young men in the south during 1987-90, the WAC reconstituted itself, with broader participation, to form a new coalition—the Mothers and Daughters of Lanka (MDL). This new coalition strove hard to mobilise women to speak out against human rights violations by both the state and the militants, and launched a signature campaign in 1989 to 'Stop All Killings Now' (see *Sun,* 14 September 1989). Many groups represented in the MDL, including Women for Peace, set up trauma counselling centres and programmes to help women and children to cope with psychological problems arising from the 'disappearance' of relatives, the witnessing of various forms of violence, the experience of displacement, and the trauma of rape, domestic violence and other kinds of sexual abuse. Several representatives of this coalition also visited Jaffna in November 1989 to participate in a march protesting the LTTE killing of feminist Rajani Thiranagama a month earlier. The indiscriminate arrest of many Tamil civilian women in the city of Colombo due to increased vigilance against LTTE infiltrators into the city in the 1990s was also protested by this group.

Since the 1990s, many Sri Lankan feminists have consistently sought to link women's rights with human rights, in keeping with international feminist trends particularly well captured by the popular slogan 'Women's Rights Are Human Rights'. They have campaigned on this issue using posters and pamphlets, the latter including English reprints as well as translations of the pioneering work of US feminist Charlotte Bunch on this subject. The Vienna Declaration in 1993 at the World Conference for Human Rights which proclaimed that the 'human rights of women and of the girl child are an inalienable, integral and indivisible part of universal human rights' provided a great fillip to this campaign.

Mothers' Fronts

The 1980s and 1990s further witnessed the political mobilisation of 'motherhood' in the context of the civil war in the north and east as well as the second JVP uprising in the south. In 1984, the Mothers' Front was formed in Jaffna to protest the mass arrest of Tamil youth by the Sri Lankan state. This organisation was controlled by and consisted of women from all classes. Feminist Rajani Thiranagama has documented how these women 'mobilised mass rallies, and picketed public officials demanding the removal of military occupation [by the Sri Lankan state]' (Hoole et al., 1990). It was not only the spirit, observed Thiranagama, but also the enormous numbers that this group was able to mobilise which 'spoke loudly of the high point to which such mass organisations, especially of women [could] rise' *(ibid.)*. Though the members of the Mothers' Front had spontaneously mobilised their maternal identity in the face of state repression, they were also quick to criticise the blatant manipulation of such an identity when Tamil militant groups put up posters inciting women to have more babies in order to further the cause of separatism (quoted in Jayawardena, 1985b).

The Mothers' Front also inspired Tamil women in the east to begin their own branch. In 1986, the eastern Mothers' Front took to the streets with rice pounders to prevent a massacre of members of the Tamil Eelam Liberation Organisation (TELO) by the LTTE (Hensman, 1992). In 1987, one of its members, Annai Pupathi, fasted to death to protest the presence of the Indian Peace Keeping Force (IPKF). She was subsequently immortalised by the LTTE (it was common knowledge that the LTTE had forced her to keep at her fast), who now offer a scholarship in her memory. It was finally the increasing hegemony of the LTTE, and their suppression of all independent, democratic organisations that did not 'toe the line', that pushed the Mothers' Front in the north and east into political conformism and reduced its wide appeal and militancy. 'It became another Y.W.C.A.,' notes Thiranagama, and its central structure, which was mainly made up of middle-class women, finally began to confine its activities to works of charity (Hoole et al., 1990). Many members who refused to work under LTTE hegemony migrated abroad or to Colombo.

In July 1990, a Mothers' Front was formed in the south to protest the 'disappearance' of their male kin during the JVP uprising from 1987 to 1990. These women's only demand was for 'a climate where we can raise our sons to manhood, have our husbands with us and lead normal women's lives' (quoted in de

Alwis, 1998c). Their mass rallies and *deva kannalawwas* (beseeching of the gods) had a tremendous impact on Sinhala society during the two years in which this organisation was especially active. As de Alwis has argued, the seemingly unquestionable authenticity of these women's grief and their espousal of 'traditional' family values provided the southern Mothers' Front with an important space for protest at a time when feminist and human rights activists who were critical of either state or JVP violence were being killed with impunity (*ibid.*).

While many feminists in the south celebrated the successful campaign of the southern Mothers' Front and participated in its rallies, they were nevertheless split on how best to respond to such a movement, for several reasons. For example, while the Front identified itself as the largest grassroots women's movement in the country (with an estimated membership of 25,000 women), it was common knowledge that it was founded, funded and coordinated by the main opposition party in the country—the Sri Lanka Freedom Party (SLFP)—whose politbureau was predominantly middle-class and male. As members of autonomous women's groups, feminists felt very uncomfortable about working with a political party that not only did not espouse a particular feminist ideology, but in fact was perceived to be using the Mothers' Front for its own political ends (de Alwis, 1998b). Feminists were also concerned about the limited agenda of the southern Mothers' Front which precluded it from calling attention to similar issues faced by Tamil and Muslim women in the north and east of the island. Many feminists who had reservations about the Front's mobilisation of 'motherhood' felt that they would have been more willing to compromise if it had been used as a space within such a mass movement of women from different ethnic groups could have united and launched a collective critique of the violence perpetrated by the state as well as by militant groups.

In fact, the concerted energies of many women's groups in Sri Lanka have been so focused on addressing issues that arise in a context of continuous violence and carnage, that many other important struggles have had to be abandoned. Other areas needing change include, for example, the persistence of pockets of illiteracy and poverty among women in plantations, urban slums and remote rural areas; the continuance of customary laws which include provisions oppressive to women and the absence of a secular, unified code (based on the Sri Lankan constitution, CEDAW and other international covenants) expanding the choices for women in determining the body of law they wished to be judged by; the glass ceiling faced by women in employment and sexual harassment in the workplace; the absence of adequate laws against domestic violence and marital rape; the continued criminalisation of abortion (except when pregnancy is perceived to be detrimental to the mother's health); and the fining and imprisonment of prostitutes (but not their clients).

Nevertheless, it must also be acknowledged that women have visibly progressed in many areas in the fifty years since independence. Their physical qualitv of life—as seen from indices of health, maternal, mortality, education (including literacy) and life expectancy—is the best in the South Asian region, and compares favourably with other more developed parts of the world. Women's literacy has also had an important impact on later marriage, lower birth rates and access to family planning. While male domination persists in all spheres and bargaining with patriarchy continues, the struggle for women's liberation will be carried into the new millennium and the inspiration for the women's movement of the future will come from the struggles of the past.

Notes

1. We are grateful to Pradeep Jeganathan for his perceptive comments during our preliminary discussions for this chapter. Our thanks also to our anonymous reviewer for some useful suggestions.

   In this chapter, we will switch between 'Ceylon' and 'Sri Lanka' in order to retain the historical specificity of their usage. The British used the name 'Ceylon, for the island during the eighteenth, nineteenth and early half of the twentieth centuries. The island's name was changed to 'Sri Lanka' with the adoption of the 1972 constitution, post-independence.
2. We are not listing here the names of older women's organistions such as the Women's Christian Temperance Union (1862), Young Women's Christian Association

(1882), the Girls' Friendly Society (1904) and Ladies of Charity (1904), which were founded by Anglican and Catholic missionaries and were predominantly local branches of foreign organisations.

3. The limitations of social service and its particularly contingent usefulness are especially well captured in the critique of such work by the Eksath Kantha Peramuna (EKP) on the eve of independence (see de Mel et al., 1997).
4. The WFU only demanded that women who possessed a qualification of a standard equivalent to the School Leaving Certificate Examination should be given the franchise (rather than universal franchise), and were content only to focus attention on their role as a crucial vote bank rather than directly arguing for women's representations in the legislative council. Their conservatism, however, is particularly illuminating of the material as well as ideological constraints within which they lived. For an extended discussion of this group, see de Alwis (1998b: Ch. 3).
5. Though Dr Rutnam was unseated on a technical flaw in 1938, her interest in municipal politics and women candidates for the municipality continued. She went on to endorse the candidature of Mrs H.M. Gunesekera in 1938, Vivienne Goonewardena in 1949, and Ayesha Rauf (Jayawardena, 1993: 34-35).
6. Today, the representation of women in the national parliament is a mere 4.9 per cent, 3.1 per cent in the provincial councils and 1.1 per cent in local authorities (Leitan and Gunasekera, 1998: 1; see also the tables in W. de Silva, 1995: 233).
7. Unfortunately, they did not win a seat in the election which was marred by violence and vote-rigging.
8. A similar effort was initiated by the Centre for Women's Research (CENWOR) when they sent a Gender Issue paper (which was signed by about thirty NGOs) to all political parties on the eve of the 1994 elections.
9. It is an undeniable fact also that the most organisations that work among women, be it in the context of economic empowerment or social upliftment, provide opportunities at varying levels for the building of leadership skills among

women—a crucial prerequisite for political empowerment. In this regard, the Change Agent's Programme, conceived in 1978 by innovators in the State Rural Development and Research and Training Institute (and later adopted by non-governmental organisations and groups as well), has made a crucial contribution (see Jayaweera, 1989).

8

The Assessment

One of the greatest challenges is harnessing the energy and activism that many women exhibit in informal activities and translating that into their participation and influence in formal activities. This challenge is intensified by the false assumption that peace processes are gender neutral, the negative attitudes of many participants in formal peace processes toward women's involvement and by the expectation that anyone engaged in formal peace processes should understand the manner in which they are conducted (including expectations of knowledge of international legal and other standards, United Nations protocols and terminology). Many women report that they need capacity-building opportunities to acquire the expertise required to participate in formal peace processes.

One way to support capacity-building would be to facilitate women's participation in non-official talks that are carried on discreetly at the level below the formal official process, and are referred to as Track II negotiations. Officials may be included, but generally the participants are people from all sides of the conflict in the community or the diaspora who have some influence in the community. Supported by a facilitator they discuss some of the main issues of the conflict and explore possible options for addressing them. The process helps to prepare the opposing sides for the formal process. The inclusion of women in Track II negotiations would give them the training and confidence to participate in formal peace talks.

In addition, many women who choose to participate in peace marches or reconciliation efforts may choose not to participate in formal peace mechanisms because it is unclear to them how such formal strategies will affect their lives. Formal mechanisms, such as early warning may be carried out by international organizations, which are not always perceived as having the interests of local peoples in mind. Those involved in formal peace processes should devote more effort to public education campaigns that explain how early warning, peace negotiations and similar measures are not only important for formal political actors, but for civil society as a whole.

The paucity of information on the gender perspectives of formal peace processes is also problematic. While some work has been done on gender perspectives for early warning and peace negotiations, there are other important areas of the formal peace process for which little information is available at this time. For example, the potential impact of gender perspectives on preventive diplomacy or peace-building remains seriously under-researched. A comprehensive collection of data by DPA would be required on the ways in which the incorporation of gender perspectives affect formal peace processes. Research and analysis of peace processes, negotiations and sanctions regimes as well as reports to the Security Council need to fully integrate gender perspectives.

Initiatives by United Nations entities. United Nations agencies have been actively involved in efforts to promote and support women's activities in informal peace processes. There are a number of important initiatives aimed at increasing the participation of women within formal peace processes.

DPA, the Division for the Advancement of Women (DAW) and UNIFEM support women's groups and networks to foster dialogue conflict. This work is especially important for countries where the usual forums for discussion (newspapers, public forums, parliaments, etc.) are weakened or destroyed. Women's social and community networks may allow access to power holders and an opportunity to engage in dialogues in alternative forums. For example, in Guinea-Bissau, DPA's initial efforts to make contact with and bring leaders of the warring groups to the peace table failed. DPA then partnered with local women and women's organizations, which in turn made contact with leaders of warring parties through their own family ties. Through these efforts the leaders were eventually brought to the peace table.

A number of United Nations entities, including DAW, the Economic Commission for Africa (ECA), the United Nations

Development Programme (UNDP) and UNIFEM, and regional organizations, have played a supporting role in a number of women's peace groups, including the Mano River Women's Peace Network, the African Women's Committee on Peace and Development and Femmes Africa Solidarité, by providing capacity-building in conflict resolution and negotiating skills. In addition, the work of the Mano River Women's Peace Network on conflict prevention, early warning and mediation has also been supported through provisions of funds to attend regional meetings and summits. This represents a positive start to working with regional and subregional organizations in support of the efforts of civil society and women's groups in early warning and conflict prevention.

In Burundi, prior to the All Party Women's Peace Conference, UNIFEM, in cooperation with the NGOs International Alert and Search for Common Ground, provided training in conflict resolution. This training served as an opportunity for dialogue and consultation among women from various backgrounds and ethnic groups, including women of the diaspora. Similarly, in 1999, UNIFEM began a three-year initiative to support women in Kosovo in integrating gender perspectives into ongoing peace-building activities. Working in close collaboration with OSCE, the European Union and United Nations departments and agencies, the project provides leadership skills to promote the active participation of women in the economic and institutional restructuring of the province.

In parallel with the Bonn talks on Afghanistan, two meetings were held in Brussels at the urging of Afghan women. The Afghan Women's Summit for Democracy was organized by international NGOs, such as Equality Now, in collaboration with the Office of the Special Adviser on Gender Issues and Advancement of Women and UNIFEM. The Government of Belgium and UNIFEM organized a roundtable on women's leadership in Afghanistan. The Summit concluded with the adoption of the Brussels Proclamation, which addresses women's demands with respect to the peace process and reconstruction of Afghanistan, including the right to vote, equal pay and equal access to health care, education and employment; the protection of women from forced underage marriages and sexual harassment; and the active participation of Afghan women lawyers in the drafting of a new constitution that would include principles of non-discrimination.

The Afghan Women's National Consultation, held in Kabul on 8 March 2002, was another effort to involve Afghan women in the long-term peace and reconstruction process. The meeting, which was organized by the Ministry of Women's Affairs in cooperation with several United Nations agencies, adopted a plan of action that would guide ministries and international organizations on women's participation in the rehabilitation of the country as well as in all political and administrative processes. Under the leadership of the SRSG and the UNAMA Interim Gender Adviser, an Inter-Agency Network for Gender Equality was established. The Gender Adviser works closely with the Minister of Women's Affairs and considerable effort has gone into soliciting the views of women and facilitating their inclusion in the emerging political structures of Afghanistan.

The success of the peace initiatives of women's groups in Africa result from many factors. Women have recognized the value of focusing on crosscutting issues of importance to them, and organizing across religious, ethnic and political lines. In several instances, women have organized locally but first used the opportunity of international meetings to express their views on political or peace issues. To allay fears that they were not suited to negotiations, they sought support from such bodies as Africa Women's Committee on Peace and Development and Femmes Africa Solidarité to obtain the necessary skills in conflict resolution at the community and regional levels.

They have reached outside their national boundaries to make strategic alliances with regional groups and international organizations and NGOs, which could facilitate their participation in peace processes. In this way, they have put aside their differences, and made the sheer weight of their numbers felt in the peace process. They have understood the impact of unity, collective action and innovation and learned to use the media in different ways to effect change. Women interested in participating in peace processes have learned to build effective relationships and strategic partnerships with international and regional agencies, which could assist them with political and financial support.

In Afghanistan, the United Nations encouraged the parties to include women delegates in the peace negotiations. Women were full delegates in two of the four parties and advisers in the other two parties. The resulting Bonn Agreement contained an explicit commitment to the role of women in Government and created a Ministry of Women's Affairs. Two women were appointed to the Interim Administration as Minister of Women's Affairs, and Minister of Health. The Afghan Human Rights Commission, which was established according to provisions of the Bonn Agreement, is also headed by a woman.

The Bonn Agreement called for the participation of women in the Emergency Loya Jirga, a general assembly that would elect a transitional Government. In June 2002, about 200 Afghan women representing all regions took an active part in the Emergency Loya Jirga. The United Nations Assistance Mission for Afghanistan (UNAMA) in cooperation with the Ministry of Women's Affairs, provided them with training and daily support. Following the Loya Jirga, a network of 45 women delegates was created to play a leading role in women's preparations to the next Loya Jirga in 18 months.

The political mobilizing by women in the Democratic Republic of the Congo prior to the formal peace talks made it possible for them to participate as delegates of political parties and experts from civil society in the Congolese peace talks, held in Sun City, South Africa, from 25 February to 19 April 2002. All political parties to the peace talks included women delegates, with 40 women and 307 men participating. Members of Le Caucusdes Femmes participated and women were members of all five official working commissions. As a result of significant efforts, one woman was included in the commission on defence and security questions. The women acted as a unified dynamic force to keep the talks going throughout the frequent blockages in the negotiations, and formed parallel shadow commissions that met with all heads of delegations, international observers and the Special Representatives of the Secretary-General (SRSG). The United Nations Mission in the Democratic Republic of the Congo (MONUC) gender unit supported the efforts of civil society in the peace process, and Radio. Okapi (United Nations radio) served as a discussion forum to highlight the ideas and views of women throughout the peace process.

The systematic exclusion of women from official peace processes has detrimental effects on the long-term sustainability of a settlement because all voices and interests are not heard. In Bosnia and Herzegovina, even though the international community was aware of the violence and marginalization that women and girls had experienced during the conflict and the responsibilities they would be shouldering during the conflict and reconstruction, there were no women on the negotiation teams. In the Ram-bouillet negotiations prior to the Kosovo bombings only one woman was present, despite the active participation of women's organizations in the nonviolent movement in Serbia. In Colombia, the one woman involved in peace talks resigned from the process as a result of being harassed by other negotiators, guerillas and the press.

Women who are involved in negotiating peace agreements, are more likely to advance issues that are of importance to women and girls. The participation of women in the Guatemalan process, for example, resulted in specific commitments to women, such as access to housing, credit, land and other productive resources; the obligation of the Government to implement a national health programme for women and girls; commitments to reunite families and locate children and orphans; a review of the national legislation with the purpose of eradicating all forms of discrimination against women, and penalizing sexual harassment; a guarantee of the participation of women at all decision-making in local, regional and national bodies, on equal terms with men; and the creation of the National Women's Forum and the Office for the Defense of Indigenous Women, in order to promote women's participation and rights.

However, the presence of women peace negotiators is not a guarantee that gender equality issues will be placed on the peace agenda. This was demonstrated in El Salvador, where although approximately 30 per cent of the Farabundo Marti National Liberation (FMLN) negotiators were women, gender equality was not included in the peace agreements. The El Salvador peace agreements included discriminatory provisions in the accords, such as barring women to varying degrees from reconstruction programmes, with far-reaching consequences for adolescent girls, women and their dependants.

If a peace agreement fails to note specifically the importance of gender equality, any measures proposed to promote gender equality in the implementation phase can be interpreted as beyond the scope of the peace mandate. As analysis of the Dayton Peace Accords shows, provisions that are gender-neutral may create obstacles to achieving equality and nondiscrimination in post-conflict situations. In its enumeration of rights, the Dayton Accords did mention the right to marry, but did not promote the inclusion of women in the highest levels of the new Government, with the result that from the beginning women were under-represented in Government and administrative and economic positions.

Explicit attention to gender equality in peace agreements could include human rights provisions in new constitutions, implementation of special efforts to enable women's participation in elections, measures to promote the participation and involvement of women in decision-making, laws against sexual violence, and plans to prosecute perpetrators of gender-based violence. For example, women have demanded the provision of medical and social services to women and girls. The pursuit of gender-sensitive justice and land reform, protection against discrimination, and specific protections for poor, indigenous or ethnic minority women and girls are other central issues.

Proposals to have a gender focus in development strategies, including in relation to access to credit and housing, inheritance rights, education and health programmes, including reproductive health, have also been sought by women activists in different countries.

Peace-building. Peace-building is defined as a means of preventing the outbreak, recurrence or continuation of armed conflict and therefore encompasses a wide range of political, developmental, humanitarian and human rights mechanisms". A range of short-term or long-term actions can be adopted to meet the needs of societies falling into or emerging from conflict. To be successful, the process of peace-building should be locally owned and focused on social transformation and the re-establishment of trust through the participation of the national authorities as well as the local population, including women. The process should be designed to meet the specific needs of the country or region, and address the immediate security and humanitarian needs as well as the root causes of actual and potential crises.

Without specific attention to and understanding of gender relations and inequalities, women can be excluded from peace-building initiatives and as a result, their needs may not be met. The incorporation of gender perspectives into peace-building efforts includes explicit support of both established and nascent women's organizations working to become part of newly created political structures. It requires that international institutions working on peace-building are aware of the different priorities and resources of women and men, as well as boys and girls. Networking with women and women's organizations can facilitate mediation efforts, reconciliation and dialogue. Some women's organizations, such as the Mano River Women's Peace Network, have established sub-regional and regional contacts and expertise that can be drawn upon to provide information and facilitate capacity-building at regional and sub-regional levels.

Responses and Challenges

Within the United Nations, the Department of Political Affairs (DPA) is the designated focal point for peace-building and has a mandate to identify potential or actual conflicts, to monitor political developments world-wide, and to provide early warning of impending conflicts and analyzes of options for preventive action. In 1998, DPA established a Conflict Prevention Team to provide an intra-departmental forum for the development of preventive action options. Within DPA, desk officers develop country profiles on their respective countries and then monitor developments over time. DPA serves as the Convener of the Executive Committee on Peace and Security which was established in 1997 to deal with issues of system-wide preventive action. The Secretary-General's Special Adviser on Gender Issues and Advancement of Women is a member of this Committee. Other mechanisms within the United Nations system can also be brought to bear in early warning and conflict prevention, such as the reports of Special Rapporteurs and Representatives on human rights.

In 2001, DPA developed the United Nations Plan of Action on Peace-building as a practical guide for the United

Nations system in the formulation and implementation of peace-building strategies. Peace-building missions are meant to be temporary catalytic and facilitating mechanisms and are normally small. Currently there are four peace- building missions: the United Nations Peace-building Support Mission in Central African Republic (BONUCA); the United Nations Peace-building Support Office in Guinea-Bissau (UNOGBIS); the United Nations Peace-building Support Office in Liberia (UNOL) in Liberia and the United Nations Tajikistan Office of Peace-building (UNTOP). Their political responsibilities involve: protection of nascent democratic institutions; crisis management; political mediation; and provision of good offices.

As part of its peace-building efforts, DPA is sometimes involved in the political education of local elected representatives and in strengthening the role of local leaders. These activities can involve the training of women as voters and candidates for public office. An important element of human rights monitoring also includes monitoring violations of the human rights of women, as noted in the Plan of Action. This monitoring would indicate not only the extent to which latent violence may reappear, but also the extent to which new democratic institutions are taking root in the local population.

Informal Peace Processes. International organizations have not always recognized or capitalized on women's involvement in informal peace processes, since these are often small-scale initiatives concentrated at the local level. Public marches or cross-community development projects are not viewed as central to the peace process, even though they may be very effective in changing people's attitudes, opening up opportunities for more formal peace processes and acting as important catalysts for change. Women involved in informal peace processes may themselves not be focused on gaining the attention of official actors or intervening in the formal peace process. They often view their own activities as focused on questions of survival or equal rights, and may regard themselves as apolitical. One of the challenges for all international actors involved in formal peace processes is to become familiar with the variety of peace-related activism carried out by women at grass-roots level.

A challenge for those involved in informal peace processes is finding the momentum to continue their activism and involvement once the immediate goal of cessation of hostilities has been accomplished. Many groups of women who respond to conflict have larger agendas than peace alone, and their activism can generate multiple offshoot organizations. In other instances, once armed conflict ceases and people turn their attention to recovery, some organized efforts for peace-building simply dissipate.

Women involved in informal peace processes have identified lack of access to sources of funding as a major constraint to the achievement of their goals. Women's grass-roots organizations in situations of armed conflict receive little financial assistance from local or national actors, and many are largely dependent on international NGOs and international governmental and inter-governmental institutions. Procedures for obtaining funding are complicated and protracted. There may also be conflicting priorities between donors and local groups. Women cite leadership training and skills training programmes, in such areas as peace education, trauma healing and counseling, as essential for carrying out their peace work.

Formal Peace Processes. Women and women's groups involved in organizing for peace have identified the need to be included at all levels of decision-making of formal peace processes as critical to the achievement of their goals. If the United Nations were to lead by example in terms of representation of women, local women would have a better chance of being included in formal peace processes.

One of the greatest challenges is harnessing the energy and activism that many women exhibit in informal activities and translating that into their participation and influence in formal activities. This challenge is intensified by the false assumption that peace processes are gender neutral, the negative attitudes of many participants in formal peace processes toward women's involvement and by the expectation that anyone engaged in formal peace processes should understand the manner in which they are conducted (including expectations of knowledge of international legal and other standards, United Nations protocols and terminology). Many women report that they need capacity-building opportunities to acquire the expertise required to participate in formal peace processes.

One way to support capacity-building would be to facilitate women's participation in non-official talks that are carried on discreetly at the level below the formal official process, and are referred to as Track II negotiations. Officials may be included, but generally the participants are people from all sides of the conflict in the community or the diaspora who have some influence in the community. Supported by a facilitator they discuss some of the main issues of the conflict and explore possible options for addressing them. The process helps to prepare the opposing sides for the formal process. The inclusion of women in Track II negotiations would give them the training and confidence to participate in formal peace talks.

In addition, many women who choose to participate in peace marches or reconciliation efforts may choose not to participate in formal peace mechanisms because it is unclear to them how such formal strategies will affect their lives. Formal mechanisms, such as early warning may be carried out by international organizations, which are not always perceived as having the interests of local peoples in mind. Those involved in formal peace processes should devote more effort to public education campaigns that explain how early warning, peace negotiations and similar measures are not only important for formal political actors, but for civil society as a whole.

The paucity of information on the gender perspectives of formal peace processes is also problematic. While some work has been done on gender perspectives for early warning and peace negotiations, there are other important areas of the formal peace process for which little information is available at this time. For example, the potential impact of gender perspectives on preventive diplomacy or peace-building remains seriously under-researched. A comprehensive collection of data by DPA would be required on the ways in which the incorporation of gender perspectives affect formal peace processes. Research and analysis of peace processes, negotiations and sanctions regimes as well as reports to the Security Council need to fully integrate gender perspectives.

Initiatives by United Nations entities. United Nations agencies have been actively involved in efforts to promote and support women's activities in informal peace processes. There are a number of important initiatives aimed at increasing the participation of women within formal peace processes.

DPA, the Division for the Advancement of Women (DAW) and UNIFEM support women's groups and networks to foster dialogue conflict. This work is especially important for countries where the usual forums for discussion (newspapers, public forums, parliaments, etc.) are weakened or destroyed. Women's social and community networks may allow access to power holders and an opportunity to engage in dialogues in alternative forums. For example, in Guinea-Bissau, DPA's initial efforts to make contact with and bring leaders of the warring groups to the peace table failed. DPA then partnered with local women and women's organizations, which in turn made contact with leaders of warring parties through their own family ties. Through these efforts the leaders were eventually brought to the peace table.

A number of United Nations entities, including DAW, the Economic Commission for Africa (ECA), the United Nations Development Programme (UNDP) and UNIFEM, and regional organizations, have played a supporting role in a number of women's peace groups, including the Mano River Women's Peace Network, the African Women's Committee on Peace and Development and Femmes Africa Solidarité, by providing capacity-building in conflict resolution and negotiating skills. In addition, the work of the Mano River Women's Peace Network on conflict prevention, early warning and mediation has also been supported through provisions of funds to attend regional meetings and summits. This represents a positive start to working with regional and subregional organizations in support of the efforts of civil society and women's groups in early warning and conflict prevention.

In Burundi, prior to the All Party Women's Peace Conference, UNIFEM, in cooperation with the NGOs International Alert and Search for Common Ground, provided training in conflict resolution. This training served as an opportunity for dialogue and consultation among women from various backgrounds and ethnic groups, including women of the diaspora. Similarly, in 1999, UNIFEM began a three-year initiative to support women in Kosovo in integrating gender perspectives into ongoing peace-building activities. Working in close collaboration with OSCE, the European Union and United Nations departments and agencies, the project provides leadership skills to promote the active participation of women in the economic and institutional restructuring of the province.

In parallel with the Bonn talks on Afghanistan, two meetings were held in Brussels at the urging of Afghan women. The Afghan Women's Summit for Democracy was organized by international NGOs, such as Equality Now, in collaboration with the Office of the Special Adviser on Gender Issues and Advancement of Women and UNIFEM. The Government of Belgium and UNIFEM organized a roundtable on women's leadership in Afghanistan. The Summit concluded with the adoption of the Brussels Proclamation, which addresses women's demands with respect to the peace process and reconstruction of Afghanistan, including the right to vote, equal pay and equal access to health care, education and employment; the protection of women from forced underage marriages and sexual harassment; and the active participation of Afghan women lawyers in the drafting of a new constitution that would include principles of non-discrimination.

The Afghan Women's National Consultation, held in Kabul on 8 March 2002, was another effort to involve Afghan women in the long-term peace and reconstruction process. The meeting, which was organized by the Ministry of Women's Affairs in cooperation with several United Nations agencies, adopted a plan of action that would guide ministries and international organizations on women's participation in the rehabilitation of the country as well as in all political and administrative processes. Under the leadership of the SRSG and the UNAMA Interim Gender Adviser, an Inter-Agency Network for Gender Equality was established. The Gender Adviser works closely with the Minister of Women's Affairs and considerable effort has gone into soliciting the views of women and facilitating their inclusion in the emerging political structures of Afghanistan.

The success of the peace initiatives of women's groups in Africa result from many factors. Women have recognized the value of focusing on crosscutting issues of importance to them, and organizing across religious, ethnic and political lines. In several instances, women have organized locally but first used the opportunity of international meetings to express their views on political or peace issues. To allay fears that they were not suited to negotiations, they sought support from such bodies as Africa Women's Committee on Peace and Development and Femmes Africa Solidarité to obtain the necessary skills in conflict resolution at the community and regional levels.

They have reached outside their national boundaries to make strategic alliances with regional groups and international organizations and NGOs, which could facilitate their participation in peace processes. In this way, they have put aside their differences, and made the sheer weight of their numbers felt in the peace process. They have understood the impact of unity, collective action and innovation and learned to use the media in different ways to effect change. Women interested in participating in peace processes have learned to build effective relationships and strategic partnerships with international and regional agencies, which could assist them with political and financial support.

The gender roles framework (GRF) derives from insights and concerns of the early WID approach, in particular the above-mentioned project appraisals. Developed by researchers at the Harvard Institute of International Development in collaboration with the Women in Development Office of USAID, the framework has become widely used in other mainstream development institutions. Its theoretical underpinning is provided by 'sex role theory' that informs liberal feminism.

Many of the shortcomings that critics have identified in the gender roles framework are thus a reiteration of those directed at sex role theory. The framework takes as its starting point the view that the household is not an undifferentiated unit with a common production and consumption function. Households are seen as systems of resource allocation themselves. Gender equity is defined in terms of individual access to and control over resources; women's (actual and potential) productive contributions provide the rationale for allocating resources to them. Gender equity and economic efficiency are thus synergistic.

'Gender analysis' is described as a diagnostic tool for planners to overcome inefficient resource allocation. While GRF focuses on what men and women do-the gender division of labour-it does not restrict itself to a discussion of activities/roles alone. It also highlights gender differences in access to and control over income and resources. It then considers the implications of these divisions and differences for project design. In sum, it aims to highlight the key differences between the incentives and constraints under which men and women work.

The insights gained from this analysis are then used for tailoring planned interventions (credit, education, training, etc.) in such a way as to improve overall productivity. An example of the GRF approach is Cloud's analytical framework for agricultural projects. The first step involves developing an activity profile for the individuals performing different productive activities by asking an open-ended series of questions about the division of labour within the household. The second step overlaps with the first but places more focus on access to and control over resources (land, technology, labour, capital, etc.) and benefits (income, assets, etc.).

In each phase, planners are encouraged to ask questions about the impact of project components on women's time availability as well as on their access to and control over productive resources and benefits. If, for example, a project places new labour demands on adult women, planners are encouraged to ask about how that will impact on their existing productive and reproductive activities, their leisure time, and on the responsibilities of other household members. Might daughters, for example, be withdrawn from school in order to take over their mothers' reproductive responsibilities as a result of adult women's increased agricultural work burden? The emphasis on women's time constraints also figures prominently in the Development Planning Unit (DPU) framework, which is also based on the concept of gender roles. The gender roles framework thus provides important data on the distribution of roles and resources within the household.

The systematic enquiry into men's and women's activities attempts to overcome the ideologies and stereotypes that render invisible women's work. Armed with such information, planners and policy-makers are in a position to avoid some of the mistakes that resulted in project failures. While the attempt to differentiate activities and resources along gender lines thus goes a long way in meeting the need for a gender-sensitive planning methodology, the framework falls short in several respects, most of which stem from the way in which the gender division of labour is conceptualized. By treating the gender division of labour primarily as a relationship of separation, the gender roles framework tends to neglect its 'social connectedness'.

While the gender division of labour involves men and women undertaking different activities, it also entails an intricate and changing system of co-operation and exchange - one that is potentially conflictual. In fact, the allocation of responsibilities for household maintenance is as important a family process as the allocation of resources. Even in the sub-Saharan African context where women and men engage in a limited degree of independent farming, women's outputs have often been seen as a source of accumulation, as well as a buffer for fluctuations in men's incomes.

Moreover, while the management of responsibilities has tended to be gender-specific (e.g., men pay for children's school fees while women buy foodstuffs), specialization has never been complete. Rather, responsibilities tend to oscillate according to each sex's ability to cope with its own sphere, and its ability either to tap into the other or to shift the responsibilities. For example, where the revenues from men's cash crops have dropped, women have had to intensify their productive activities (e.g., beer brewing, trading) to assume many of men's traditional responsibilities.

Conversely, women's enhanced earning capacity very often means that they will end up making a more significant contribution to the household budget as men's contributions are re-directed to other uses (personal consumption, productive investment, etc.). By neglecting the concrete relations between men and women, the framework fails to raise questions about how change is brought about in men's and women's roles in production and in the division of responsibilities between them. The GRF makes a useful distinction between access to resources and control over them, directing the planner's attention to issues of power and control as an important aspect of gender relations. In so doing, it raises a question about development interventions which seek to direct resources to women (e.g., credit schemes): namely, will women be able to exercise any meaningful control over them? However, by restricting its analysis of power to tangible resources (e.g., land, credit, cash), the GRF gender analysis fails to highlight the role of 'intangible' resources-contacts, information, political clout-which also impact on power relations. Often women's extra-household relations-through informal associations or grassroots organizations that pursue empowerment-strengthen their authority over decisions that affect their lives (vis-à-vis their husbands, vis-à-vis employers). These 'intangible' resources are important to take into account if development interventions are to be informed by a full understanding of the factors contributing to gender inequalities in power.

The key assumption underpinning GRF is that women have not been able to benefit from 'development' because planning efforts have failed to recognize fully women's actual and potential contribution to the development process. Logically then, if planners' prejudices (or ignorance) are rectified and women are 'integrated' into development interventions, they-like men-can benefit from the process. GRF thus views development as a process that is inherently benign-one from which everyone can benefit. Moreover, according to GRF, if gender issues are correctly identified and incorporated within development interventions, then project effectiveness will increase; 'both economic growth and social justice call for increased attention to the integration of women into the development process'.

There are two main problems with this approach. First, the assumption that economic development has been generally beneficial, except for its negative impact on women, ignores the wealth of evidence documenting the polarizing outcomes of development interventions for men. The introduction of new technologies, for example, has often worked to the advantage of some groups-frequently those with assets and political clout-while alienating others from their sources of livelihood. Similarly, the intensification of commercial agriculture has often increased class differentiation; in many contexts the small farmers have been squeezed by rising input prices and land alienation. It is typically the more affluent social groups-those with secure access to land, irrigation water and marketing outlets as well as political contacts-who have been in a position to reap the benefits of growth.

A better recognition of these social processes would cast some doubt on GRF's optimistic assumption of the benefits of 'integration' for women. Linked to this first pitfall is the tendency of this framework to overlook the complex ways in which gender and class hierarchies cross-cut each other. GRF often assumes that women constitute a homogeneous category with shared interests which planners can easily identify and act upon. While there are a large number of issues on which women's interests may converge (e.g., child custody; sexual harassment), there are enough points of divergence to make the task of the planner using GRF a difficult one. There is in fact very little in the GRF literature which prepares the planner for such conflicts of interest.

A good example is the introduction of post-harvest rice milling technology in Bangladesh which eased the unpaid work burdens of female family members, but in so doing jeopardized one of the few employment opportunities open to women from landless households seeking wage labour. Finally, the above example points to another major oversight in GRF: the neglect of political factors underpinning policy-making. Will planners alter their policy priorities (e.g., curtail the spread of electric rice mills) if they have accurate information (e.g., that a significant number of poor, landless women are losing their only employment option)?

There is nothing in GRF to explain the political forces informing policy-making, since the entire policy process is explained as a rational, technical exercise executed by 'essentially benign and neutral agents'. Landless female labourers have very little political weight in most national contexts (even if they are organized, which they rarely are). It is thus very unlikely that they can exert enough pressure on policy-makers to shape policies in a way that meets their interests.

GRF: Institutional Scope

The analytical and conceptual focus of GRF is 'intra-household dynamics'-the gender division of labour and gender differences in access to and control over resources. Underpinning the understanding of the household is a bargaining model which offsets the bias towards concepts of a unitary household and male heads as sole decision-makers and sources of information.

While Cloud's more detailed formulation of the GRF framework makes reference to gender bias in land, capital, technology, and wage markets, these tend to be ad hoc or circular, as for example: Women's access to land is generally greater in systems of low population density; Women's lack of access to cash assets, which results from their role as unpaid family laborers and subsistence producers, when combined with constraints on their access to paid labor markets, limits their ability to invest in productivity-enhancing agricultural inputs.

In the context of wage labour markets, a brief reference is made to 'distinct male and female segments', but no explanation is offered as to how these distinct segments are created and maintained. Issues of power and control which were drawn upon to explain the intra-household inequalities do not seem to enter the domain of 'impersonal' markets. The attempt to tackle the issue of gender bias within markets lacks a clear analytical framework and conceptual underpinning. Similarly, GRF makes no attempt to understand the gendered nature of development institutions.

The planner is assumed to be a rational individual-'essentially benign and neutral'. Planning and policy-making institutions (governments, international agencies) remain outside the framework and no reference is made to the complex ways in which male bias has become institutionalized within these organizations. Nor is any emphasis placed on the need to change the working procedures and organizational goals and mandates of these institutions to make them more gender-egalitarian. The problem of male bias in policy-making is essentially one of error, lack of information, or short-sightedness. In short, the GRF framework offers no guidelines or analytical tools for extending the gender analysis from the household to other institutions. As a result, issues of gender bias and female subordination become almost synonymous with the household, while other institutions escape scrutiny.

GRF: Development Interventions

The gender roles framework is distinctly pitched at the project level. The attempt to put together this framework was in fact a direct response to project failures extensively documented in critical WID evaluations of development projects. The task that GRF set out to accomplish was to provide project staff with 'a new set of conceptual and analytical perspectives and skills in order to deal explicitly, effectively and efficiently with women-related issues in the spectrum of projects in which they become involved'.

One of the main weaknesses of the GRF, highlighted by development agencies that have used the framework, is its focus on community-based projects. According to CIDA, 'the insights and tools that GRF offered were difficult to adapt to the policy and program level'. While this may have been true, several analyses of gender and macro-economic policy have been developed using an understanding of gender very similar to the GRF approach.

In these models gender analysis is essentially about disaggregating existing macro-economic variables by gender: women, for example, specialize in non-tradables while men specialize in tradables (activities which are being prioritized under adjustment). The disaggregation is meant to highlight the way in which labour reallocation problems, caused by rigidities in gender roles, can constrain adjustment policies.

Organizations which have used the GRF methodology or have had training in the methodology include: USAID, CIDA, UNDP, IDRC and the World Bank. Illustrations of GRF can be found in the Kumarian Press handbooks, which draw on USAID-funded projects and have been used for training by USAID and other agencies: Gender Roles in Develop-ment Projects, and Working Together: Gender Analysis in Agriculture. Moreover, elements of GRF, such as its access and control profile, have been taken up by agencies which do not embrace the entire training framework. Organizations which have relied from the beginning on GRF, such as USAID and CIDA, have in recent years tried to expand the analytical scope of their training modules beyond the project, endeavouring to provide practitioners with tools that can facilitate gender analysis at the programme and policy levels.

As in the case of GRF, planning is seen as an essentially rational, top-down process; equipped with information (both quantitative and qualitative), planners (disembodied, rational agents) are in a better position to design and implement development interventions. In the case of USAID's Gender Analysis Tool Kit there is no mention of participatory methods of data gathering and development planning. USAID's Gender Analysis Tool Kit includes several tools that help practitioners analyze national-level quantitative data in order to identify 'relevant gender issues that have an impact on development goals'.

Gender analysis is essentially about disaggregating national data sets by gender (e.g., sex ratios, life expectancy, infant/child mortality), and analyzing their possible implications for economic growth, human resource development, population and health policies. Within this framework gender issues impact development goals in three ways:

a) to contradict one or more goals;
b) to act as a constraint on the achievement of one or more goals; or
c) to act as a catalyst to help achieve one or more goals.

For example, fertility reduction is identified as a primary goal. Thus national demographic and health surveys are analyzed (disaggregating average ideal family size of husband and wife, decision-making powers of husband and wife) in order to devise policies that can make family-planning strategies more effective. The emphasis on disaggregating data by gender parallels GRF's emphasis on disaggregating activities and access/control by gender. In both cases gender analysis is meant to facilitate the achievement of pre-determined development goals and priorities. In both cases gender issues become relevant to development if they are potentially affected by development interventions, or could act as either constraints or catalysts in the accomplishment of development goals.

The DPU Framework (Gender Planning)

The DPU Framework, so-called because it was developed by Carolyn Moser at the Department of Planning Unit at London University, is widely used within development institutions. While an analysis of women's triple roles constitutes its key analytical building block, any assessment also must include a consideration of its two other components: practical and strategic gender needs; and the schematization of policy approaches to women in the development context. The lack of an overarching conceptual/theoretical framework to integrate its different components renders the training module something akin to an eclectic 'tool kit' rather than a coherent framework.

Nevertheless, what gives the tool kit some unity is its political message: the need to use development interventions to transform unequal gender relations. The DPU Framework, like GRF, takes as its starting point the fact that roles are gender-differentiated. In order to highlight the multiple demands on women's time in low-income households, distinctions are made among women's productive, reproductive and community managing roles-hence, triple roles.

By using categories that are easy to understand and employ (if not analytically robust), Moser provides a useful mental grid that enables planners to include all that women do-even if the activity is 'invisible' because it is not valued in the market place (e.g., reproductive work) or because it is not culturally accepted (e.g., productive work). The framework's second major component is the distinction between practical and strategic gender needs. This distinction draws the attention of the practitioner to the transformatory potential of development planning.

Moser developed a 'triple roles' schema to draw planners' attention to the way in which the gender division of labour places a range of demands on women's time and impacts their ability to participate in planned interventions. The 'productive role' comprises market production and subsistence/home production, both of which generate an income (in cash or kind) and have an exchange value. The 'reproductive role' refers to the childbearing/rearing responsibilities and domestic tasks done by women that are required to reproduce and maintain the labour force. The 'community management role' involves women's activities at the community level, as an extension of their reproductive role, in order to ensure the provision and maintenance of collective consumption resources (e.g., water, health care, education). The triple roles schema claims to be more than a description of what men and women do. Deriving from an extensive literature and research on gender relations, the framework takes the view that the gender division of labour embodies and perpetuates women's subordination.

While women and men within the household engage in all three areas of activities (productive, reproductive and community management), the division of labour is rarely even. Although women are also involved in productive work, reproductive and community management work falls heavily on them because of their gender-ascribed roles. Whereas work carried out by men is valued, either directly or indirectly through paid remuneration, increased status or political power, women's community management and reproductive roles are not valued because they are seen as 'natural' and non-productive.

This means that a large part of women's work is made invisible, unrecognized by men in the community and by planners who are assigned the task of assessing women's needs. By providing a relatively simple schema which draws attention to multiple roles of women, the framework enables planners to understand that women's needs are often different from men's, and that meeting those needs may entail specific planning requirements. The triple roles schema goes beyond GRF's focus on the household to recognize the way in which many aspects of household survival and reproduction are located in the community. This is a particularly important and timely insight. With cutbacks in state provision for basic social services such as water and health, it is often women who take on the responsibility at the community level for the allocation of scarce resources to ensure household survival. It is often also women who put pressure on local or state institutions for the provision of infrastructure. However, by focusing on roles, the triple roles schema, like GRF, appears to be an imprecise tool for illuminating gender relations.

As regards productive and reproductive roles, the emphasis in the framework remains on what women do and what they produce (income and human resources). It is only with the definition of community roles that the framework begins to draw attention to 'intangible resources' (claims, status, authority) and the social relations through which such resources are produced (community rather than household based). Even so, as Kabeer points out, the triple role schema pays insufficient attention to 'the fact that most resources can be produced in a variety of institutional locations (households, markets, states and communities) so that the same resources may be produced through very different social relations'.

Practical Gender Needs and Strategic Gender Needs

Another important part of the DPU framework's conceptualization of gender is the distinction made between practical and strategic gender needs. According to Moser practical gender needs are those needs deriving from the concrete conditions women experience based on their position within the gender division of labour. Practical gender needs thus arise and are articulated by women themselves in response to some immediate perceived need, based on the existing gender division of labour, for such basic items as food, shelter, health care and water.

Such needs relate to women's triple roles in that they arise out of the multiple roles assigned to women through the gender division of labour (food provisioning, child care, community management of basic services, etc.). In contrast, strategic gender needs refer to those needs deriving from an analysis of women's subordination to men and the formulation of an alternative, more equal organization of society. Examples include: abolition of the sexual division of labour, establishment of political and economic equality, freedom of choice over childbearing, an end to male violence against women, etc. As Moser points out, meeting women's practical gender needs may help to lessen the burdens on women deriving from their triple roles, but it does not challenge the gender division of labour.

Because planners identify and respond primarily to practical gender needs, they are often responsible for preserving and reinforcing existing gender inequalities. The distinction between practical and strategic needs can help planners to think about more challenging interventions. For example, whereas the provision of dressmaking training can meet a practical gender need for employment, training women in areas traditionally identified as 'men's work' can help to break down existing occupational segregation, a strategic gender need. While this conceptualization of practical and strategic gender needs moves beyond the GRF in suggesting possibilities for a more transformatory planning agenda, it nevertheless tends to downplay the conflictual aspect of gender relations. Men, too, have practical and strategic gender needs, often opposed to those of women, which may account for male resistance to transformatory efforts. As noted below, such concerns have been incorporated into some of the training packages built around the DPU approach.

View of Development

It is difficult to categorize the way in which the DPU framework views development, since it seems to draw neither on a liberal reading of society and economy-as does the gender roles framework-nor on a structuralist understanding of social processes and social change-as in the social relations framework. However, a number of assumptions seem to be implicit in the DPU framework, which suggest a 'populist' and eclectic approach to development. These are:

— growth fails to 'trickle down' to the poor; in the name of 'efficiency', structural adjustment policies have imposed severe social costs on the poor
— 'poor' and 'low-income' households are those development should serve
— the reproductive economy plays a major role in achieving human well-being
— bottom-up and participatory planning are beneficial to development interventions.

There is no discussion of rules, resources, practices and hierarchies of command and control that constitute households, markets and development agencies as social institutions through which social inequalities are constructed and reproduced. The discussions of poverty and subordination are thus somewhat 'abstracted' from the institutional contexts in which they take place. To some extent, as critics have pointed out, the framework's failure to provide an understanding of the social processes through which women experience subordination and poverty can be attributed to the framework's preoccupation with roles (as opposed to social relations).

Similarly, the framework's attempt to differentiate social groups seems to lack analytical rigour.

The category 'low-income households'-identified as the target group for development interventions-is not well-defined. The emphasis on 'income' as the criteria for identifying the poor suggests a conventional market approach to poverty, which contains both measurement and institutional biases. Yet, the criticism of structural adjustment policies (that they shift costs from the paid to the unpaid economy) suggests an awareness of the limitations of market-led growth. Finally, the emphasis on 'women in low-income households' also reflects continuing gender bias; as feminist scholarship has pointed out, women's well-being cannot be easily read off the overall status of the households to which they belong.

Institutional Scope

The focus of this framework is at the household, and to some extent, the community level, with little analysis of the institutions through which gender disadvantage is perpetuated. The discussion of strategic gender needs within state institutions is limited to pointing out that the state has failed to meet women's strategic gender interests: no analysis of the gendered nature of the state is developed. Similarly, while the recognition that gender power relations impact on how development institutions operate is implicit in the DPU framework, there is no attempt to analyze the gendered nature of development institutions themselves.

The description of the different policy approaches to women (welfare, equity, anti-poverty, efficiency and empowerment), however, draws attention to the fact that different types of policies have appealed to different types of institutions, a point that other analyses have explored further. These gaps can be attributed in part to the conceptualization of the DPU framework. According to Moser, its basis is gender planning, rather than gender analysis. Methodological tools are constructed around the language and procedures of planners. Despite the assertion that the success of gender planning depends on the participation of organized women's groups, the framework says little about how planning processes can be made more participatory or how a process of 'negotiated debate' can be initiated. Overall, the focus remains on 'top-down' interventions, albeit more gender-responsive.

More recently, however, efforts have been made to translate DPU's commitment to participatory gender planning into diagnostic and operational tools. The aim is to help ensure that a cross-section of community groups or 'political constituencies' is represented in the formulation, implementation and evaluation of policies, programmes and projects. Unlike some of the training approaches based upon it, the DPU framework distinguishes among the 'professional', the 'personal' and the 'political', describing gender planning training as a 'professional' activity. It focuses on gender training as a means to acquire 'technical skills' needed to improve professional competence.

Overall, the approach and language are designed to diffuse hostility of those who find 'feminism' an unacceptable encroachment on 'objective' planning processes (the framework's focus on 'low-income' women can also be seen in this light). But through the different tools, particularly the distinction between practical and strategic gen der needs, the framework also hopes to initiate a re-examination of 'personal' as well as 'political' positions on the issue of women's subordination.

Development Interventions

Like the GRF, the DPU framework focuses primarily on project level interventions; however, it goes beyond the GRF in looking at sectoral level interventions as well. Through the case study method, for example, the DPU framework demonstrates that by collecting data on the basis of the triple role schema and distinguishing between practical gender needs and strategic gender needs, it is possible to identify the planning needs of women in various sectors, including transport, employment and training, and housing.

Applications

The DPU methodology has been used by the African Technical Department of the World Bank, Christian Aid, Oxfam UK; ODA, NORAD, FAO, ILO, UNIFEM, Sida and CUSO. Two examples of adapting the framework to meet the needs of specific organizations are the Oxfam Gender Training Manual and Gender Training Analysis, by Save the Children, America.

The Oxfam Gender Training Manual. Like many of the training packages developed in recent years, the Oxfam Gender

Training Manual is eclectic, combining a range of training approaches. Although essentially an adaptation of the DPU gender-planning methodology, it contains a number of distinctive features. The discussion of practical and strategic gender needs raises questions about the gender needs and interest of men: Is it in their strategic interests to maintain the status quo and their position of dominance? Or is it more strategic to work for a more egalitarian society, for the empowerment of women, for more balanced relationships, etc.?

Such questions help to draw attention to gender conflict (as well as co-operation) and to the need for changing attitudes at the personal level. In fact, the structure of the handbook moves from 'gender awareness and self-awareness' activities designed to promote a re-thinking of personal attitudes and behaviour to activities designed to improve planners' professional analytical skills in project formulation and monitoring.

The Oxfam approach seeks to concretize the goal of 'participatory', 'bottom-up' development. Examples and case studies are drawn from the range of development and humanitarian relief activities in which the organization and its affiliates participate. Its audience is seen as non-governmental organizations (NGOs) and grassroots organizations, which also impacts on its methodology. Thus the manual emphasizes participation in project formulation and monitoring. Analyses of data-collection methods, such as Participatory Research Analysis (PRA), stress that data gathering must be gender-sensitive to be truly participatory.

Similarly, a component on working with men and women is designed primarily to help NGOs facilitate women's involvement in needs assessment at the grassroots level. Implicit in the activities is an understanding of gender power relations which make it difficult for women to articulate their needs.

Gender Relations Analysis, Save the Children, America. The Gender Relations Analysis Guide also emphasizes the 'personal' and the importance of challenging attitudes and stereotypes about gender differences held by decision-makers within organizations. The main objective appears to be overall gender awareness sensitization. The concept of women's triple roles and the distinction between practical and strategic needs are seen as tools to collect gender-disaggregated data and to develop more gender-sensitive projects.

Although the training model does not assume a project context, and takes as one of its guiding principles the goal of the equal capacity of women and men to influence and change current economic, political and social norms, the gender-sensitization activities in the training package provide few tools to understand how gender inequalities are constituted and reproduced within institutions beyond the household and community levels.

Added to the Gender Relations Analysis is a component on the conceptualization of power. Following CIDA's four-fold classification of power, the aim to is move from an understanding of power as a zero-sum game to non-conflictual understandings, including power to (empowerment at the individual level), power with (collective use of power), and power within (internal strength). Yet unlike the Oxfam manual, the package makes no reference to the hostility and resistance (from both men and women) likely to be encountered in challenging existing gender roles and relations.

The training provides guidelines on evaluating projects to promote men's and women's knowledge and capacity to negotiate for rights and to change existing decision-making patterns, but there is no mention of how beneficiaries can be brought into the project formulation process and how that process can be made more participatory, nor does there appear to be provision for advocacy training for grassroots women and men. The objective is to enable technical and management practitioners to identify the needs of beneficiaries.

Social Relations Framework

The social relations framework (SRF) describes an analytical approach developed at the Institute for Development Studies, Sussex (UK), derived from social relations analysis. Many of its assumptions appear to have come out of the Subordination of Women (SOW) Workshop in the mid-1970s, which criticized the Women in Development (WID) approach on several grounds: rooted in liberal individualism it tended to isolate women as a separate and often homogeneous category, it was 'predominantly descriptive', as well as 'equivocal in its identification and analysis of women's subordination'. The SOW Workshop set out an alternative approach, informed by a Marxist analysis of social change (without succumbing to the structural determinism of many Marxist accounts) and a feminist analysis of patriarchy. Its work on the social relations of gender, along with the scholarship and practice of feminists from developing and developed countries, provided the conceptual framework for what is often referred to as the Gender and Development (GAD) approach. The social relations framework is constructed around many of the insights of this work. It takes into account both the relations of production and the interrelated range of relations through which human needs are met, 'the social relations of everyday life'.

This ensemble of relations governs the processes of production, reproduction, distribution and consumption, and operates through a broad range of institutions: the household, the community, the market and the state. Gender relations refer specifically to those dimensions of social relations that create and reproduce differences in the positioning of men and women in social processes. In this perspective, gender is always intertwined with other social relations: gender, class, ethnicity, age, religion, caste, etc. cross-cut one another. Thus 'a gender analysis must be embedded within a broader social-relations framework'. This means that in any given context, different axes of inequality assume different levels of analytical importance. Not only must similarities and differences among women be taken into consideration; in some contexts gender may not be the key factor of analysis.

SRF: Conceptualization of Gender

By drawing attention to the range of social processes and institutions through which social inequalities are constructed and reproduced, the SRF avoids 'abstracting' women from the institutional contexts in which they experience their lives. From the perspective of the SRF, the rules, resources, practices and hierarchies of command and control of any institution must be analyzed in order to uncover how gender is constituted as a relationship of inequality within it. Like the gender roles framework, such an analysis highlights gender-differentiated roles and responsibilities as well as gender divisions in access to and control over resources.

However, several assumptions distinguish the SRF from the gender roles framework. First, whereas the gender roles framework conceptualizes the gender division of labour as essentially a form of social separation (assigning women and men different roles and responsibilities), the SRF sees the gender division of labour as a form of social connection, making it essential for women and men to engage in relationships of co-operation and exchange. This interdependence is not, however, symmetrical. The unequal division of resources and responsibilities means that gender relations involve conflict as well as co-operation.

Second, and related to the first, because conventional economic planning considers primarily individualized production and material resources, it undervalues the more fluid social or 'relational' resources such as rights, obligations and claims.

The 'moral economy' often involves relationships that entail loss of status and autonomy in exchange for some measure of security. For women, the gender relations of family and kinship frequently embody a trade-off between security and autonomy.

Within the SRF, then, culturally constructed rules about the different capacities and aptitudes of men and women not only determine gender differentiated roles and responsibilities, they also underpin their differentiated claims, rights and obligations. In order to understand women's economic decision-making patterns and their use of labour time, it is necessary to determine how women perceive their interests and to consider how these relate to their position within the family and the household-insights that cannot be read off a disaggregation of the gender division of roles. Where resources are directed to women, for example, an effort must be made to consider whether, in subverting existing gender relations, targeted interventions will ultimately enhance women's status or, by undermining certain familial or community rights to which they were traditionally entitled, place them in a more vulnerable position.

This view implies potential for transformation where those with a stake in change are prepared to challenge existing gender relations. Thus, in addition to supporting the view that information about existing gender roles and relations is an important prerequisite for gender-aware policy and planning, proponents of the SRF take a normative view of the need to change existing gender relations.

SRF: View of Development

Analyses put forward by the SOW in the 1970s provide a framework for understanding the view of development which is implicit in the SRF. Unlike WID scholarship, which characterized women as being left out of thedevelopment process, according to members of the SOW 'it is precisely the relati ons through which women are "integrated" into the development process which need to be problematized and investigated'.

In other words, this approach challenged the benign, universalistic, vision of development inherent in the WID approach and attempted to locate gender relations and women's subordination within the processes unleashed by market-led development.

Through a structuralist analysis of class and gender relations, attention was drawn to the highly varied, and often polarizing, implications of development, especially in the context of the spread of the global market economy. For example, building on a Marxist analysis of women's position as a reserve army of labour, such an approach pointed to the exploitative nature of the new international division of labour, whereby women in developing countries were being recruited into multinational factories as cheap, docile workers.

The analysis also highlighted the role women's unpaid work played in underpinning market-led development (through the production and maintenance of human life), despite the failure of traditional economic approaches to value reproductive work. In its view of development, SRF thus problematizes both the narrow focus on economic growth and the hierarchy of production over reproduction within mainstream development discourse.

The framework takes the final goal of development to be the achievement of human well-being, which is taken to encompass certain basic goals: survival, security and autonomy. From this perspective, production is defined as encompassing all activities that produce the means by which these final goals are met, including the reproduction and care of human beings. The redistributive implications (in terms of power and resources) of achieving the final goal of development (defined as human well-being), and the likelihood of resistance to redistributive policies, are also made explicit in this approach.

The logic of the framework entails a shift in terrain from the primarily technical concerns of policy makers and planners to the political arena per se. The centrality of the power dimension of gender relations brings the importance of women's 'empowerment' to the forefront. From this perspective development interventions need to be designed in ways that have transformatory potential, in other words, that help build up the enabling infrastructures necessary for the process of women's self-empowerment. One example given in this context is the provision of space, resources and time to allow women to articulate their own interests (through social action groups and grassroots movements) rather than having them identified and met on their behalf by planners.

Much of this hinges on the openness of development institutions to the 'bottom-up' flow of information (participatory planning) and their receptivity to transformative ideas about gender-again raising the issue of institutional change implicit in the SRF. It should be noted, however, that the SRF also seems to reflect a certain 'agnosticism' about the market.

The implication is that there is a need to evaluate the market both from the point of view of the possibilities and problems it raises for women, particularly for different groups of women-insights that a social relations analysis can help to illuminate. A case in point concerns interpretations of women's employment in export-oriented industries. While much feminist scholarship has focused on the exploitative nature of women's employment in export industries (in terms of wage discrimination, labour relations, working conditions, not to mention factors accounting for women's entry into wage labour), a recent study of the impact of women's wages on intra-household power relations in urban Bangladesh offers some interesting findings on the empowering potential of waged employment for young women garment workers, enabling them to renegotiate the terms ofunsatisfactory relationships or to walk out of, or not enter into, relationships which undermine their agency.

SRF: Institutional Scope

In the SRF perspective, 'gender-awareness in policy and planning requires a prior analysis of the social relations of production within relevant institutions of family, market, state and community in order to understand how gender and other inequalities are created and reproduced through their separate and combined interactions'. Since power relations between men and women are conceptualized as the product of institutional practice, the SRF takes the position that overcoming gender-based inequalities involves institutional transformation at all these levels.

To take the example of credit programmes, an analysis of gender relations within different institutional contexts would show how supposedly gender-neutral policies of state and financial institutions, through collateral requirements and the need for literacy and time to understand complicated loan procedures, etc., make it difficult for poor women to get access to credit. Where institutional practice is changed to give women access to resources, a social relations approach would point to the complicated dynamics of control when women borrowers bring credit into the household: even where they are unable to retain control over resources allocated to them, there may be more indirect gains to their status and autonomy by virtue of their newly acquired loans.

Another salient feature of the SRF institutional focus is that development agencies are seen as implicated in the reproduction of gender and other social inequalities. Thus, not only do policy-makers need to be 'conscientized' to critical dimensions of gender relations and interests, but more importantly, unless women empower themselves to identify and establish their gender needs and interests as legitimate policy concerns within the bureaucratic planning process, these concerns are unlikely to be met. Again, this reflects the view that planning is a political as well as a technical process.

SRF: Development Interventions

The social relations framework suggests that all planning, from macro-economic policy to micro-level interventions, must be informed by an understanding of the social relations through which production is organized and human needs are met. As a planning tool, the SRF provides no 'quick fixes' for overcoming gender inequality, nor much guidance on the specific types of interventions that would promote gender equity. What it does provide is a framework for a sensitive reading of the intricate social relations through which women and men live their lives, the insights of which can aid development planners in tailoring interventions more appropriately.

SRF: Applications

The social relations framework refers to a training approach developed by researchers and trainers at the Institute for Development Studies, the main features of which have been described in Kabeer and Kabeer and Subrahmanian Elements of the social relations framework have also been picked up by CIDA in its Gender and Development Briefing Module.

While this analytical framework attempts to assist planners in developing policy interventions, it is a much more complex framework than training methodologies that focus primarily on data disaggregation or checklists of activities. Although a seven-point 'gender audit for development interventions' has been developed, presumably to be used at all levels of development interventions (from the macro to the micro), the audit itself is a good example of the challenge of capturing the analytical complexities of social relations analysis in a checklist: many of the questions parallel those that are used in the GRF and the DPU approach.

Feminist Economics: Taking Gender Analysis to the Macro-Economic Level

The body of work commonly referred to as 'feminist economics' is only just beginning to emerge and define itself as a discipline within economics. Some of those who define themselves as feminist economists, such as Ingrid Palmer, work within the neo-classical paradigm, while others, such as Diane Elson and Nancy Folbre, draw on a variety of critical approaches (structuralist, Marxist and political economy) which challenge the neo-classical perspective.

Neo-Classical Feminist Economics: Gender and Adjustment

The literature examined here is drawn from economic analyses of adjustment and gender. The novelty of this genre lies in the way it conceptualizes gender using neo-classical tools of analysis (factor market rigidities, informational biases, market distortions), juxtaposed against an appreciation of intra-household inequalities and bargaining (similar to the GRF). More significantly, the analysis of gender relations is systematically linked to the design of structural adjustment programmes. Rather than a focus on how structural adjustment programmes have affected the welfare of women and children, their concern is to show how gender biases and rigidities affect adjustment policies, and can ultimately frustrate them. 'Gender analysis' is thereby taken well beyond the project focus of the GRF and into the realm of macro-economic policy-making.

Gender and Adjustment: the Models

What is the main argument here? Adjustment, neo-classical economists would agree, is essentially about inducing the inter-sectoral flow of resources (especially labour and credit) from non-tradables to tradables in order to alter what are seen as original misallocations of resources between sectors. If resources, however, are not mobile between sectors, raising prices of tradables is not likely to bring about the desired flow ('supply response'). Palmer and Collier point out that resources (especially female labour) may be allocated between sectors in a skewed and inefficient manner due to various constraints which arise from gender roles and inequitable gender relations.

The same constraints, they add, may reduce the mobility of resources between sectors, and leave them 'stuck' in the production of non-tradables, thereby reducing the desired supply response. Collier locates four distinct processes, based on underlying 'social conventions', that account for why women face differential constraints upon economic activity. The first is discrimination outside the household-in labour and credit markets. The second is that role models (in production) are gender-specific, i.e., girls copy women, while boys copy men. If a new economic opportunity is initially taken up by men, therefore, it may be diffused over the male population by a mechanism that will not transmit it to the female population.

The third is that within the household rights and obligations between husband and wife are asymmetric, such that women have little incentive to increase their labour input. The final element is the 'burden of reproduction', with its attendant demands on women's health and time. Palmer identifies similar processes, although intra-household markets and bargaining are more prominent in her analysis, while 'role copying' is largely absent.

Within households, she argues, at least in the African context, there are markets - albeit rigged ones. The social aspects of gender impose their own definitions of correct exchange, which tend to reflect bargaining power and status, and inevitably mean that the terms of trade are biased against women. This can be described as an asymmetry of obligations and responsibilities between women and men. What are the implications for public policy? According to Collier, if private sector labour and credit markets and private processes of information dissemination all make it likely that women will be less mobile than men, existing public mechanisms should have an offsetting bias.

If these rigidities could be overcome through public interventions (e.g., by redressing the male bias in financial markets, in education and in extension services, and re-targeting payments made by public marketing channels), women would be able to participate more fully in the production of tradables, the booming sector under structural adjustment. This would reduce gender inequity, as well as reducing economic stagnation-hence the convergence between gender equity and economic efficiency. Palmer also recommends legislative and institutional reform of the public sector in the short to medium term.

But she takes the efficiency argument a step further and questions the presumed efficiency of the smallholder that underpins adjustment policy support for the 'small farm' (via land titling and agricultural services). If male small-holders were to hire female labour, she asserts, their presumed superior efficiency would become questionable. Thus, encouraging alternative rural employment for women (e.g., in plantations) can be a desirable means of freeing their labour from family production where it is used lavishly, and of forcing a proper costing of labour on the family farm manager. Palmer's recommendations for achieving long-term dynamic efficiency also include opening up the non-biological elements of women's reproductive labour to market forces ('a calculus of costs'): 'tap water and electrification of homes means a paid workforce in public utilities. Creches mean professional, paid child-minders'. This, she argues, would not only reduce the amount of unpaid work women have to do, but would also increase efficiency in the reproduction of human capital.

Gender and Adjustment: Conceptualization of Gender

Gender and adjustment models share a number of key assumptions with the GRF in terms of their understanding of gender.

— In both, an important aspect of gender analysis involves looking at what men and women do-gender-differentiated roles. Collier's model combines the disaggregation of agents by gender with a sectoral disaggregation of activities-between tradables and non-tradables-which is critical to structural adjustment.

— There is a clear recognition in both that women's 'burden' of reproductive work acts as a constraint on their ability to engage in productive activities. The gender and adjustment literature, like the GRF, highlights constraints on women's time as an important factor that planners/policy-makers need to take into account if they want to achieve their desired policy objectives. As noted below, feminist economics offers quite a different interpretation of reproductive work.

— Both models highlight intra-household gender differences in access to and control over resources and income. In both, these differences are the basis for analyzing the incentives and constraints under which men and women work; women, for example, may withhold labour from their husbands' agricultural enterprises because they have no access to the proceeds.

— Both GRF and the gender and adjustment literature attempt to theorize gender using economic tools of analysis: bargaining models are used to explain the processes of intra-household decision-making for labour and resource allocation. The recognition of bargaining and conflict within the household, in particular, goes a long way in meeting the feminist demand that power relations be explicitly recognized in analyses of gender.

What Important Gender Issues Are Left Out?

Gender and adjustment models share a number of problems in the way gender is conceptualized.

— Collier's emphasis on role copying as an explanation of gender segmentation in the labour market (and the gender division of labour more generally) is problematic. Calling segmentation a voluntary process (girls copy women, boys copy men) provides a misleading picture of how these gender-differentiated roles (and segments of the labour market) are created and maintained; there is no mention, for example, of the ways in which the more powerful agents construct and maintain theboundaries between male and female sectors-sometimes using brute force.

— Similarly, by explaining gender asymmetries in rights and obligations in terms of 'social convention' the model provides an extremely static picture. These asymmetries are not simply given by society, as the term 'social convention' seems to imply. They are in fact constantly created and re-created through the everyday relations between men and women; they are actively mobilized by those with power against those without power.

Women's obligation to use their incomes/savings to feed the family in some social settings is not just a social given. It is through conjugal conflicts underpinned by power asymmetries that the more powerful household members (adult men) are able to shift these responsibilities onto women while they maintain personal control over other income flows.

Gender and Adjustment: View of Development

In general, according to this literature the policy agenda being promoted through structural adjustment programmes is inherently benign-one from which everyone can benefit. In other words, markets are a reliable means of mobilizing resources for production, and (implicitly) an effective means of meeting needs. In this regard, the approach adopted is, to use Jahan's terminology, 'integrationist'. There are obvious problems with this approach. One of the main shortcomings of Collier's work is that it does not explicitly deal with the non-monetized, reproductive sphere, i.e., the social and material processes through which the human population is maintained and renewed on a daily and inter-generational basis.

Reproductive work enters the equation only insofar as it constrains women's ability to contribute labour to the production of tradables. It therefore goes along with conventional macro-economic analyses which ignore the un-monetized sphere of human reproduction. In much of feminist macro-economics, by contrast, social reproduction is seen as a necessary activity which underpins both the production of tradables and the promotion of human well-being. The export sector is not always booming, as the adjustment literature seems to assume. Low returns to export crops often persist despite adjustment measures because of rising input prices, credit shortages and falling international prices. For example, the cocoa boom in Nigeria and Ghana burst long ago with the collapse of international prices, environmental problems and rising input costs.

Moreover, expansion of traditional exports has limitations from a long-term price perspective. Many researchers and agencies such as UNICEF and UNCTAD believe that the fall in commodity prices in the 1980s was partly linked to the expansion in agricultural output that accompanied the introduction of the new incentive structure.

Gender and Adjustment: Institutional Scope. Gender analysis is focused at the household level (using bargaining models); while there are references to gender bias within markets, the literature does not provide a robust analytical framework for understanding the gender hierarchies within markets. Other institutions (states, development agencies) escape gender scrutiny entirely.

Households. The Gender and Adjustment literature (especially Palmer's work) draws heavily on anthropological/feminist writings which look at intra-household dynamics. The model of the household that informs Palmer's and Collier's work is not a single unit with a joint utility function. Rather, like the GRF, it rests on an analysis of gender relations that includes ge nder asymmetries in rights (e.g., access to crop revenues) and obligations (e.g., labour exchanges between husband and wife). Nor is the 'burden' of reproduction equally shared between husband and wife (although for Collier, this does not seem to pose a problem in itself; it is a 'constraint' only insofar as it impedes women's ability to engage in production of tradables).

Markets. When it comes to middle-level market institutions, the Gender and Adjustment model is less analytical and more descriptive. Collier, for example, refers to gender bias in credit and land markets, but offers no analysis (or models) for understanding how these biases are created and maintained, beyond the observation that 'role copying' plays a critical role in creating male and female segments within the labour market. The conceptualization of markets is one of the main problems in Palmer's work, too. While her critique of gender discrimination within private credit markets, for example, appears to describe how 'real' credit markets operate, some of her policy recommendations are clearly framed in the realm of 'abstract' markets (i.e., idealized models), as for example her endorsement of large-scale commercial agriculture.

The solution to the under-valuation of women's labour in small-holder agriculture, in this analysis, is to encourage female employment in the large-scale commercial sector since it would provide a 'proper costing' of their labour. This, however, ignores the fact, pointed out by feminist critical economics, that definitions of labour (female, migrant, skilled, etc.) are built into the way markets operate. Thus even though a female labourer does not work on a commercial estate in her capacity as 'wife', her labour is still defined as 'female', thereby carrying her subordinate status with her into the workplace. While gender hierarchies can be challenged via political action, the assumption that markets can automatically provide a 'proper costing' of female labour ignores the need for public action to regulate them.

Development Agencies. Finally, a rather benign view of 'public policy' and development agencies is implicit in these models. Both Palmer and Collier rely on public policy to off-set biases in the private sector (households, markets), failing to consider that these public agencies themselves tend to institutionalize the power asymmetries attached to gender difference, and are poor instruments for implementing gender policies. The framing of adjustment as a case of 'misguided policies' (i.e., policy-makers working with the wrong conceptual guides) and the excessive reliance on top-down planning to 'set things right' ignores the fact that policy-making institutions are themselves 'gendered' and that they often respond to political pressures.

Gender and Adjustment: Development Interventions. Despite their shortcomings, the Gender and Adjustment models represent an innovative departure in the literature on women and development. They provide a systematic way of thinking about gender using economic tools of analysis, as well as a way of assessing the impact of gender differences on macro-economic concerns. The policy implications are therefore pitched at the macro-economic level, which opens up a new level of development practice to gender scrutiny.

Gender and Adjustment: Applications. While it is perhaps too soon to look for applications of the gender and adjustment literature, given its relative recent appearance, a number of embryonic efforts are currently being made-primarily in the form of 'technical notes' and 'advisory notes'- to bring this type of gender analysis into the realm of policy-making.

The obvious example of such efforts is the Africa Department of the World Bank's Paradigm Postponed: Gender and Adjustment in Sub-Saharan Africa. Adopting elements of Palmer's and Collier's approaches, the study draws attention to the major gender biases instructural adjustment packages-biases that result from the invisibility of women's work; from asymmetrical rights and obligations between men and women defined by the gender division of labour; and from the linkages between the paid and the unpaid economic sectors.

The study does not contest the benefits of market-led growth-the policy goal which adjustment is meant to facilitate-but highlights the gender biases that need to be removed if structural adjustment policies are to achieve their intended goals (supply response in the tradable sector). While not yet adopted as official World Bank policy, the study has been used by gender advocates in their discussions with mainstream economists in the institution.

Feminist Critical Economics. Although feminist critical economics is becoming more familiar to policy-making institutions, it has not yet been translated into a discrete gender-training framework. Since it provides a number of useful analytical tools which policy-makers can use for gender analysis at the programme and policy levels, we summarize some of its main analytical threads and examine points of convergence and divergence with neoclassical approaches. The neo-classical paradigm is criticized for its male bias at the micro-, meso- and macro-levels, which it treats as fully integrated: the macro-level views the economy in terms of total marketed output and total expenditure; these monetary aggregates are the coherent result of the activities of millions of individuals (at the micro-level) integrated by the institutions of the meso level (markets, firms).

While male bias at the meso- and macro-level arise from omitting gender, at the micro-level male bias is rooted in the way gender is conceptualized.

The micro-level. A central premise of neo-classical economics is its characterization of individuals as utility maximizers with well-defined choice sets and preference orderings. Differences and inequalities between males and females can be accommodated as long as they can be conceptualized as a matter of differences in preference and resource endowments.

Thus differences in women's and men's labour allocations (where women allocate more time to housework and less time to the wage labour market) are explained in terms of the lower returns to women's labour market activities and their 'preference' for housework.

Similarly, inequalities between men's and women's leisure time and access to food and medical care are explained in voluntary terms-differing preferences and women's greater taste for altruism. There is no space in this model for conflict, power and preferences that are socially-constructed rather than exogenously given-'the socially entrenched asymmetries in rules and resources that enable some categories of individuals to constrain and shape the options and actions of others'.

The meso-level. Gender bias at the meso- and macro-levels takes on a different form: since the meso-level structures (markets, firms) and monetary aggregates (GNP, exports, etc.) are not seen as 'male' or 'female', gender analysis is considered to be irrelevant.

This in fact is a premise that neo-classical economics shares with critical economic approaches (e.g., structuralist approaches). Looking at the meso-level institutions first, neo-classical economics sees markets as essentially gender-neutral and ultimately empowering for women.

Markets can become contaminated with male bias as a result of extraneous factors such as prejudice. In the labour market, for example, neo-classical economics does admit the possibility that 'pure' discrimination might exist-as an irrational 'taste' on the part of employers-but sees it as self-correcting within the logic of markets and so offers no guidelines for its eradication.

Feminist critical economics starts from the understanding that market institutions are not 'intrinsically gendered' in the way that family and marriage are, but nevertheless become 'bearers of gender'; gender relations shape the relations between men and women as they engage in market transactions.

In other words, while commercial relations between buyers and sellers, or employers and employees, are not intrinsically gendered in the way that conjugal and kinship relations are, the social positionings of employer and employee, or buyer and seller, vis-à-vis each other are conditioned by gender hierarchies and norms. Even though a female labourer does not work in a commercial estate or factory as 'wife' (in the way that she does on her husband's farm), her labour is defined as 'female', thereby carrying her subordinate status with her into the workplace.

The literature on female employment both in the commercial agricultural sector and in industrial establishments demonstrates how social norms about 'femininity', 'women's work' and 'wifely dependence' operate within these so-called impersonal markets to create separate male and female spheres and distinct gender hierarchies.

Similarly, even if women entrepreneurs enjoy the same access to capital and technical skills as their male counterparts, they may still face a disadvantage in the market place due to their exclusion from the business-social networks through which vital information is exchanged and 'good will' is built.

The macro-level. Macro-economics is concerned with monetary aggregates, the output of human effort that money can mobilize which gets counted in the gross national product, in savings and investments, in exports and imports and in public expenditure and public revenue.

Absent from this picture is the entire area of production referred to as the 'reproductive economy'-the unpaid production of human resources-which underpins the paid economy and is in turn dependent on it. It is now widely appreciated that the failure to take account of the unpaid reproductive labour of child care, housework and care for other adults both in measuring the level of aggregate output (GNP calculations, for example) and in analyzing the determinants of aggregate output renders much of women's work invisible.

'Male bias' at the macro-level thus stems from the way the macro-economy is conceptualized, and the activities and values that are left out. But this omission is not simply due to complexities of measurement; it also reflects some assumptions built into the model, with serious implications for the formulation of macro-economic policies.

One of the most dangerous assumptions that is implicit within the neo-classical view of the macro-economy is that the reproductive economy will continue to function irrespective of the changes in the rest of the economy. In other words, it is assumed that women will continue to supply all the labour needed to ensure the satisfactory reproduction of human beings, compensating for all the shortfalls in purchased inputs required to sustain human resources.

If, for example, public sector investment in infrastructure is cut, causing deterioration in rural water supplies, the assumption is that the members of the household (usually women) will undertake the arduous work of carrying water from distant bore holes to their homes in order to ensure that the needs of their households are met. Or if wages are reduced, the assumption is that the household (again, mainly women) will produce some of the products and services that were previously purchased (health care, repairing clothes) to compensate for the shortfall in cash resources available to the household. Feminist economists have argued that women's labour is not infinitely elastic; the breaking point might be reached where the household is no longer able to reproduce itself, with serious implications for the paid economy. If daughters are withdrawn from school to help with the reproductive work of their mothers, or if women are unable to contribute labour to their paid activities because of the urgent need to attend sick children, this is likely to have a negative affect on the balance of payments-through shortfalls in human skills and through the diversion of public resources to the tasks of policing and repairing the damaged fabric of society.

The key issue at the macro level is thus the interdependence between the output that macro analysis does take into account-marketed output-and the output that macro analysis does not take into account-the unmarketed services that are critical for human resources production.

This is a gender issue because responsibility for coping with this interdependence is socially constructed as women's much more than men's. The male bias in macro theory results from ignoring this gendered interdependence, with outcomes that are biased against women, and detrimental to development.

Feminist Critical Economics: Conceptualization of Gender. Feminist economics challenges the conceptualization of the gender division of labour in neo-classical micro-economics, particularly 'new household economics', as the outcome of free choices of economic agents specializing according to their innate comparative advantage. From the neo-classical perspective, gender differentiation is depicted as generally rational, efficient, and mutually advantageous to men and women, with women undertaking unpaid domestic labour because of their preferences and skills.

The neo-classical perspective does not attempt to explain how such skill differentiation comes about. Like the Social Relations Framework, feminist economics seeks to move beyond a gender disaggregation of roles and activities to emphasize the power relations underpinning the gender division of labour. Questions are asked about how social institu- tions and norms shape or constrain individual 'choices' in ways that perpetuate gender inequalities. A bargaining model of the household draws attention to the household as a site of 'co-operation' and 'conflict': women and men may co-operate to increase the household capabilities as a whole, but there is likely to be conflict over the control and allocation of resources, with women in a weaker bargaining position vis-à-vis men. For feminist economics, then, gender differentiation derives from structural inequalities rather than free choices of economic agents: 'it may be seen as the profoundly unequal accommodation reached between individuals who occupy very different social positions with very different degrees of social power'.

Feminist Critical Economics: Institutional Scope. As noted, feminist critical economics applies a gender analysis across a range of institutional contexts (households, communities, markets and states). Its approach to gender analysis of economics at the micro-, meso- and macro-level is particularly useful. Its analysis of how markets act as 'bearers of gender' helps to illuminate women's disadvantaged position in market transactions. The conceptualization of the interdependence between the productive and the reproductive economy (and the male bias in measuring aggregate outputs which renders women's work invisible), is a major contribution to the effort to take gender analysis to the macro-level.

Bibliography

Arjun Appadurai, Frank J. Korom & Margarent A. Mills, (eds.), *Gender, Genre and Power in South Asia,* Philadelphia: Univ. of Pensylvania Press.

Athukorala, Prema-Chandra (ed.), *The Economic Development of South Asia,* Cheltenham: Edward Elgar Publishing, 2002

Benneti, Gay, *A Family in Sri Lanka,* Minnea Polis, Lenner Publications, 1985.

Government of Sri Lanka, "National Plan of Action for Women in Sri Lanka–Towards Gender Equity", Ministry of Transport, Environment and Women's Affairs, 1995.

Hasna Begum, *Women in the Development World: Thoughts and Ideas,* NY: Apt Books, 1990.

Hilsdon, Anne-Marie; Machintyre, Martha & Mackie, Vera and Stivens, Maila (eds.), *Human Rights and Gender Politics: Asia-Pacific Perspectives.* London; New York: Routledge. p. 60.

Hudson, Valerie M & den Boer, Andrea, A Surplus of Men, A Deficit of Peace: Security and Sex Ratios in Asia's Largest States, In *International Security,* 26(4), 2002.

Kumari Jayawardena & Swarna Jayaweera, (eds.), *A Profile on Sri Lanka: A Stuidy: The Integration of Women in Development Planning,* Sri Lanka, Colombo: Women's Education Centre, 1986.

Kumari Jayawardena, *Feminism and Nationalism in the Third World,* London: Zed press, 1986.

Maithereyi Krishnaraj and Karuna Chanana, (eds.), *Gender and the Household Domain: Social and Cultural Dimensions,* Newbury Park: Sage Publications, 1989.

Mallick, Ross, Development, Ethnicity and Human Rights in South Asia, New Delhi: Sage Publications, 1998.

Quibria, M.G. (ed.), *Rural Poverty in Developing Asia,* Volume 1: Bangladesh, India and Sri Lanka, Manila, Philippines: Asian Development Bank, March 1994.

Savitri Goonesekhere, *The Legal Status of the Female in Sri Lankan Law on Family Relations,* Colombo: Gunasena, 1980.

Sirima Kiribamune & Vidyamali Samarasinghe, (eds.), *Women at Corssroads: A Sri Lankan Perspective,* New Delhi: International Centre for Ethnic Studies, 1990.

Swarna Jayaweera, *Gender and Education in Sri Lanka: Women, Schooling, Work,* Colombo: Centre for Women's Research, 1991.

Sam arasekara, ohanapala, *Take a Trip to Sri Lanka,* New York: Franklin Watts, 1987.

UNDP, Human Development Report, Oxford University Press, New York, 1997.

World Bank, the South Asia Regional Gender Action Plan. Washington, D.C., 1997.

Wanasundera, Nauda P., *Cultries of the World: Sri Lanka,* Singapore-Kuala Lumpur: Times Books International, 1991.

Wanasuudera, Noudr P., *Cultures of the World: Sri Lanka,* Singapore-Kuala Lumpur: Times Books International, 1991.

Index

F

Q

S

U